GUILT, SHAME, AND FEAR: RELATIONALITY ACROSS CULTURES

By Geoffrey Beech, PhD

Guilt, Shame, and Fear: Relationality Across Cultures

By Geoffrey Beech

Lifeworld Education
6 Kalimna Close
LAKE HAVEN NSW 2263
geoff@lifeworld.com.au

ISBN 978-1-64669-566-9

Dedication

This book is dedicated both to my first wife, Michelle, who stood with me through the doctoral process, even as her health failed, and to my current wife, Elizabeth, who has been a great source of encouragement and whose knowledge of Bolivia and the Bolivian people has been of great value.

Table of Contents

CHAPTER 1

Introduction and research context

A preface

The research topic covered in this book is of significant complexity, and the issues covered in it pertain to academic areas including cross-cultural studies, sociology, anthropology, linguistics, ethics, and organisational leadership. The research project outlined below merely considers a sampling, as it were, from across these areas, and other researchers may wish to deal with the research topic based on their more focused areas of expertise. It is the combination of these areas, however, that has provided the background for the research and allowed for the variety and richness of the findings. The material that follows has been extracted from a doctoral thesis with some technical sections removed and then modified a little, hopefully to make it more readable. The original thesis may be accessed at:
https://researchbank.acu.edu.au/theses/336/.

The research context

Bolivia, located in the centre of South America, is landlocked and bordered by Brazil, Peru, Chile, Argentina and Paraguay. The country, approximately the size of New South Wales and Victoria in Australia (Texas and New Mexico in the USA) combined, includes a section of the Andes Mountains and high plains (over 4000 metres), descending to the lowlands that are a part of the Amazon Basin. The geography is significant for this study in that each of the geographical regions—the high country, the "valleys" in the centre of Bolivia, and the lowlands—has, in general terms, a different indigenous language and its own subculture. The city of Cochabamba lies in a high valley surrounded by the *Cordillera Central* of the Andes Mountains. Cochabamba has a population of over one million, including many communities living on the edge of the city and a number of communities that had once been small towns that are now a part of the metropolis. The rural participants in this research who came from rural settings were mostly from villages in the Cochabamba hinterland. The research problem is associated with these two subculture groups within Bolivia.

Leaders in Bolivia make decisions within cultural contexts as well as within the context of their particular organisation and network of relationships. Given the cultural contexts of the two subculture groups in this research, the question may then be asked as to whether cultural and worldview differences influence the decisions that leaders make. In particular, this research examines the potential influence of pairs of affective domain components (shame, guilt, fear, honour, innocence and a sense of power) on decision-making, the priorities given to these in different subcultures, and their possible cultural or worldview origins.

The project addressed a lack of a comprehensive understanding of what is termed here the avoidance-pursuit pair phenomenon that has been identified as existing across cultures in the work of Blaschke (2001), Hegeman (2006a and 2006b) and Muller (2000 & 2006a). In addition, this research examines the worldview and cultural origins of the prioritisations of the avoidance-pursuit pairs and their components. This requires linking the prioritised avoidance-pursuit pairs with evidence of fundamental values and belief systems and identifying any coherence with the subcultures of the participants. This research sought to fill a particular lacuna that exists because no research has been done on the valuation or prioritisation of the avoidance-pursuit pairs in different subcultures within a Bolivian context.

Much of the cross-cultural leadership research that has been carried out in recent years has related to commerce and industry. This particular research examined the cross-cultural distinctions pertaining to more general leadership. It therefore has application at the various levels of leadership, including various organisations or institutions, so that the results of the research have a general application to improving the understanding of decisions and actions of individuals within different cultures.

While there is very limited literature regarding the existence of the full suite of avoidance-pursuit pairs used in this research, there is considerable literature surrounding their individual components, as discussed in Chapter 2. In general, the research that has been done in this area has centred on the recognition by Westerners of the importance of shame and honour in collectivist, most often Asian, cultures (Benedict, 1946; Yau-fai Ho, 1976; Uskul, Oyserman and Schwarz, 2009). In particular, the need for these studies has arisen from the growing economic interaction between Asian countries and the West (Lieber, Fung & Leiung, 2006; Dahl, 2004; Littrell, 2002; House, Wright & Aditya, 1996). Robert House (with Hanges, Javidan, Dorfman & Gupta, 2004) and Geert Hofstede (1984) have studied leadership across cultures but the studies have been driven often by Western, industrial models and the impact on the decision-making of leaders of the avoidance-pursuit pair prioritisation has not been considered.

The research was undertaken in order to answer the research question:

What worldview and cultural factors influence the prioritisation of affective domain avoidance-pursuit pairs and do they affect the ethical decision-making of leaders in different subcultures—in this case, in Bolivia?

In order to answer the research question the following subsidiary questions were posed:

> What defines and differentiates the two Bolivian subcultures in this research?
> How does leadership function within these cultures?
> How do leaders make decisions?
> What determines the "right thing to do" in the decision-making process?
> What priorities do the members of the subcultures place on the avoidance-pursuit pair components (guilt, shame, fear as opposed to justice/innocence, honour and power)?
> Do the prioritisations of the pair components indicate culturally-based pair prioritisations?
> What are the worldview and cultural sources of the prioritisations?

The purpose of the study was therefore to confirm the existence and influence of the prioritisation of the affective domain avoidance-pursuit pairs and their potential impact on the decision-making of leaders in and around Cochabamba, Bolivia, and to identify the worldview and cultural antecedents of this prioritisation. The assumptions generated from the literature that was examined in this research were: That the pair components (guilt, innocence, shame, honour, fear and power) are identifiable as being important to the people in the two subculture groups studied and that there is an observable sub-cultural variation in the levels of importance attributed to them and to their pairs: guilt-innocence, shame-honour and fear-power. Also, these priorities, which may impact decision-making, flow from culturally embedded worldview sources, including religious beliefs. From the literature, it was also assumed that the prioritisation of the avoidance-pursuit pairs affects the decision-making of leaders.

The basis for the research was that if value systems were embedded in worldview assumptions and the decisions we make depend on our values, then we may ask whether the making of ethical decisions, or the determination of the "right thing to do", varies between cultures. Cultures provide the lifeworld contexts for culture members, and according to Naugle (2002), these lifeworlds give birth to worldviews or the presuppositional, interpretive frameworks that individuals use to give coherence to what they perceive and believe. Specifically, this research examines the question of how these decisions may be influenced by a framework, derived from the literature, of affective domain avoidance-pursuit pairs and how any differences that may be caused may be linked to worldview and culture. From the literature, it was hypothesised that in this research context, the people living in the city of Cochabamba would place a high value on shame and honour, and the people from rural communities on fear and power, with a particular relationship to the metaphysical. It was also hypothesised that the influence for hundreds of years of the Catholic Church and, in more recent times, of the evangelical church, would lead many people, particularly in the city where their influence is strongest, to place a high value on guilt and innocence.

Global media coverage of the responses of individuals from a variety of cultures to news events demonstrates that, in some cases, those in other cultures do not seem to act or think the same way that we in "the West" do. To our way of thinking, decisions made, or actions and reactions, in other cultures may even appear at times to be illogical or constitute *non sequiturs*. We accept that others may believe different things or see the world differently from the way we do, but it is difficult for us to accurately interpret how these influences their decisions and actions. This research project was undertaken in order to explore this problem.

Limited though it is, the extant literature in this field (Blaschke, 2001; Hegeman, 2006a, 2006b; & Muller, 2000, 2006a) hypothesised the existence of what are here defined as avoidance-pursuit pairs. While these authors use various terms, the expression "avoidance-pursuit pairs" was chosen because they appear to exist as the juxtaposition of the desire to avoid guilt and pursue innocence (justice or rightness), to avoid shame and pursue honour (or glory), and to avoid fear and pursue power (or powers). The literature mentioned indicated that, for example, individuals in one culture may act based on decisions that have been made with regard to the priority of guilt and justice or perceptions of innocence, while within another culture, shame and honour may be seen as being more important.

A qualitative methodology was used in this research, based on a case study using participants who were leaders from the distinct sub-cultural groups. The leaders came from a range of organisational contexts, including religious, education, politics,

4

business and non-government organisations and the data on which the research was based comprised the reflections of leaders on their cultures, leadership and decision-making processes. The contexts within which the participants lived and worked were known, at least to some extent, by the researcher.

As globalisation, international communication, trade, tourism and even terrorism increase, it would appear that there is a very significant need for a better understanding of the forces behind the making of decisions by those from cultures other than our own. The lack of such an understanding that exists in this regard would appear to have been the result of the use of monocultural models.

According to Fessler (2004), "cross-cultural comparisons can . . . illuminate the manner in which cultures differentially highlight, ignore, and group various facets of emotional experience" (p. 207). This research adds significantly to the understanding of the decision-making processes of leaders in different cultures by approaching the problem from a qualitatively different stance: one based on a broader and deeper understanding of culturally informed worldviews and their effect on decisions and actions. By doing so, this research has significance in terms of contributing to cross-cultural understanding not only in situations such as city and rural Bolivia, but is also applicable to contrasting cultural situations within Australia and other cultures. This may include cultures in other countries or the cultures of those who are first-generation migrants to Australia.

The participants

The participants who provided the interview data in this research were chosen from leaders within Bolivian communities or organisations. The choice of participants in leadership positions was made because it was presumed that leaders would be more likely to think more deeply about the decisions they made, as their decisions could have a profound influence on the organisation or community and on the lives of those for whom they were responsible. Two subculture groups of participants were involved in this research.[1] The first group was drawn from leaders within the city of Cochabamba, Bolivia. The city is relatively cosmopolitan, with a considerable Hispanic influence, and has seen significant modernisation in recent years. All of the participants from this subculture would have access to computers and mobile phones, and many would have travelled extensively. The participants in the second subculture come from, or work in, village communities in the mountains away from the city. Leaders in this

---

[1] Bolivia is a country with many cultures. In this research, the term subculture is used specifically with reference to one found in the city (the largely Hispanic, urban subculture of the city of Cochabamba) and one in the rural areas surrounding Cochabamba (a Quechua *campesino* culture). It is recognised, however, that this is a generalisation in that neither of these cultures is "pure" in that each has influenced the other to some degree.

group mostly live in simple adobe or stone houses in very small village communities, where generally there is no access to electricity or other utilities, though they travel to the city to sell their produce or negotiate aid for their communities.

These two subcultures represent distinct belief systems that have historical bases in the life-world contexts of pre-Columbian ideological conceptualisations and practices, and the distinct European Roman Catholic perspectives and practices introduced in the Spanish Conquest (Batista Gumucio, 1978; Thomas, 2010a). They also have very different lifeworld settings and therefore distinct worldviews. These distinctions provide a very adequate setting for the exploration of the research problem. This exploration was conducted within, or flowing out of, a range of contexts including that of the researcher, the cultural history of the groups and the worldview beliefs that the groups hold.

The researcher's context

For most of the time from October 1989 till June 2005, the researcher worked as a missionary educator in the city of Cochabamba. His roles in Bolivia included the principalship of an international school for missionary and Bolivian children and working in a consultancy role with Bolivian educators, mainly in evangelical, private schools and universities. In each of these positions, he was able to meet with leaders in the Bolivian community both socially and in work-related situations. Some of the participants were therefore known to him prior to the commencement of this research, and in particular, the participants designated as key informants were well known. This research may therefore be seen as having both etic and emic components: having the perspectives of an outsider and an insider with regard to the culture (Den Hartog et al., 1999).

Within Bolivia, his work took him to most of the *Departamentos* [Departments, similar to States] in the country and to most of the significant cities where he was able to meet with educators and other leaders, see schools and other institutions in operation, and meet with representatives from the Ministry and Departments of Education as well as other political leaders and those working with non-government organisations. Very frequent, informal discussions were held during this time with government officials, academics and school principals regarding leadership, particularly educational leadership, in the country. His work also involved travel outside Bolivia, including visits to Peru, Paraguay, Argentina, Brazil, Mexico and Guatemala, for meetings with educators in those countries to discuss a variety of educational programs.

This experience was important for this research for several reasons. Living within the Bolivian culture enabled him to develop friendships and contacts in many areas of the education sector, with a number of politicians at local, state and federal levels, and with leaders in the country's business community, enabling him to start to understand how they function in leadership. The length of time spent in the country enabled him to learn the language to a level of conversational competence and, through numerous hours of casual conversation with Bolivians from many areas within the country, to learn a good deal about not only the culture of Bolivia in a general sense, but also of some of the sub-cultural distinctives. In doing this, an understanding of some of the cross-cultural differences between Western and Bolivian thinking was developed.

Western and Bolivian cross-cultural understanding

Coming from a Western mindset, it was important to recognise this when considering questions of worldview and patterns of culturally directed reasoning of other cultures. Philosophy in the West, based largely on Greek thinking, has provided us with our basis for understanding and a framework for interpretation and has meant that our understanding of the thinking patterns of other cultures has been substantially influenced. Commenting on the hegemony of Western thinking, Hallinger and Leithwood (1996) wrote:

> The nineteenth and twentieth centuries have been so dominated by Western paradigms that the intellectual traditions and practices of other cultures are often judged without questioning the implicit assumptions embedded in Western cultures. The tendency for Western knowledge to overshadow the intellectual traditions of other cultures has become even more acute in recent decades. (p. 101)

Heidegger (1975) said in 1943 that the term *Western Philosophy* was a tautology because "there is no other philosophy than Western. 'Philosophy' is in its essence so primordially Western that it carries the foundation of the history of the West" (p. 3). According to Reyes and Mendieta (2001), "the light of [Western] philosophy has eclipsed other lights; it has also blinded us to other visions of the world" (p. 249). This Western philosophy, Reyes and Mendieta continued, finds definition in Hegel's use of the term *Weltgeist*, or universal spirit, that was fundamentally European, Germanic, and protestant. Some significance for this research may be drawn from this study involving Hispanic subjects, as Reyes and Mendieta wrote:

> Spain, as is well known, did not even from afar touch the mantel of this spirit because, for Hegel, Europe ended in the Pyrenees. Latin America also does not come out too well. News of great pre-Hispanic cultures in Mexico and Peru had reached Hegel's ears. But these did not have to be taken seriously, says Hegel, because the day that the *Weltgeist* approaches them they are bound to melt like a sugar cube. Mexico and Peru belong to pre-history and if they

want to enter history they will have to follow the trail marked by the *Weltgeist*. (p. 253)

For Hegel (1975), Latin American culture presented itself as "purely natural" and fundamentally impotent, judging by the destruction of the cultures in the face of the European conquests, or, as he put it, "the breath of European activity" (p. 163). These conquest activities brought with them foreign languages that have since been adopted as national languages in Latin America, and this strongly influenced the cultures and worldviews of the people. Last century, the European philosophers Wittgenstein, Whorf and Gadamer all spoke of the close linkage between language and worldview (Horn, 2005; Kienpointner, 1996) and this compounds the problems inherent in communicating cross-culturally.

At the most basic level, difficulties in cross-cultural communication and understanding suffer not only from this difference of interpretive frameworks but also as a result of language differences. The differences arise in both a lack of translatable correspondence and in the thought patterns that have developed the language. As Lotman's theory (Lotman & Uspenski, 1978) indicated, a language cannot exist if it is not steeped in a cultural context, and a culture cannot exist without the structure of natural language at its core. One example that illustrates the differences in language and philosophical or logical framework is the fact that in Spanish, double negatives are an acceptable form of expression. Another is seen in the use of reflexive Spanish verbal expressions, such as *se rompió,* or *it broke itself.* This example makes little sense outside a culture that may save face or reduce shame by imputing responsibility to inanimate objects.

For this research, it was felt to be important that an effort be made to interpret the cognitive and affective processes of others who function according to different philosophical and worldview frameworks. To do this required an understanding of at least some of the lifeworld circumstances of the participants and was facilitated by an understanding on the part of the participant of some of my lifeworld. An illustration of the fact that the participants in the research also would recognise this problem of the impact of worldview difference on communication is given in a comment by Thomas (2010c) regarding an interview in his research:

> One young Aymara leader, who had all the characteristics of charisma and *gallardía* [gallantry, dash] that are so culturally admired, once responded to me in the middle of a difficult discussion, *"el indio en mí está respondiendo al gringo en ti"* ["the Indian in me is responding to the gringo in you"]. (April 22, para. 5)

Historical context of Bolivian subcultures

The characteristics of the subcultures have developed over time and must be understood within the context of their historical development. Bolivia's history has played an important role in the development of the multiple subcultures in the country and, therefore, the development of respective worldviews and ethical frameworks. What today is known as Bolivia has a long history of human settlement involving numerous large and small ethnic groups. Some of these groups, such as those of the ancient Incan and Tiahuanacan Empires, formed long-standing and sophisticated civilisations. The early Quechua empire, led by Incas (rulers), once extended from Ecuador into northern Chile and eastward towards Argentina, eventually dominating the Aymaran empire, though the Aymaras retained their language and much of their culture (Klein, 2003, p. 18). The eastern lowlands of the country were home to the Moxos people.

These three significant people groups were invaded and conquered by the Spanish *conquistadores* [conquerors] over a period of time from 1532 to early 1560s (Klein, 2003) and the three hundred and thirty year reign of the Incas came to an end. The Incas had developed a political power system based on inheritance and this formed a rigorously maintained classed society[2] that used religion to bind the classes together (D'Altroy, 2003).

The Spanish invasion brought with it a different class order, one based on pre-existing Spanish classes and on race as well as military power and religion. The Spaniards attempted to extend the Quechua language across Lower and Upper Bolivia—Peru and Bolivia—(Klein, 2003), but the language that has now been adopted as the lingua franca of the country is Spanish. Through the education system, the Bolivian government has tried to incorporate the original languages into all schools and universities in a drive towards a universally bilingual education, as expressed in the new constitution (Congreso Nacional de Bolivia, 2008). At present, however, many of the people lacking schooling, particularly women in rural communities, have little or no Spanish, while Quechua and Aymara may be heard frequently in the cities— particularly in marketplaces.[3] So, despite four hundred years of Hispanic dominance, the various people groups in Bolivia have maintained a degree of identity, though there exists a wide diversity within each of the groups as in any culture. Some understanding

---

[2] This classed society was a "peasant society living in agricultural communities as opposed to a tribal society with [a] high emphasis on egalitarianism and kinship" (Thomas, 2010a).

[3] Derks,(2010) made a point regarding this gender inequality:

> Despite the progress in women's rights at a national level, there are still large gender inequalities. For instance, according to the national census that was help in 2001, 80.65 percent of the Bolivian women over 15 years old were able to read and write, whereas 93.06 percent of the men over 15 were literate. There are considerable differences between the rural and urban areas, as in the rural areas 62.09 percent of the women were able to read and write (against 85.58 percent of the men). (p. 8)

of the cultural and ethnic distinctions is essential in order to understand the full context and significance of this research.

The ethic subcultures and people groups

The history and geography of Bolivia that have contributed to the cultural heterogeneity have ensured that Bolivia is a multi-ethnic, multi-cultural and, according to the government, a *pluri-lingual* country. The significant groups for this research are the Quechua and the *Mestizos*—those of mixed indigenous and Spanish blood. As well as migrants from a number of countries, there are some descendants of the Spanish *conquistadores,* but they are relatively few in number. Any cultural study involving Bolivians must consider the origins, history and religion of these groups as the assumptions and presuppositions from which their knowledge proceeds are founded on the ontological perspectives of the cultures.

Quechuas and Aymaras live in rural as well as urban areas, though often in the cities, there are no clear boundaries or evidence of ethnic identity in their dress or physical features. The Quechuas were the primary people group of the Incan Empire and are now the most numerous of the non-Hispanic cultural groups in Bolivia. The Aymara community has its centre in the very high country surrounding Lake Titicaca— on the border of Bolivia and Peru—and in northern Chile. While many of the Quechua and Aymara live in the *campo* [rural areas] and speak their own languages, many are bilingual and also speak Spanish. Living in the *campo* identifies them in Latin America as *campesinos*—a term of deprecation for much of the country's post-colonisation history. The *mestizos* live primarily in the cities and speak Spanish—though many also speak an indigenous language. [4] Europeans and others live mostly in the cities and speak Spanish as a second language. The people groups of Bolivia, therefore, tend to have relatively distinct histories, languages, geographic contexts and cultural distinctives, though, as Thomas (2010) noted, many Bolivians would lie on a continuum between the city and country subcultures. In general terms, however, the distinguishing factors will have provided the lifeworld situations that have been responsible for each subculture's distinct worldview, which demonstrates a relationship to their cultural origins.[5]

---

[4] The process of *mestizaje*, of becoming a *mestizo*, is a dynamic one that results in changes from census to census as languages are lost from one generation to the next and as migration to the city occurs (Thomas, 2010).

[5] Participant 23 explained some of the sub-cultural distinctions and spoke of the distinct ways some words are pronounced by different social groups in Bolivia as well as the lack of understanding that exists at least on the part of the city community members in this research of the *campesinos.*

10

The Quechuas and their worldview

In order to understand the decision-making of leaders in this research, it is important to have some understanding of the leadership culture of the dominant, non-Hispanic people group in the Cochabamba valley: the Quechuas. The culture of the Quechua appears to date from around 2600 BC (Schlecht, 2004) and grew to be the dominant culture prior to the Spanish conquest. While most *Cochabambinos* [citizens of Cochabamba] would have a mixed ethnic heritage, the influence of the Quechua culture has been particularly significant. Quechua culture is evident in the dress of many of the people who have migrated from rural areas, in the Quechua language that is widely spoken in the city, and in the inclusion of Quechua terms in the Spanish spoken in the city.

Within Quechua ontology and teleology lies the conceptualisation of two classes of supernatural cosmological entities and one or more classes of supernatural terrestrial forces (Schaedel, 1988) that require placation, but Schaedel noted that the differentiation between the supernatural entities was not necessarily hierarchical. Rather, the Quechua beliefs were founded on a holistic view of their surroundings, and where distinctions are made, the definition is usually in terms of "balanced pair opposites" (Schaedel, 1988, p. 770). This concept also extended to the physical realm to emphasise a distinction but a parity between, for example, left and right or male and female.

Revolving around this concept are the three customary principles of the Quechua people, which, according to Tamayo Flores (1992), are:

1. *Reciprocity:* encompasses the principle of equity and provides the basis for negotiation and exchange between humans and with the deity *Pachamama.* (*Pachamama* may be translated as Mother Earth or Earth Mother, though there are strong links to fertility—soil and belly—and to temporality—hour or era).

2. *Duality:* indicates that everything has an opposite which complements it; behaviour cannot be individualistic, for example, in the union between man and woman, and that other systems or paradigms can be accepted.

3. *Equilibrium:* refers to balance and harmony, in both nature and society—e.g., respect for the '*Pachamama*' and other deities; resolving conflicts to restore social harmony; and complementarities (e.g., between ecological niches). Equilibrium needs to be observed in applying customary laws, all of which are essentially derived from this principle.

The leadership of the Incan Empire was necessarily highly vertically structured, sophisticated and complex but Schaedel (1988) wrote that there was little evidence in the Quechua language of a strong vocabulary surrounding superordination and subordination or of the distinctions normally made in a class-oriented society. Schaedel presumes that this could be due to the development of the language in pre-Inca times and those words that do express hierarchies appear to have been introduced following the Incan and Spanish conquests. The vocabulary and expressions that do exist to distinguish communities are "essentially ceremonial ("traditional") and not economic or political" (p. 772). The leadership arising within this pre-Incan framework appears to have been not for the purpose of control but for the "passing on of ingredients that unite them" (Schaedel, 1988, p. 772). Archaeological evidence around the southern portion of Lake Titicaca from 600–1200 AD indicates the existence of a complex society comprised of capitals and sub-capitals operating as a theocratic paramount chiefdom.[6]

Following the Spanish conquest, the social structures and relationships changed substantially to include a system of patronage. According to Vila de Prado (2003), this system was based on the symbolic kinship concept of *compadrazgo* [relationship between godparents] whereby the indigenous people adopted the role of *ahijados* [godchildren] of their Spanish godparents who were from a considerably better socio-economic class and the relationship was used as a controlling mechanism within the society. Notwithstanding this, in effect, many of the indigenous people were forced to live in a state of indentured slavery to wealthy *caciques* [local political leaders] in Bolivia and Peru (Pedraza, n.d.). The existence of this system had an effect on the demands for the implementation of universal education, and its concomitant enculturation, in the rural areas:

> The *mestizos* demanded education as a means for social mobility, the Indians demanded it in order to obtain citizenship and defend their property rights over their lands. These demands were directed to rulers in whose discourse "education" was regarded as one of the most powerful ingredients for progress. (Vila de Prado, 2003, p. 15)

The implementation of a universal education was important in order to provide a degree of uniformity in the country. Through it Spanish could be taught, providing a basis for communication between the different groups. This communication assists with governance and trade as well as internal migration. It also allows the different groups to be more actively involved in local, state and federal government, through which they are able to impose worldview constructions from their culture on the broader community. According to a number of Bolivian friends of the researcher, this is

---

[6] Schaedel (1988) made this observation on the basis of "the first book-length Andean document written in an Andean language" (Murra, 1970, p. 3) which containing legends and tales. Schaedel commenting on work by Murra (1970) said that "a detailed reading of the manuscript, the most comprehensive ethnohistoric document available on Andean world view, provides full support for a nonauthoritarian cosmology" (p. 773).

something that is particularly evident in the operation of the current "indigenous" government.

The Aymaras and their worldview

Even though there are many fewer Aymaras in Cochabamba than in the higher country of Bolivia, their influence is still felt by the participants in this research, in that the group has great significance in the country as a whole, particularly due to the influence of the present government. Many features of the Aymaran culture and religious beliefs and practices have been adopted by the Quechua-based *mestizo* culture of the Cochabamba region. The Aymaras are Amerindians who descended from the members of the Tiwanaku civilisation on the shores of Lake Titicaca, where they were the first to domesticate and cultivate potatoes. While they were overtaken by the Incan Empire, the Incas were never able to impose their Quechua language on those who lived in the Aymara heartland around the lake (Pedraza, n.d.). They were eventually conquered by the Spanish, and according to Pedraza[7]:

> During the time of the colony, the condition of the Aymaras and that of all the other natives was worse even than that of the African slaves; since the latter were at least attributed some value in money, while the Indians ('la indiada'), could be obtained for free. Millions of Aymaras and other indigenous people died, abused by the 'encomenderos' [agents], who acted with consent of Spain's political and ecclesiastical authorities. (para. 11)

The religious context of the Aymaras is important in the worldview formation of Bolivians. The ancient religion of the Aymaras involved ancestor veneration—as they believed that once dead, each person became a god—and the worship of deities around an agricultural context. Pedraza (n.d.) wrote:

> The old Aymara God *Thunupa* is the central icon found on the stone sculpture known as '*Puerta del Sol*' in Tiwanaku [Tiuanacu], and is the personification of certain agents in nature, such as the sun and wind, rain and hail, which can

---

[7] Thomas (2010a) commented on the relationship between the Quechua and Aymara cultures in the high plains of Bolivia where they co-exist, as follows:

> The origins of people who now speak Quechua and Aymara and even other indigenous languages in the altiplano are ancient, but I understand that Quechua is also an imposed language and culture by the Incas, much in the way the Assyrians resettled the people they conquered in new areas in order to break allegiances and to control them . . . . Because of the history of Catholic evangelism on the altiplano, many of the Quechua communities were originally Aymara, and culturally they are indistinguishable from Aymara communities. Andean anthropologists speak of one culture with two languages. But it is noteworthy that the Aymara and the various Quechua languages do not have a common origin.

affect agricultural yield for better or for worse. One other aspect of this manifestation of faith was, as it still is today, the Goddess *Pachamama* (mother earth), provider of food and pastures. This Mother and Goddess demanded sacrifices, the foetus of the llama being her favourite request. Worship to the ancestors on the other hand, was made manifest materially, in the construction of shrines, which served also as tombs, and which varied in complexity depending on the status of the deceased . . . . The Aymara people thought of their Gods as their protectors, and they identified them with the hills around about (*Awki, Achachila*). This expression of faith has prevailed to the present day, in that each hill found locally is given an individual name and is always invoked as the local guardian. The *Anchanchu* or *Saxra* were evil Gods of the underground. Minor Gods were thought to dwell in water springs (*Phuju*). Another important aspect connected to Aymara spirituality was the practice of ritual medicine and the use of natural healing remedies by the *Yatiris* (sages) [in Western parlance these may perhaps be known as diviners]. (para. 21)

The coming of the Spaniards brought the imposition of a different form of governance with military might enforcing imported Spanish legal and bureaucratic forms, and the church enforcing its rules and authority (Pedraza, n.d.). The importation of foreign concepts of governance and religion was, however, only partially successful—particularly in rural areas where communities continued to be structured as they had been for centuries and where the indigenous religious practices were still carried out. At times these would be in the form of traditional practices and beliefs, and at others, syncretised with the beliefs and practices of the Catholic Church. An example of this accommodation of belief that was, and continues to be, practised is given by Pedraza (n. d.) as follows:

> The Spanish political and ecclesiastical authorities, tried to destroy without success, the sense of religious spirituality of the Aymara people. The Spaniards destroyed the icons, the *'Chullpas'*, etc. The brutal way in which the new religion was imposed is an unpleasant memory. But nature itself, the hills, the lakes, remained unchanged spurring the religious traditions of the Aymaras. It is right to point out however, that there were many within the Catholic Church, who opposed this wrongful process of evangelization. The Jesuits and Franciscans were within this moderate sector of the Church, and opted for accommodating or christianising the old Aymara Gods. This explains why the powerful God *Thunupa* was turned into *Apu Qullana Awki*, a handy identification as regards the religious explanation of the world's creation. An important characteristic of the God *Thunupa* however, is that he used to be identified with thunder and lightning, so that *Thunupa* is simultaneously *Apu Qullana Awki* (the world's creator), and St. Bartholomew (patron saint of lightning). One other syncretistic

adaptation, is the identification made between *Pachamama* and the Virgin. (para. 23)

Noting the importance of examining a people in the context of their history and geographical environment, La Barre (1966) wrote that the Aymara "live in an unhappy, hostile, and insecure world. Children's souls are liable to be kidnapped by place-demons in the earth; when travelling, even adults must be solicitous to placate these spirits" (p. 132). He went on to list other spiritual concerns relating to curses, bodiless, flying-head vampires, and the like. The difficulties encountered by living at high altitude while having to cope with the unseen spirit world and the variations in food production have contributed, according to La Barre, to the development of an Aymara character that he described in less than flattering terms:

> Ethnologists are in consensus concerning the temperament of the Aymara. I found the Aymara truculent, hostile, silent, suspicious, treacherous, and vindictive, masters of indirect aggression when they did not express it directly. Forbes called them "intensely suspicious and distrustful . . . [with] the most deep-rooted and inveterate hatred for their white oppressors"; Grandidier considered the Aymara "cruel"; Walle, "hard, vindictive, bellicose, rebellious, egotistical, and jealous of his liberty . . . lacking in will, except the will to hate." Squier says they are "a people notoriously morose, jealous and vindictive" and "more sullen and more cruel" than the Quechua. (p. 133)

Thomas (2010a) commented that there are cultural studies that correct this "ugly and erroneous description" such as in the work of Carter and Mamani (1982) and the work of Javier Albo, the Jesuit founder of the *Centro de Investigación y Promoción del Campesinado* [Research Centre for the Promotion of the Peasantry] in La Paz. Personal experience in Bolivia also does not fully support La Barre's (1966) portrayal of the Aymara, though under the current, Aymara-led, government, there is certainly the desire to remove all forms of colonial oppression—institutional and religious—and the *mestizo* people certainly fear what may happen under the new ruling party. When there is political tension in the country, it is very often Aymara groups from the *altiplano* and from the mine workers who close down the capital, often with violence or threats of violence. They appear to the researcher to have a very strong sense of justice and their rights, regardless of the constitutional or legal position of the issue.

One form of community leadership that is used to try to redress rights issues is the concept introduced by the Spanish of the *cabildo,* or meeting of a governing group. In Sergio Gabriel Waisman's (1998) footnotes to his translation of the famous Bolivian book, *Nataniel Aguirre*, by Juan de la Rosa (1995), he noted that the concept of the *cabildo* had been imported from Spain with the conquest and that although these groups were primarily for administering local and judicial matters, at times they became the seat of political power. A *cabildo* is a group of officials or people seen to have some importance or ability in the community and who become, in some ways, the governing body for the community. These may function alongside or, in times of political turmoil, instead of official government authorities such as mayors or state governors. When expressed in mass gatherings, they convey an expression of community-based democracy.

An analysis of Aymara folktales by La Barre (1966) showed a preoccupation with food and with relationships—particularly the inter-clan marriages which were the norm due to a dislike of marriage within the kinship group. Difficulties in relationships between *ayllus* (collections of communities) may boil over into open conflict. Perhaps the most spectacular example of this is the celebration of a violent *Tinku* [encounter], as opposed to the normal dialogue form. In early May each year, members of *ayllus* in the Northern Potosi region spend days drinking heavily and then fighting. Any bloodshed during these events is considered an oblation, and deaths are seen as sacrifices to *Pachamama*, to restore harmony and equilibrium (Thomas, 2010a), and therefore both are useful for the blessing of the next season's crops (La Barre).

According to La Barre (1966), the origins of the Aymara ethos, then, are:

1. The harsh environment
2. The social structures of the communities (*ayllus*)
3. Loyalty to the *ayllu* and defending it against the imposition of external forces
4. Up to one thousand years of rule by the Incas[8]—though Schaedel (1988) did not see this as being so important, and
5. The revolt against the Spanish, which was at times violent and which, according to La Barre, may explain the fact that Bolivia has had more revolutions per year of national life than any other country.

A variety of guerrilla groups, such as the Tupac Katati Guerrilla Army, have at times initiated violence by way of protest, though their activities have been curtailed by vigilant government forces (Kushner, 2003). When the research was undertaken, the ruling party in the Bolivian government, *Movamiento al Socialismo* (MAS) or Movement to Socialism, was driven by the *originario* [original or indigenous] peoples and was led by an Aymara president, Evo Morales Ayma, and a Vice President, Álvaro Garcia Linera, who once had been an organising member of the Tupac Katari Guerrilla Army (García Linera, Stefanoni, & Ramirez, 2009).

Hispanic Bolivians

---

[8] This statement is a considerable exaggeration. While the Incas had existed from the 12th century, the Incan Empire lasted from the establishment of the rule of Pachacuti in 1438 till the beheading of Túpac Amaru by the Spaniards in 1572 (Keen & Hayes, 2009)—one hundred and thirty four years.

16

The Spaniards have had an enormous influence on the people and their beliefs, as well as on the formation of bureaucracies and new forms of leadership. The Spaniards ruled in Bolivia from the foundation of La Paz in 1548 until the country's independence in 1825. While the conquest was neither a very rapid process nor dependent on the Spaniards alone (Restall, 2003), the surviving influence of the *conquistadores* is seen in the adoption of Spanish as an official language in Bolivia for use in many of the institutional structures in the country. Spanish influence has also included the governance and legal structures of the Spanish enforced by the conquering military and the accompanying Roman Catholic Church, and these have deeply influenced the city populations of modern Bolivia.

A small percentage of the Bolivian population has maintained a relatively pure Spanish lineage. This is a source of much pride and a significant factor in the class structure of the country. In general terms, these people have formed the "old money" base for the economy, and while most of their wealth has been eroded by successive revolutions and inadequate replacement of funding sources in changing economies, they still retain much of their upper-class status.

Because Bolivia is a classed society, the current president, while ruler of the country, would still be considered by the upper-class Bolivians to be a *campesino* or peasant (Archondo, 2006). Even if he were to have come from generations of wealthy families with considerable political power, he would still retain his peasant social class status. While the term *campesino* has been used in a pejorative sense, it still does not have the strong negative connotation of the term *indio* or Indian. This term is used to describe people from the tribal indigenous groups in the Amazon basin, though in an insulting way, it may be used of a Quechua or Aymara *campesino*. Some years ago, this racism in theory and practice (Vila de Prado, 2003) led an Aymara man who was later to become Vice President of the country, to change his Aymara name to a Hispanic one in order to obtain a place in a government university.

The status of individuals in Bolivian society, and the honour ascribed to them, are linked strongly to their names. A Quechua name, such as Mamani, while meaning 'condor' in Aymara and being linked to leadership, will always be seen by the Hispanic community as being *campesino,* and the bearer will automatically hold a different social status from someone with a Spanish surname, such as Quiroga or Saavedra. The importance of social distinctions is also reflected in the Spanish use of both paternal and maternal surnames (for example, Tomás Quiroga (paternal name) Saavedra (maternal name)), which is evidence of birth to an officially recognised marriage (Thomas, 2010a). The addition of the maternal surname helps in the more accurate positioning of a person within the social structure of the country.

Mestizos **Bolivians**

Most of the participants in this research come from a group that has arisen from a merging of cultures and races. As indicated in the interviews with the participants, this mixed-race group added considerably to the Spanish-speaking social group as its members endeavoured to speak the language of the Spanish overlords, live in cities and dress in "western" clothes to distance themselves from the rural indigenous groups. The mediation and translation roles of the *mestizo* groups have played an important role in Bolivian society, but the suffrage of a group of such considerable size has helped to legitimate their position in the culture (Vila de Prado, 2003).

From experience in the country and discussions with the participants, it seems that the move to the city and away from a strict adherence to traditional customs also included changes in religious practices. In the city, there were large churches to attend, with resident trained clergy and laity. This differs considerably from country communities, where they were often served by peripatetic priests and where syncretism or traditional religions were practised more widely. Also, while evangelical missionaries have worked in some isolated village areas for over a century, in the cities, there are many large protestant churches and up to twenty per cent of the population who would say that they are now evangelicals.

The primary influence of Hispanic culture is in the urban areas, whereas the rural areas have retained much of their original culture as well as their languages. Western, or foreign influence has been mostly in the cities, though there is some influence also in the rural communities as transport and communications improve across the country. The animistic religious beliefs in Bolivia stem from the communities in the rural areas, whereas the cities, influenced by the Spaniards, have a much stronger Roman Catholic presence. The growth of evangelical belief has coincided with the more recent influence on the country of foreigners, and particularly Western mission agencies.

Religious contexts

The main cultural components in Bolivia, as well as the sources and influence of the three main religious belief systems:
- The colonising Spanish influence and Catholicism
- The indigenous peoples' influence and animism
- Western influence and evangelicalism

The religious contexts of the participants in the research may be seen to inform ethical considerations (Muller, 2006a) and therefore influence decision-making. The changing vista of religious practice and beliefs in Bolivia in more recent times is reflected somewhat in the evolution of the nation's constitution. This is illustrated in the following relevant articles drawn from (a) the first constitution drawn up for the new Republic by the liberator Simón Bolívar in 1825, (b) a version of the articles common to constitutions since 1878 (Vargas Rivas, n.d.) and (c) the new constitution promulgated 8th February 2008.

(a) Article 6: The Apostolic, Roman Catholic religion is the state religion, to the exclusion of all other public worship. The government will protect it and respect it, recognising the principle that conscience is not governed by human power (Congreso Nacional de la República de Bolivia, 1826).

(b) Article 3: The State recognises and upholds the Apostolic, Roman Catholic Church. The state guarantees the public exercise of any form of worship. The relationship with the Catholic Church is governed by covenants and agreements between the Bolivian State and the Holy See (Congreso Nacional de Bolivia, 2004).

(c) Article 4: The State respects and guarantees freedom of religion and spiritual beliefs, in accordance with the worldviews [of the different sectors in the society]. The state is independent of religion.

Article 21.3: [Bolivian men and women have the right] to liberty of thought, spirituality, religion and worship, expressed in individual or collective forms and for legal purposes (Congreso Nacional de Bolivia, 2008).

It is interesting to note that while Catholicism was enshrined originally in the constitution as the official religion of the country, and this led to considerable persecution of those with other religious beliefs, the attitude of the church in Spain was less limiting. The local interpretation of the state religion, therefore, had a local flavour. The Catholic Encyclopaedia (1907) stated that at that time Article 2 of the Constitution of Bolivia said: "The State recognises and supports the Roman Apostolic Catholic religion, the public exercise of any other worship being prohibited, except in the colonies, where it is tolerated." The growing number of churches since the mid-twentieth century would suggest that there has been a considerable increase in the size of other groups—Evangelicals, Pentecostals and sects of various types—and the amended constitution allows freedom of worship and reflects the reality of diverse religious practice in the country. The intent of the constitutional change, however, was also to support the traditional worship practices of indigenous communities. This significant change in the Bolivian constitution has allowed, among other things, for the development of independent schools practising a range of faiths. The schools from which most of the educational leaders for this study come are private, evangelical schools.

The religious context of the people of Bolivia, including their beliefs, worldview presuppositions, and understanding of truth and knowledge, relates to a particular epistemology that framed the understanding of this research.

An epistemological context for the research

Ways of knowing are important in any setting, and a framework is proposed here for considering the epistemological background within which understanding in different cultures may be seen. Given the importance of relationships in this research, a relational epistemological basis was deemed to be important. This perspective takes into consideration the relational context of the researcher, participants and others. This is most fitting for this research for several reasons. In the first place, the researcher was known to a number of the participants—some of them for many years. The knowledge exchange between participant and researcher is therefore contextualised within a personal relationship, and this relationship may be of particular importance when dealing with participants from collectivist cultures, as Mok and Martinson (2000) found within a Chinese context. A second reason is that the participants commented on the decision-making and actions of others: a process involving both the collectivist cultural context of "others" and the relational context of the participant to them. A third consideration is that the gathered data pertain to the relationship the participants have to their cultures, and the analysis must also consider the pertinence of the researcher's relationship with his culture, as well as to the subcultures of the participants. In some ways, such a relational epistemology resembles a return to an Augustinian, Neoplatonic, triadic structure, recognising a reality distinct from the individual-object physical reality (c.f., Plato's forms). The proposed structure, however, goes much further, including a more complete inclusion of knowable objects and their relationships. In this research, therefore, epistemologically, knowledge and relationality are linked in a similar way to that described by Shults (1997):

> A "relationalist" structure of rationality . . . takes the tensional reality of subject and object in knowing as a relational unity that precedes the description of either side. We may think, for example, of Martin Buber's comment that it is in the "between" that spans subjectivity and objectivity that truth is found. By framing the situation in this way, this structure of rationality can recognize the contextual, provisional nature of the "subjective" side of knowledge, but simultaneously affirm the real (or true) existence of the "objective" side of knowledge. It is *out of* the relationality itself, out of the tensional unity of subject and object in the knowing event, that rational judgments are constructed. (p. 31)

With relationships being such an important component of this research, at a cross-cultural level, the epistemic encounter we might have with an object is seen to involve the full connectedness of that object: with the knower, with other knowers, with the rest of the created order and with an acknowledged Creator. Cross-culturally, the ontological source, or perceived Creator, in this sense refers to an individual's or to a culture's perceptions of origins of being. The philosopher Herman Dooyeweerd (1960) referred to the idea of an *absolute origin* that would be held by individuals and cultures. This may represent, for example, the Hindu pantheon of gods, the God of the Abrahamic faiths, natural laws or Darwinian evolutionism, or, pertinent to this research, deities such as the Andean *Wirracocha* and his attendant *Inti* and *Pachamama*. This perspective is of particular importance for this research if links are to be discovered between the ranking of the avoidance-pursuit pairs and cultural-religious distinctives, as indicated in the literature—particularly by Muller (2006a), Hegeman (2006) and Blaschke (2001). Given this relational epistemology structure, the participants may be seen to make decisions within a network of relationships that includes the object of the decision, others and other cultures, their recognised perception of an ontological source and the pertinent components of the physical environment. This provides a link between the decisions that are made, the relationship structures of the participants, and their worldviews: all features of the research question being explored.

Added to the observation and inter-relationship of externals, this framework also recognises Herman Dooyeweerd's considered importance of the thinker in the thought process (Hart, 1985; Hayward, 2005) and an attempt to overcome the "traditional dualisms between thinker and agent . . ." (Denzin & Lincoln, 2005, p. 152). The researcher had some form of relationship with each participant, with others within the culture, perhaps with the lifeworld of the participant, and with other objects that inhabit the participant's lifeworld; however, the researcher may or may not have the same perceived ontological source as a particular participant.

With specific reference to the type of knowledge that may be typical of "indigenous" thinking, such as that of the participants in this research from the *campo*, Battiste and Henderson (2000) draw attention to the importance for them of the connections between the ontological sources and the physical environment:

> Perhaps the closest one can get to describing unity in Indigenous knowledge is that knowledge is the expression of the vibrant relationships between people, their ecosystems, and the other living beings and spirits that share their lands .
> . . . All aspects of this knowledge are interrelated and cannot be separated from the traditional territories of the people concerned. Similarly, there is no need to separate reality into categories of living and nonliving, or renewable and nonrenewable. (p. 42).

A further perspective on the relatedness of knowledge that is pertinent to this research is that while in English the verb "to know" is used to signify a variety of knowings—such as of a perception, awareness of, cognisance, memorization, understanding or acquaintance with—in Spanish, as in other languages such as French, there is a distinction drawn between the two primary verbs used for 'to know'.

The Spanish *saber* (and the French counterpart, *savoir*) signifies to know a fact; whereas *conocer* (French *connaître*) signifies personal knowledge or of something that is known well—for example, to *know* someone, or to *know* the street where I have lived for some time. At this simple level, then, the use of participants' vocabulary in the responses in this research indicates not only what datum is known but also the type and depth of the knowledge: an indication of denoted knowledge and connoted knowledge. The researcher's relationship with the participants thus added depth to the research: "Friendships may bias data collection; but they may also contribute an even more potent voice, that gained through rapport" (Glesne, 1989 quoted in Schram, 2006, p. 139).

A second linguistic phenomenon that supports the use of a relational epistemology is the use of the personal form of the pronoun *you* as found in Spanish (and French as well as other languages) but not in English. In general terms, Spanish, particularly that spoken around Cochabamba, differentiates between *you* used in different relational contexts—both in the use of the personal pronoun and in the associated verb form used. If the person to whom one is speaking is unknown, not well known, or in a formal or fictive relationship, then the formal pronoun *usted* is used, but if the person is well known, then *tu* is used, along with the appropriate verb forms. *Tu* is always used within a family context, and *usted* is used when speaking to someone of perceived higher social rank, while *tu* may be used when speaking with someone of perceived lower rank. In formal contexts, such as formal meetings, the formal *usted* is used even though outside the meeting *tu* may be used.

These language differences concern at least a weak form of the Sapir-Whorf hypothesis[9] regarding the interrelationship of language and thought, and thence culture. Cobern (1995) explained this concept in the following way:

> Language and thought are closely related. As stated in the Sapir-Whorf hypothesis, "habitual modes of thought of a group are functionally related to the structure of the language of the group" (Morrill, 1975, p. xx). In other words, how one thinks is related to the language in which one thinks; thus, how one thinks must also be related to language literacy. If a person studies a second language, particularly if the second language is of a totally different linguistic origin (e.g., English and Japanese), becoming literate in that second language also means coming to understand a different view of the world (though it does not necessarily mean adopting a different worldview). (pp. 5–6)

---

[9] While the Sapir-Whorf hypothesis has come under considerable criticism, in recent years experimental psychologists have found evidence that would seem to support it (Meteyard, Bahrami & Vigliocco (2007); Bedny, Caramazza, Grossman, Pascual-Leone, & Saxe (2008); Lupyan (2008a); Lupyan (2008b)).

The participants in this research live mostly in non-English environments, and many speak more than one language, so there exist Whorfian complexities (Cobern, 1995) due to the combination of languages and cultures that are being navigated: English, Spanish and Quechua. A few of those participating in this research were purely monolingual. The researcher and some of the participants speak English and Spanish; other participants speak Spanish and Quechua.[10] Several participants would claim to speak only Spanish but would have some Quechua vocabulary, such as greetings and the names of market goods. Translation between the three languages, therefore, becomes problematic. This is particularly the case for the Quechua participants who would think in Quechua and speak in Spanish, with their comments being translated by the researcher into English.

Further, the conversation within a collectivist cultural context is also to be considered. The interpretation of the interview data from Bolivia, given by members of cultures that are primarily collectivist, such as Latin American cultures (House et al., 2004), must reflect the collective nature of their cultures. According to Gadamer, a hermeneutical event is part of a *sensus communis* rather than occurring in subjective isolation (Triplett, 2002), being determined by the language and values of a particular community and acquired by being part of that particular culture (Thiselton, 1992). It is important, therefore, to recognise that within the cultural and linguistic milieu already mentioned, the process of understanding is a "conversation" and "participants in a conversation 'belong' to and with each other, 'belong' to and with the subject of their communication" (Weinsheimer & Marshall, 1998, p. xvi). This is pertinent as the interviewer-interviewee setting provides a conversational context for understanding the participant's belonging relationship to their community and also the connection to the decisions he or she makes.

A final need for the use of a relational epistemology framework is that animistic peoples, like those inhabiting the Andes regions, have a holistic view of the universe and a relational epistemology (Bird-David, 1999). The holism derives from the tendency of some cultures to see "dividuals" (human beings connected or related to everything else) as opposed to the Western concept of "individuals" (Sabine, 2006; Munro, 2005; Snyder, 2002; Strathern, 1988). Experience in the culture suggests that these people see the connectedness of all things in a much more natural way than Westerners can.

---

[10] Spanish, as a Mediterranean langauge with a Latin base, has many similarities to English. Quechua and Aymara a distinct languages that have no linguistic connection to each other or to Spanish or English apart from a limited vocabulary of terms that have been borrowed from the other languages.

That said, this relational framework functions within a range of contexts, as has been mentioned, and one context that is of particular importance within a country such as Bolivia, which has had such a troubled past, is the political context.

The Bolivian political context

The leadership of such a culturally diverse nation has not been without considerable difficulty, especially when each sub-cultural group has its own leadership model that has evolved over millennia. As with so many Latin American countries, the political turmoil that has been such a noteworthy feature of Bolivia has had a very significant influence on the leadership styles that have developed and also that have been required at times. Simón Bolívar, the soldier-statesman who "liberated" seven of the Latin American countries from Spanish rule nearly two centuries ago, wrote a month before his death:

> First, for us America is ungovernable; second, he who serves a revolution ploughs the sea; third, the only thing one can do in America is emigrate; fourth, this land will inevitably fall into the hands of the unbridled masses, to pass later to petty, almost indiscernible tyrants of all colours and races; fifth, devoured by all kinds of crimes and consumed by the ferocity as we are, Europeans will not deign to conquer us; sixth, if it were possible for a part of the world to return to primeval chaos, America would do it. (Bolívar, 2003, p. 146)

Bolívar's expression of dismay as he looked back on his time as a leader in Latin America, and Bolivia's first president, was still within a context of feudalism. During most of the last century, Bolivia was led by governments or military juntas that ruled by either strong right or left-wing persuasions. The fear of one side of the other has been a significant part of the Bolivian psyche. Within these contexts, therefore, the study of leadership, leader-follower relationships and what Evers and Lakomski (1995) referred to as the normative decision-making processes of leaders may have about it a very different flavour from that found within a Western context.

The historical and political frameworks within which Bolivia has existed have meant that there has been both much abuse by leaders and also times when near anarchy has prevailed. This has also affected the way people see the role of leadership. A study by Gamarra (2003), for example, found that almost one quarter of Bolivians said that the country requires "hard line" leaders who would preserve law and order. In recent times, one can see in the constant, often violent, demonstrations and in the overthrowing of presidents, that many groups of citizens see their democratic right as being the ability to enforce their own desires through populist dissent.

For much of the country's history, military dictators enforced their rule, often as brutal as their neighbours in Chile, Argentina and Paraguay, or perhaps more so. The left-wing governments traditionally received backing from Cuba and Russia, while attempts were made by the USA to maintain right-wing governments, even, according to Joseph November (2000), to the insertion by the FBI of the Nazi war criminal Klaus Barbie as a member of the Bolivian Secret Police. These extremes in the political leadership of the country have led to a deep distrust and even fear of those in power or leadership. This appears to have encouraged the mass movements against governments or against government decisions, where hundreds of thousands flock to the federal and state capitals to demand change, often rioting, even though at times some may be killed in the process—for example, in the "Water Wars" of 2000 (Olivera & Lewis, 2004). These demonstrations are so frequent within the country that they rarely receive attention from the foreign press.

At a local level, institutional or political leadership has tended to follow the models developed in the traditional rural communities in the *campo*, the bureaucratic and hierarchical models imported from the Spanish bureaucracy and the Spanish Catholic Church, or models recently imported from outside the country. Increasingly, images of other possible leadership models are becoming available via the media.

Modernisation and globalisation contexts

Bolivia, particularly urban Bolivia, has been affected increasingly by the modernising forces of the Western, developed world. A vast array of imported goods may be procured now in supermarkets and other outlets in the country. While these goods are beyond the economic reach of much of the population, their presence is evident in the shop windows and in the growing proportion of late-model cars and trucks on the country's roads.

The greatest effect, however, is probably to be seen in the proliferation of Western media products such as movies and television programs. Some of these are shown in English, some in English with sub-titles and some with dubbed Spanish. Theatres and home television sets have introduced a visual world beyond the reality of the lifeworlds of Bolivians. Many of the very poorest, including those in rural areas where there is a television reception, have been affected by this media. This has been at least partly responsible for the paradoxical situation where foreign goods have become desirable and foreign fashions sought after, but at the same time, there still exists, particularly amongst those supporting revolution, a suspicion, resentment, or even hatred for the foreign powers that produce the media content (Manos Fuera de Venezuela, 2008).

Educational leadership context

Schools, having a role in the formation of young people, including their beliefs and culture, must contend also with this changing background of globalising influences on students. This context, as well as the others, influences teachers and educational leaders. Of the different leadership settings in this research, the largest group of leaders interviewed were school principals with responsibility for the effective functioning of educational institutions. Bolivia's economic problems and political instability have hampered education development. Education in Bolivia has been influenced historically largely by European models, commencing with the Spaniards and education systems initiated by the Catholic Church following the conquest, and later by French and other European models that prevailed in the public school arena. In more recent times, there has been the introduction of private schools, including evangelical schools governed by independent boards, though necessarily complying with government regulations. The educational leaders, therefore, have contexts involving their country, leadership, education, and educational leadership.

Educational leaders are significant in that they lie at the juxtaposition of institutional bureaucracy and a popular motivation for significant change. The most important influences for change in the thinking of education systems in the past century have come from the continuing influence of the Catholic Church and the strong ideological influence of left-wing and often politicised ideologies. Because many of the educational priorities have been given to literacy amongst the poor and because of the ideologies that dominated the education profession, education has been seen as a grassroots endeavour to foment a class struggle. Perhaps the most outspoken of the advocates of this Latin American class struggle in education, Paulo Freire, illustrated this when he said:

> There is a qualitative difference when the leaders of the working class discover something that is very obvious, that is, that the education that the dominant classes offer to the working classes necessarily is the education that reproduces the working class as such. I don't want to say that *every time* the education that the ruling class offers to the working class reproduces the working class as such. Maybe sometimes education does not get this result, but the *ideological* intention of the ruling class could not be another one. If it was another one, we could no longer understand the contradictions in social life. (Bell, Gavanta & Peters, 1990, pp. 212–213)

Paulson and Tidwell (1990) referred to this as a *correspondence principle* where, for Latin American schools, "schooling corresponds to and reproduces the inequality required by the capitalist state" (p. 714). Education in Bolivia remained so impoverished and entrenched in a class system and almost impenetrable bureaucracy for centuries that it saw little real change until recently. As Healy (1994) wrote at the end of the last century: "For years, Bolivia's presidents have thrown up their hands in despair at the condition of the country's schools, wondering what, if anything, could be done to bring the educational system into the twentieth century" (p. 32).

The integration of effective leadership within these conditions has also been hampered by perceived incompetence and corruption.

> The diverse problems of schools are often attributed to ignorance, incompetence, or malevolence on the part of those responsible for educational governance . . . . As educational systems fail to accomplish worthy goals, or to accord sufficient importance to objectives preferred by influential constituencies, reformers demand changes in the institutions of educational governance, in the hope that new institutions will place braver, wiser, and nobler persons in charge of children's schooling. (Plank & Boyd, 1990, p. 4587)

At the same time, texts on leadership for this new generation of educational leaders contain ideas primarily, and perhaps inappropriately, sourced in the Western world, particularly in the United States.

Toward the end of the last century, a plan to reform the education system was introduced (Ministerio de Educación, 1994). With considerable funding in the form of aid from outside the country. This *Reforma Educativa* [Educational Reform] set out to restructure the entire system, with a devolution of power in decision-making processes, moving the pedagogical model from a rote learning mode to a constructivist paradigm, including parent involvement in the educational process, and the introduction of books in the form of classroom libraries. (Prior to this, in the early 1990s, a principal had told the researcher that his school's library consisted of a dictionary and a Bible, both of which were under lock and key in his office.) The Education Reform Law #1565, which was finally approved on 7th July, 1994, was designed to force schools to leave behind these traditional educational models that had been in vogue for over a century (Contreras & Simoni, 2003).

This led to a move by the government to promulgate an Education Reform Law (*Ministerio de Educación*, 1994) which stated that education was the highest function of the state (though teachers have been always poorly paid and schools inadequately resourced) and that education should be universal, democratic, multicultural, revolutionary, coeducational, progressive, scientific, promote justice, promote the development of the country and democracy and bring the country together (*Ministerio de Educación*, 1994).

More recently, with the reform process having moved through most levels of the schooling system, the present government has moved to "*decolonizar*" [decolonise] schooling, or move schooling further away from its Spanish conquest roots (*Los Tiempos*, 2006). At the same time, due to the impact of the media and the interchange of people studying in other countries, the effects of globalisation are also being felt also on the leadership of schools (Cano Tiznado, 2001) as school leaders, particularly of private schools, endeavour to gain advantage for their schools for economic and prestige reasons.

Leaders in Bolivia's schools, however, have been developed through years of classroom practice within a different regime from that currently in place. They find themselves managing schools where the teachers exhibit behaviour patterns similar to those in other contexts on the continent. Montero-Sieburth (1992) wrote of a qualitative study by Avalos in Colombia, Venezuela and Bolivia, in which they described teachers as acting as benevolent dictators who had poor expectations of students' abilities. These expectations appeared to relate to the socio-economic status of the students. Lessons typically involved rote learning and copying, with students being given poor-quality feedback. In this context, "Teachers often suspect innovation out of fear that change will involve greater demands on their time, more content preparation, and strict evaluations" (p. 185).

The education system, however, continues to be plagued by challenges such as the low salaries paid to educators, and with the consequence that teachers known to the researcher find that they must teach effectively, at least two full days each school day through the use of morning, afternoon and evening shifts, in order to survive financially. Corruption also seems to be endemic and strikes that may last weeks or months have not been uncommon, although they are becoming less frequent.

At the same time, the schools in Bolivia express a great deal of pride through their school uniforms, bands, the way the teachers dress, and the way the students and teachers march in the many civic parades. In addition, there is a strong desire on the part of the Department of Education officers and many school principals to be seen to be following current international trends in education and leadership practices. This applies not only to government schools but also to private schools, including the growing number of evangelical schools.

Bolivian evangelical schools

As several of the school principal participants in this research were responsible for evangelical, independent schools, some explanation is given here of their context. While government schools function under the direct authority of the Department of Education, the private, evangelical schools have intermediary governance structures. The particular schools from which the principals in this research were drawn fall into four general categories. First, there are the schools that historically have belonged to particular evangelical denominations or churches. These schools are governed by school boards selected, or elected, by their particular church from those with an interest in education. The second group includes schools that are interdenominational, having been formed by a group of churches. These first two classes of schools often have, or have had, the support of foreign missionary agencies. This support has diminished over the years so that, for the most part, these schools are mostly now independent of foreign financial or administrative support. Another type of private school found in Bolivia is one that has been started and managed by private individuals. These schools are usually run with a profit motive, but the motives may be broader and include schools run by individuals who also see the school as a spiritual ministry or as community aid.

Yet another type of school is the *convenio* [agreement] school. These schools are government schools that are managed by churches or foreign missionary groups. The government places teachers in these schools—often with input from the school administration—and pays wages and basic infrastructure costs while the group with which the government has the *convenio* appoints the administrative staff, oversees the administration and provides funding for the modernisation and improvement of facilities and equipment.

The schools in Bolivia, following international leads, are required by law to adhere to government education policy as proclaimed by a national Ministry of Education and a local (state) level Department of Education. The private schools are also governed by their own school board. Within the school, the Principal of a private school often acts as a CEO and in country schools, may be a professional from outside education. The Principal relates as a leader to Deputy Principals, Heads of Department, teaching and ancillary staff, as well as to the students and the parent community.

While the schools established to cater for the evangelical community in Bolivia would, generally, endeavour to train the students to have an evangelical worldview, the Catholic schools were established, naturally, to train students in a Catholic worldview for their community. This is contrasted with the position of the government, which not only controls state schools but also controls the curriculum in independent schools. The government will also use education in order to infuse the next generation of Bolivian citizens with its particular worldview in order to ensure that the particular value system to which the government adheres will be perpetuated (Luykx, 1999). There are, therefore, two worldview systems being promoted in these independent, evangelical and Catholic schools—each with its own set of values and applied morality that reside within the Bolivian systems of values and ethics.

Bolivian values and ethics contexts

The making of decisions by leaders requires a valuation of alternatives according to a culturally and individually determined system of values. Biggert and Hamilton (1987) commented that in order to have effective management, an understanding of one's own core values as well as those of society was important. A fuller discussion of values and ethics is undertaken in the next chapter, but there are two contextual issues relating to values and culture that may be mentioned here: *machismo* and corruption. To one degree or another, these issues may have a direct effect on many of the decisions that leaders make within the Bolivian culture.

i. Machismo

Many of the informants in this research are women in leadership positions. As such, they have to contend with social constructions such as *machismo*. *Machismo* is often associated with Latin masculinity and may play a part in the decision-making processes of leaders where decisions regarding the treatment of the opposite sex are considered. While the myth of authoritarian, swaggering, Latin masculinity is common around the world, including in Latin American countries, the reality is that the relationship between the sexes is rather more complex than this model would imply. It is true, however, that apart from the widespread physical abuse of women, other forms of male domination are to be seen in the subcultures. For example, women in poorer sectors of society are often left to carry heavy loads while their partners walk ahead of them. In many sub-sectors of society, there is also an expected infidelity and sexual permissiveness afforded to men. This may be seen in practices in the city of Cochabamba, such as *el viernes del Soltero,* where married men declare themselves to be single on Friday evenings (Lavaud, 1998).

A study by Torres, Solberg and Carlson (2002) found, however, that the authoritarian, emotionally restrictive and controlling *machismo* model was representative of only around ten per cent of Latin men. In fact, in the experience of the researcher, as illustrated in the list of participants in this research, many women take leadership in businesses, education and politics. But while many men in Bolivian culture do take a domineering role, at times perhaps physically and verbally abusing their families, it is the women who are often the strength of the family and who control the finances. Interestingly, there is a common saying in Bolivia that "mothers make *machismo*" because while being abused by their husbands or partners, they dote on their sons, spoiling them in such a way that they will replicate the excesses of their fathers.

ii. Corruption

Any consideration of the decision-making of leaders in Bolivia inevitably encounters questions of corruption and morality. At the time of the research, according to Transparency International (2009), the level of corruption in Bolivia, as perceived by Bolivians, placed the country in 102nd position out of 180 countries. This was quite an improvement from the 2004 figures of 122 out of 145 (Transparency International, 2004). [2018 figures place Bolivia at 132/180.] As with many developing countries, corruption is endemic and plays an important role in the decision-making processes in the country. While being corrupt is seen generally to be wrong, it is also seen as something that is inevitable in society.

Experience with individuals and organisations in Bolivia has led the researcher to identify three types of corruption that are commonly available to institutional leaders: nepotism, *coima,* and *muñeca.* Nepotism, in a country that places a particularly high value on familial relationships and extended families, is very commonly reported in the press, relating particularly to politics, and particularly local politics. While being condemned as being wrong or not desirable, because it is seen as lacking a sense of fairness, within a collectivist culture where trust outside the in-group is rare or non-existent, the hiring of members of one's in-group is an obvious, logical, and often necessary course of action (Plueddeman, 2009). In business circles, it does appear to be common and would be considered good business practice, and the concept of a family business is strong. Nepotism in education may involve the appointment of relatives to posts in departmental headquarters, and at the school level, it could mean, in private schools, the appointment of relatives as teachers or in other positions.

Coima, or the direct payment of bribes, appears to the researcher to be more common than nepotism and is mentioned more in the popular press. Rumours circulate constantly through the community regarding bribes in government departments and in business. Indeed, it is expected that something will have to be paid to expedite almost every bureaucratic process. In private schools, some public schools and in the universities, especially those with good reputations and restricted enrolments, parents would be willing to pay well for a place for their child.

The attitude of Bolivian institutions to the corrupt officials who insist on being paid extra for their special services varies greatly. From the researcher's experience with NGOs and schools in Bolivia, it appears that many simply pay while others will try to avoid payment on either economic or moral grounds. Corruption of this sort is illegal and railed against in the media, but has almost universal application.

Muñeca is a rather different form of corruption that relies on networks of relationships to guarantee a desired outcome. An example of *muñeca* might be found in circumstances where a school principal may need a particular approval from the local department of education offices. The approval being sought could be for something that is illegal, legal or even an entitlement, but because the bureaucratic wheels turn painfully slowly, the principal may choose to 'jump the queue' by using relationships. In this example, the principal may have a friend who is a friend of someone in a senior position in the department of education, and through this relationship, the favour might be acquired.

CHAPTER 2

Theory from the Literature

This chapter indicates the literature associated with worldview and cultural factors that may influence the prioritisation of avoidance-pursuit pairs and the effect they may have on the ethical decision-making of leaders in different subcultures in Bolivia. The overview of the literature seeks to provide the theoretical structure and setting for the research. In consideration of the research question and the subsidiary questions, the literature was reviewed across the following fields:

- The avoidance-pursuit pairs and their components: Guilt-justice (or innocence), shame-honour and fear-power
- The subcultures of the research setting
- Cultures identified as pertaining to particular prioritisations of the avoidance-pursuit pairs
- Worldviews and values
- Ethical decision-making
- Leadership within the Bolivian contexts

To accomplish this, first, the culturally embedded, affective domain avoidance-pursuit pairs and their components were identified in the literature, as well as research that relates to cultures that have been seen to emphasise a particular pair, along with the importance of relationships and collectivism in some cultures. This work is also linked to the concepts of worldviews and values, and how these are important in the consideration of leadership, particularly leadership as experienced by the participants in the research context. Ethical issues and considerations of what might constitute the "right thing to do" in decision-making are then discussed. Finally, leadership within a

Bolivian context is discussed, including reference to international leadership research by the GLOBE Project (House, Hanges, Javidan, Dorfman & Gupta, 2004) and by Geert Hofstede (2006).

Leaders across all cultures and societies are called upon to make decisions, and this has been researched extensively within a range of contexts. These decisions are made on the basis of ethical frameworks and moral determinations of what is deemed to be the right and proper thing to do within a given situation. The literature suggests that the ethics and morality behind the decision-making process are influenced by the culture that has formed the leader's worldview and that the influence of culture has therefore given rise to the consideration, particularly by anthropologists, of forms of culturally relative ethics, and in this case, descriptive relativistic ethics (Sower, 2003).

The culturally imbued, affective domain avoidance-pursuit pairs

During the twentieth century, particularly the last half of the century, a number of anthropologists, sociologists and missiologists encountered a phenomenon that in this research is referred to as culturally imbued, affective domain avoidance-pursuit pairs. These are believed to be related to the distinctives of cultures and appear to be deeply embedded in the worldviews of all individuals (Muller, 2006a). One part of the avoidance-pursuit pair phenomenon was studied initially by Ruth Benedict (1946), who observed post-World War II Japanese culture in order to locate the cultural source of the significant differences that existed between the Japanese and North Americans. In his foreword to the Mariner Books Edition of Benedict's main work on the subject in 1946, Ian Buruma said:

> Perhaps nothing in *The Chrysanthemum and the Sword* attracted more interest than Benedict's discussion of shame and guilt. She was intrigued by the fact that the Japanese were extremely sensitive to others' opinions and less concerned with internalised, standardized rules about right and wrong. Dozens of scholarly articles, stimulated by her questions, defined and redefined the relationship between Japanese guilt and shame. (p. xi)

Later in the century, others, principally missiologists, added more culturally imbued avoidance-pursuit pairs to Benedict's shame and honour pair, noting in particular the importance of fear and power in animistic cultures in West Africa (Blaschke, 2002; Hegeman, 2006; Muller, 2006a) and of guilt and innocence within many Western cultures (Muller, 2006). A fourth dimension was proposed by Hegeman (2006) as gaining importance in the increasingly Epicurean Western cultures: that of emotional pain and pleasure.

Defining the avoidance-pursuit pairs

Despite the work of the last century, defining and locating these avoidance-pursuit pairs within cultural and worldview frameworks seems to remain a difficult task. DeSilva (1999) defined honour and shame as social values. Hegeman (2006) defined his four avoidance-pursuit pairs as "axes" and used the terms "four axes of cultural values" or values axes, labelling them as "values of highest pursuit" (Hegeman, 2006, p. 1). Muller (2006a) preferred to use the term *cultural dimensions,* though his conceptualisation of their valuation was similar to that used by Hegeman (2006). For the purposes of this research, the avoidance-pursuit pairs will be defined as culturally imbued, affective avoidance-pursuit pairs. This definition places them within individual worldviews, being derived from the commonable core of cultural value and belief systems.[11] Each avoidance-pursuit pair implies aspirational and affective components: desire and distaste for the distinct poles that work with volition to influence decision-making and consequent actions. These pairs are seen in the literature to be given different values in different cultures (Muller, 2006a).

Within the definitions of the avoidance-pursuit pairs also lies the concept of duality, and therefore they may appear to be related in some ways to a structuralist concept of binary opposites (Fogarty, 2005). For example, they satisfactorily fall within our human (or at least Western) desire to think in terms of opposites, they are shared culturally, they create meaning, each pole helps to define its opposite, and one side is seen as being more desirable than the other. On the other hand, however, these particular opposites do not appear to be only Western constructions (apparently being common to at least most cultures), and the majority of cultures would, presumably, see the negative poles as being very undesirable and the positive poles as desirable. The exploration of the valuation and operation of the entities is not generated out of any desire to find a central position. In each case, one pole describes a condition to be eagerly sought and one to be abhorred.

We might note that Dodd (1997) proposed a different set of pairs that represented cultures:

> shame based <====> guilt based
>
> task oriented <===> people oriented
>
> secular oriented <===> spiritual oriented
>
> doing based <===> being based

While these may describe orientations and important distinctions between cultures, they differ from the avoidance-pursuit pairs discussed in this research in that only the

---

[11] The term, commonable core, is used here to represent those values and beliefs that are held in common by community members and to which all have access.

first of Dodd's (1997) dimensions relates to the affective domain. In this research, apart from what Dodds refers to as shame-based and guilt-based cultural differences, the third fear-based avoidance-pursuit pair is also considered.

The nature of the avoidance-pursuit pairs

The pairs appear to be given valuations both personally and culturally in two directions: there is a preference between the two poles of each axis, and there is a preference for one axis over the others. The pair that has the highest value for a culture or for an individual, either in general or at a specific moment in time, Hegeman (2006b) refers to as being a "value of highest pursuit" (para. 2) and will play a significant role in the framing of moral action and the direction of the decision-making process. This conceptualisation recognises that all three of the avoidance-pursuit pairs are present in every person's worldview and presumably in all cultures, but different cultures will prioritise them differently. The unconscious action of choosing the priority order of the avoidance-pursuit pairs will vary not only from one culture to another but may also vary from one person to another as "values are established by judgements—by judging things, qualities, events or actions from a personal point of view" (Roubiczek, 1969, p. 219). Because the avoidance-pursuit pairs are embedded in worldviews through cultures, their operation may often not be observed by the individual. As with the Baatonu studied by Hegeman (2006a), "their own assumed wider values seem 'normal,' that is, culturally correct, orthodox, reasonable, right and wise" (p. 3).

Muller (2006a) saw the pairs as "planes on which worldview function" (p. 69), rather than within worldviews, and claimed that the avoidance of emotional pain and the seeking of pleasure was a pair that was equally distributed across all cultures (Muller, 2006b). Hegeman (2006a) used an example from his research in West Africa to justify his inclusion of the fourth pair, saying that in his research, the expatriate community in Benin did not appear to adhere to the three primary axes. Instead, "It would appear that the highest values pursued by streams of visiting and working Westerners is to live supremely for adventure, for pleasure, for exotic satisfaction, for self-consumption and then chiefly for themselves" (p. 6). This research, within Bolivian contexts, does not include an examination of European or Western worldviews, and therefore, it was felt that the fourth pair could be disregarded, though further research with participants from postmodern Western cultures may give important insights into this area.

It must be stated, however, that rather than one avoidance-pursuit pair dominating all of a culture and defining it, Hegeman (2006a) presented the avoidance-pursuit pairs as being flexible and changeable, operating in varying degrees in all human beings but in each case in a primary to quaternary ranking. These valuations also operate collectively and vary within families, communities and cultural or ethno-political groups.

As this research relied heavily on a model proposed by Hegeman (2006a), it was important that consideration be given to the qualifications Hegeman added to the explication of his model, saying that the axes (pairs) co-exist in all societies to some extent but that one axis (pair) will stand out above the others. He stated that "the four axes of values of highest pursuit are therefore integral to all worldviews in which one axis is the primary leader" (p. 7).

Hegeman (2006a) felt that the personal or cultural sub-valuations were a useful tool for the analysis of the orientations of individuals to the principal ethics framework of their culture.

> Values of highest pursuit differ significantly among them because within each person, all four value tracks are ranked in their unique way in ordering their pursuits. There are primary, secondary, tertiary and quaternary value pursuits in each person, and this order varies richly in each person. This flexibility allows for remarkable diversity, and indeed, if glory and honour are placed first, then six variants alone are possible, and 18 more when all possibilities are conjugated. (p. 12)

While Benedict's (1946) designation of cultures as being shame-based or guilt-based has been used for much of last century and "many experts, though not all, find it helpful to think of societies as either guilt based or shame based" (Elmer, 2002, p. 171), as Hegeman (2006a) has indicated, it may be an unhelpful distinction. Of course, it would be expected that cultures sensitive to the concept of shame would react negatively to the suggestion that they were in some way inferior because of a "shame" orientation. The avoidance-pursuit pairs, however, are bipolar and as such each has a second pole. It may therefore be preferable to refer to the cultural differences by their aspiration to justice, honour, power or pleasure (Hegeman, 2006a).

Any research involving ethics, worldviews and cultural distinctions must consider the importance of the researchers' own cultural preferences that may blind or blinker them from seeing all perspectives. Regarding Ruth Benedict's own research, Laniak (1998) commented that: "Many Japanese scholars of Japanese society hotly disagreed with her [Benedict's] cultural categorisations. She had overlooked the presence of guilt in the East. She had also underestimated and undervalued the category of shame in the West" (p. 25). Muller (2006a) added to this argument by speaking of the effect on Western researchers of the orientation of their cultures to the guilt-innocence "axis" or pair. He claimed, in particular, that this pair dominates our Western cultures. He argued that our culture, or cultures, see things in terms of "the good guys vs. the bad guys" (p. 152) and that this is so familiar to us that it is not questioned and we have difficulty even imaging a world where right versus wrong is not an accepted principle underlying our actions.

Western cultures and guilt and innocence

Several reasons are given by Muller (2006a) for the ascendancy of this avoidance-pursuit pair in Western culture, leading to an effect on both the researcher and the participants in this research. First, Muller (2006a) believes, there are sources of thinking and legal principles that have dominated a number of cultures, particularly Western ones. These sources were the *Ius romana,* Roman law, the Greek concepts of *Νόμος* (law) and the Platonic concept of an ordered republic. From these Greco-Roman cultures, there arose a way of thinking about things as being "right" and "wrong" as determined by written laws that are universal within the culture or nation. Added to these would be the Jewish Torah, particularly the Decalogue and the Levitical and Deuteronomic codes, as throughout Christendom they have affected Western cultures significantly. It may be presumed that these will have had an effect in the Latin American and Bolivian cultures through the early influence of the Roman Empire in Spain and later through the Roman Catholic Church, given the high proportion of Roman Catholics in the country (94% in 1965, according to Wilde (2007)).

> From an ancient Roman perspective, in On the Laws Book 2.4, Cicero said: Therefore, they called that aboriginal and supreme law the mind of God, enjoining or forbidding each separate thing in accordance with reason. On which account it is that this law, which the gods have bestowed upon the human race, is so justly applauded. (Thatcher, 1907, p. 216)

This link between the law and the divine might be thought to be significant in cultures such as the Bolivian ones that have deep spiritual roots and have been strongly influenced over millennia by the teachings of Christendom. Christendom has also been affected by the Jewish Law, such as that recorded in the book of Deuteronomy as having been given directly by God:

> 27:1 Moses and the elders of Israel commanded the people: "Keep all these commands that I give you today. 2 When you have crossed the Jordan into the land the Lord your God is giving you, set up some large stones and coat them with plaster. 3 Write on them all the words of this law when you have crossed over to enter the land the Lord your God is giving you, a land flowing with milk and honey, just as the Lord, the God of your fathers, promised you. (Bible: New International Version, 1978)

Muller (2006a) has pointed to the influence of a number of Christian theologians and church leaders whose background had been strongly influenced by the law as perceived by the Romans, Greeks and Jews: from St Paul to Calvin. Muller (2006a) differentiated between the Western and Eastern influences of the Church, claiming that Eastern theologians such as Irenaeus, Origen, Athenasius, Ephraim of Syria and Chrysostom appeared to have operated from a different avoidance-pursuit pair—giving much less emphasis, for example, to the sin-justification (guilt-innocence pair) messages of the Western theologians. An extension of this line of thought is seen in non-Western cultures in the connection of honour-led cultures of Arab extraction and other Asian cultures, including the Japanese culture (DeSilva, 1999; Muller, 2000). This distinction has been credited by Muller as having made a significant contribution to the struggle Islamic cultures have as they try to relate to the justice-oriented cultures of the West. Because of the centuries of Middle Eastern influence of the Moors in Spain, this perhaps also has affected Bolivian culture through the Spanish conquest as there are many similarities between relationship structures, collectivism and an emphasis on shame and honour.

To help understand these cultural distinctions, we may examine the distinctions between guilt and shame. McElwain and Korabik (2005) observed that feelings of remorse are felt when individuals have done wrong, or imagine they have, and believe they should have acted differently based on internally held standards. Guilt, the noted, relates to specific behaviours, whereas shame refers to "negative evaluations an individual makes about her entire self" (para. 4). These moral dimensions of feelings of guilt and shame, or disgrace (deSilva, 1999) have fairly obvious links with religious beliefs. In order to understand this connection to religion, in general and with possible application to the research in Bolivia, one can examine the connections drawn in other cultures. Muller (2000) noted the link in his work in West Africa and the Middle East and also quoted a 1999 article in the Jordan Times, which said in part:

> Guilt culture is due largely to Christianity. A shame culture is one in which individuals are kept from transgressing the social order by fear of public disgrace. On the other hand, in a guilt culture, one's own moral attitudes and fear of retribution in the distant future are what enforce the ethical behaviour of a member of that society. (pp. 161–162)

In terms of Islamic worldviews that are aligned to the shame-honour avoidance-pursuit pair, Muller (2006b) further commented in a personal email (19th April, 2006):

> Islam emerged from an almost exclusive shame/honour worldview, and is going through inner turmoil as it tries to adapt itself, or accommodate itself to the west. So far guilt/innocence based cultures in the west and Islam seem to have mostly clashed with Islam or ignored it. Thus, people struggling with honour/shame issues often find meaning in Islam. Anyone struggling with a guilt issue will find little in Islam, other than denial. (para. 2)

The implication that may be drawn from these observations is that every individual wishing to examine aspects of a culture with a different avoidance-pursuit pair priority order, for example, Westerners seeking to understand Bolivian culture, will be confronted with this problem. Any Western researcher endeavouring to understand decisions made by a Bolivian animist based on an ethical framework that is directed by a possible orientation to the fear-power avoidance-pursuit pair must recognise the potential inherent difficulties. It would appear to be problematic for anyone to enter into the logic of an ethic based on a different pair, as has been demonstrated by such incidents as those reported in the international media concerning comments by Pope Benedict XVI regarding the actions of the Prophet Mohammed and the subsequent response of the Islamic community (CNN, 2006). To either party, their words or actions seem to be appropriate and yet the comments on the other side of the argument appear to make no sense whatsoever. In this case, it seems to be because the Islamic culture in question holds a worldview that values honour and eschews shame.

A note regarding guilt and the law under colonial governments

While guilt and religion are strongly connected within many cultures, guilt is also obviously connected to law. Under colonial governments, such as those in Bolivia for most of the past five hundred years, these laws may be imposed, perhaps even brutally, but they do not have their origins within the cultural and historical framework of the *originario* [original, indigenous] people of the country, such as the Quechua and Aymara people. It could be that attitudes to colonial laws may be similar in Bolivia as those seen in Australia and other countries that have been colonised. Of English colonial rule in Australia, Miller (2004) remarked that "Aboriginal lore has largely been replaced by white law" (p 140). Maclean (2009) wrote of the meaning of the Warlpiri word *jukurrpa* being law, but also meaning story or dreaming (in the Aboriginal sense of that word), and Lang and Catzikiris (n.d.) also mention Aboriginal traditional lore as coming from the Dreaming [Aboriginal legends] and guides all aspects of traditional life. The Dreaming stories, Maclean wrote, guided behaviour as well as providing a structure for society and ceremonies. The law, or lore, of the *originario* people is therefore something that is profoundly embedded in their culture and self-definition. The importance of lore in *originario* communities is explained by Dodson (1995):

> This 'lore' was described as a body of codes and prescriptions-usually unwritten—which was a defining criterion for peoples who had not, In the scale of humankind yet attained the status of proper, civilised societies which had law. This notion of Indigenous peoples' 'lore' was another of the colonisers legitimising charters for their denial of our fundamental rights—a denial based on the perceived superiority of Western legal, social, economic and political systems. (para. 5)

The new, foreign laws are to be obeyed (Lang & Catzikiris, n.d.), but they are not "owned" by the people as the traditional lore is, and this may have significant consequences. While law has often been seen within Western contexts as a civilising instrument, Williams (1992) claimed that it "was also the West's most vital and effective instrument of empire during its genocidal conquest and colonisation of the non-Western peoples of the New World, the American Indians" (p. 6). Speaking of indigenous people under British colonisation in Trinidad and Australian Bird and Jindibah (1996) said that "each is, or has been, subjected to criminalisation in numbers significantly disproportionate to the other racial/ethnic groups that constitute(d) their societies" (p. 39). Viewed in this light, it may be expected that the Bolivian people would have a different view of the law and breaking the law because they do not own it as lore. This would be reflected in the importance placed by them on guilt.

Honour and shame cultures

If shame and honour have a significant role in Bolivian culture, then this significance will have its origins in either the indigenous culture of the Incas and, or, their predecessors, or in the Spanish conquest, or both. The determination of honour as an aspirational social value has a long history, as depicted in the earliest stories of the Old Testament and also, in a definitive form, in the writings of the Greeks. Aristotle made reference to the importance of honour and shame for the ancient Greeks in his Nicomachean Ethics (3.7 & 3.8).

The significance of honour from a Latin American, Hispanic, perspective is seen in a comment by Seed (1992) regarding marriage arrangements made in colonial Mexico: "honour is perhaps the most distinctive of all Spanish cultural traits" (p. 61). Seed further developed this thought with the following historical context:

> From the medieval laws known as the *Partidas* through the literature of the Golden Age, the theme was repeatedly sounded that honour was the supreme social virtue. The spell of honour and its ascendancy over the Spanish mirrored in an often-quoted remark by Lope de Vega: "The cases of honour are the best [for the theatre]/ because they move all people powerfully." It was more important than love ("Honour should be preferred to love") and more essential than money . . . . Honour was worth fighting for and dying for: as Cervantes summed up several centuries of tradition, "The man without honour is worse than dead." (pp. 61–62)

The context of this last quote, from Cervantes' (1605) most famous novel, *El ingenioso hidalgo don Quixote de la Mancha* (or more commonly known as Don Quixote) is, "if I have to try to take away your honour, clearly I take your life away because a man without honour is worse that a dead man" (p. 277). Lothario then asks the question of Anselmo, "Do you want to be dishonoured and therefore without life?"

(p. 277).[12] This powerful European sentiment, as Seed explained, arrived in Latin America with the Spanish conquest.

Of course, honour is not restricted to Spanish and Latin American cultures. Within a broader context, honour has been seen to be of primary importance in other cultures as directing the sense of the "correct thing to do" for many. In her study of Japanese culture, Ruth Benedict (1946) acknowledged that the Japanese reacted "as strongly as any Puritan" (p. 222) to the accumulation of private guilt, but that the statements that expressed their reactions to guilt pointed to the importance of shame. Adding to this distinction, Benedict believed that in what she termed guilt cultures, there was the option of confession. In cultures that have shame as a major sanction, to confess something is to bring it out into the open, thus bringing shame. Benedict claimed that this was the reason why, while guilt cultures tended to look for private expiation, shame cultures relied on public good luck ceremonies. According to Benedict, this emphasis on shame rather than guilt did not mean that there is only a concern for public expression: "Shame, they say, is the root of virtue. A man who is sensitive to it will carry out the rules of good behaviour" (p. 224). Shame, therefore, is usually contextualised within the wider community, or collectivity, in which the individual lives.

More recent research by Lieber, Fung and Lueng (2006) concerning shame in Chinese settings found that the shame subscale that emerged in their analysis showed the following features:

> Shame must be understood as an important aspect of Chinese people's emotional lives and central to guiding behaviour in many social settings (Fung, 1999; Fung et al., 2003). A functional sense of shame motivates displays of appropriate behaviour and expression, alerts the individual to social cues that dictate behaviour parameters, and serves as a moral base on which behaviour and expression can be evaluated. (p. 144)

It is this motivation that determines the culture-linked decision-making considered in this research, and that may be found in contexts other than Asia. As Chambers (1999) noted, within the society in Arequipa, a city in neighbouring Peru with a similar historical and pluri-cultural background to those found in Cochabamba, "the dominant idea was honour" (p. 160). The social aspect of honour and shame points particularly

---

[12] An interesting example of the importance of honour in some cultures could be seen during the North American invasion of Iraq in 2003. As the North American "shock and awe" campaign surged across Iraq and neared Baghdad, Mohammed Said al-Sahhaf, the Iraqi Information Minister, was seen on television informing the world that "Iraq will not be defeated, Iraq has now already achieved victory—apart from some technicalities" (Weissberg, 2004, p. 173). His comments were ridiculed in the Western media as being blatant lies and the West could not understand why he should have made such outrageous comments. Sahhaf, however, was from a shame-honour culture where saving face was an imperative (Muller, 2006) and he was later quoted as saying, "I did my duty to the last minute" (Hammond, 2003, para. 14).

to cultures that have been identified as collectivist. These include many cultures in Asian as well as Latin American and Mediterranean countries that have been described as being collectivist and distinctions are made between collectivist and individualist western cultures in many studies including those by House et al. (2004), Hofstede (1984) and Triandis (1988). The cultures identified as being collectivist in these studies include those noted by Muller (2000), Hegeman (2004) and Blaschke (2001) as well as Latin American countries, including Bolivia.

Face and honour in collectivist cultures

The first issue here is the definition of collectivism as it applies in Bolivia. According to House et al. (2004), the Bolivian setting for this research lies within a culture that is primarily collectivist. Schwartz (2006), comparing different cultures, noted the collectivism in Latin America, particularly with reference to Bolivia and Peru, which had been least exposed to European culture. Schwartz explained the concept of collectivism in terms of group embeddedness and contrasted it with individualistic cultures that practised individualistic autonomy. These are important observations in terms of our understanding of the influence of collectivism on the mindsets and worldviews of the participants in this research.

The relational structures provided by this embeddedness give a context for the development and expression of shame by group members. By way of a cultural comparison, a linked concept in other collectivist cultures, and one that has been spoken of many times in relation to Oriental cultures, is that of saving or losing "face." Within these cultures, face is often seen as being gained or maintained on the basis of status within a group. As in Bolivia, it is the relationships with other individuals and with the group that are important, and the concept of face for an individual without reference to others is meaningless. As with the Western conceptualisation of shame, face depends on the perspectives and reactions of other persons who are, for some reason, significant to the individual. Yau-Fai Ho (1976) commented on this characteristic of cultures that emphasises its relationship to family, community or society:

> While it is not a necessity for one to strive to gain face, losing face is a serious matter which will, in varying degrees, affect one's ability to function effectively in society. Face is lost when the individual, either through his action or that of people closely related to him, fails to meet essential requirements placed upon him by virtue of the social position he occupies. (p. 867)

Within Chinese communities, the network of relationships (*guanxi*) and the dependent deontological morality rely significantly on the feelings (*ganqing*)—the affective domain—of the individuals within the culture (Gold, Guthrie, & Wank, 2002). Gold, Guthrie and Wank quoted the Chinese scholar Liang Shuming as claiming that

Chinese society is not individual-based or society-based but relationship-based, or based on the concept of *guanxi*. "The focus is not fixed on any particular individual but on the particular nature of the relations between individuals who interact with each other. The focus is placed upon the relationship" (King, 1985, p. 63). This concept is so strong in Chinese culture and has become embedded in Confucian philosophy (Leung and Wong, 2001, p. 55), so that for its study, the term *guanxi*ology has been coined (Man & Cheng, 1996).

This relationship-based philosophy and praxis implies that individual identity and fulfilment are found within the web of interpersonal relationships (Gold et al., 2002b). According to Gold et al., this contrasts with the Judeo-Christian tradition that derives identity and fulfilment from a direct spiritual relation to God. Chinese culture does not see fulfilment for an individual in isolation but, rather, in the social sphere (King, 1985)— a feature also seen in Bolivian culture. As individuals in Chinese society learn how to treat others through a process of self-cultivation (Gold et al., 2002b), they apply a key concept in Confucianism: "human heartedness" (Mei 1967, p. 328). Buttery and Wong (1999) wrote that *guanxi* is something that is not gained easily or automatically; it is something that takes deliberate action on the part of all culture members, and the relationship development process is one that takes a great deal of time. It is also true, however, that for Bolivia, China and most of the world, the effect of globalisation and modernisation has been felt and Wilson (2002) has claimed that in China *guanxi* has been "significantly recast in recent years in that it has become increasingly imbued with a commercial quality" (p. 163) and that integration into regional economies has extended the distances over which relationships now function.

Yau-fai Ho (1976) mentioned in relation to "face behaviour", which he believed to be universal (and not merely restricted to Asian cultures) and an important construct for study in the social sciences, that saving and losing face affect a community member's ability to function within the community. Benedict (1946) had written that in a culture where shame was used as a sanction, shame was a reaction to other people's criticism and that, simply, if the issue were not brought to public light, then all would be considered to be well. Alford (1999), however, argued that the distinctions between shame and guilt cultures were more complex than implied by Benedict and others. In particular, Alford referred to the Confucianist Korean collectivist culture and the expressions of shame within that culture compared with the issue of guilt in Western, individualist cultures. The differences between guilt and shame within any one culture appear to become less distinct when examined closely, and not all collectivist cultures function in this regard in the same way.

Contrasting collectivist cultures

All this having been said regarding shame and honour in Asian contexts, it should be noted that while many researchers aggregate the various cultures that are based on collectivity, others point to significant distinctions that can be made between distinct forms of collectivism. Uskul, Oyserman and Schwarz (2009), for example, distinguished between the Confucian collectivism of China that Markus and Kitayama (1991) had referred to as being focused on "harmony-modesty, fitting in, not sticking out, and not bragging" (Uskul, Oyserman, & Schwarz, 2009, p. 4) and the honour-based collectivism found in the Mediterranean region, Latin America, Africa and the Middle East. For the latter cultures, they concluded, however, that

> Within a culture of honour, the central collective dimension is maintaining a good reputation—both within the group and with regard to relationships with outgroups. Like Confucian-based cultures of modesty, cultures of honour are collective—groups and group membership matter and reputation is both gained and lost not only through one's own actions, but also through the actions of others with whom one is closely associated (typically kin but also other social groupings). Because cultures of honour are collective in focus, it is likely that at least some of the literature on cognitive consequences of collectivism is generalizable beyond East Asia. (p. 4)

This is important in this research as most of the literature on this theme relates to an Asian context, so in order to understand the function of shame and honour in Bolivia, one must examine the similarities and differences that exist between the different collectivist cultures regarding this avoidance-pursuit pair and the influence shame and honour may have on the lives of culture members.

Shame and guilt distinctions

Bernard Bass (1990) found there were contrasts in the way Latin American leaders related and functioned compared to their Anglo counterparts. He found, for example, that Hispanics tended to be collectivist, were concerned with relationships and cultural identity, worried about what other members of their community thought, and felt that getting along with others was an important ideal. Ruth Leiland (2001) argued that "cultures with an honour/shame axis tend to be group oriented, whereas cultures with a justice/guilt axis are more individualistic . . . . Belonging to the group includes attachment to, responsibility for one's fellow members" (p. 132). Ruth Benedict (1946) had earlier commented on this perspective by saying: "True shame cultures rely on external sanctions for good behaviour, not, as true guilt cultures do, on an internalised conviction of sin" (p. 223).

Discussing the link between shame and guilt in relation to perceptions of failure of employees, Hareli, Shomrat and Biger (2005) wrote that "shame and guilt are often experienced concomitantly" (p. 666) (also, Sabini & Silver, 1997) but that while there is a global negative evaluation of the self involved in the feeling of shame, "guilt entails a self criticism of one's specific action or behaviour in relation to the questionable outcome" (p. 666). They went on to write:

> Consequently, guilt is more likely than shame to lead to thoughts and actions that are centred on the potential for restoring the situation (Hartz et al., 1995). In addition, guilt is more likely to lead to disclosure of information, while shame will result in its concealment (Velayutham & Perera, 2004). (p. 666)

There are circumstances, however, that produce shame that is not necessarily related to personal guilt. In these cases, the shame is felt even though the person may not actually be guilty of anything. An example of this is seen in the shame experienced by the Serbian people due to the actions of their government (Ramet, 2007).

> Guilt has to do with the breaking of rules. With guilt one has done something wrong, one has violated a rule . . . . Shame, on the other hand, refers rather to a scale morality . . . . Secondly, the concept of shame and the notion of failure are connected with a notion of achieving an ideal, perfection, that is some kind of moral maximum. The concept of guilt and the notion of violation, however, are associated rather with a minimum demand that has not been met. Guilt is tied to fault and blame and both are connected with failing to meet demands that might reasonably be placed on everybody. Shame, in contrast, may arise not through failure to follow general rules, but to do something extraordinary. With shame, our whole moral identity is at stake. (Weijers, 2000, pp. 68–69)

Guilt, then, is a feeling of disapproval of the self in one's own eyes, while shame is the feeling that another, or others, are disapproving (Harris, Wolgrave, & Braithwaite, 2004). This may relate to some "sin" one has committed against the norms of the culture or those in close relationship (the Latin American collectivist context), or in some way falling short of these norms (the Confucian collectivist context): the concept of ἁμάρτημα, or missing the mark, in Greek (Thayer, 2007).

Being relationally based, the origin of the high valuation of the shame-honour avoidance-pursuit pair in collectivist cultures lies in the family. Research by Lieber, Fung and Lueng (2006) saw shame as a "pro-socialising" characteristic instilled in children by their parents. The Chinese context, heavily influenced by Confucianism, involves a socialisation process based on filial piety, involving obedience and the honouring of one's parents. While these precepts are transmitted in a general sense by the culture—including by education, the media, legends and religion—the primary source is parents. "It is a parent's responsibility and social obligation to train the child to be sensitive to moral and social roles and the complex meaningfulness of shame" (p. 141). The factor analysis of their Chinese Child-rearing Beliefs Questionnaire data indicated significant loadings for the items:

- Children should be shamed for disobeying rules
- Shaming children helps them to learn to behave, and
- Parents should be ashamed of their child's public misbehaviour (p. 143)

The family is also the centre where the most important language development takes place, and during the very earliest years, language and cultural understanding develop together. As mentioned, in the last century, Wittgenstein, Sapir and Whorf had posited that worldview thinking and language were linked, and more recently, Boroditsky (2009) and others have applied empirical methods to the issue, and the research seems to confirm the connection. The development of language in cultures with different avoidance-pursuit pair hierarchies is therefore of interest in this research. It was noted by Scheff (2003) that English appears to be the only modern language that has only a single word for shame. Other languages distinguish between shame meaning disgrace and everyday shame—*Schande* and *Scham* in German and *honte* and *pudeur* in French, for example. In these languages, everyday shame carries no offence, but because English has only one word, discussion of shame in English is to risk offence. Spanish also has one word for shame, *vergüenza*, though the words *deshonra* or *deshonor* meaning dishonourable may be used, and there are other words pertaining to ignominy and disgrace.

On the negative side of the avoidance-pursuit pair, there is a common, strong insult that is used by Bolivians of people who have committed crimes that are visible to the public gaze—for example, corrupt politicians or perhaps members of a notorious band of thugs. The term used is *sinvergüenza* [without shame] and is often used as a noun, as in "he is a without shame." This expression, while very similar to the English word shameless, has stronger, more negative connotations in Bolivia. Central to all of these considerations of shame and losing face is the context of relationships within which the same is felt. Relationships, therefore, may be seen as affecting the importance of shame as judged by individuals in different cultures and hence of importance in this research.

The importance of relationships

The dependence on relationships and others within a culture is an important factor when considering the avoidance-pursuit pairs. On the positive side of the shame-honour avoidance-pursuit pair, having honour, glory or prestige is obviously something that involves other cultural or group members and the "culturally constituted relationships" (Barkow, 1975, p. 553) that help to maintain self-esteem. Scheff (2003) claimed that "shame can be seen as a signal of a *threat to the bond*" (p. 239) in relationships within a group, and Virgil Aldrich (1939) wrote of an "ethics of shame" that individuals may have, based on the idea of the perception of an observing other. Expression of this concept, presumably, would be expected to be found in Bolivia due to the collectivist nature of the culture, where disapproval in the eyes of others becomes more important than disapproval in one's own eyes (Harris, Wolgrave, & Braithwaite, 2004). As shame has a relational context, the collectivist and fictive relationships are discussed below.

Collectivities and relationships

The collectivism that exists in the communities from which a number of the participants in this research came was a collectivism that, in fact, may be characterised at a country level as a collection of collectives. Each family, at least in the city and at times in the country, appeared to be held together by stronger bonds than those encountered in individualistic societies. These bonds, however, weaken significantly the further individuals are situated away from the locus of the nuclear family, having diminished strength with blood relatives to *padrinos* [godparents] and less with other *parientes simbólicos* [symbolic relatives]. Beyond these bounds, there are work-related friendships and some social friendships, but these bonds are generally much weaker, depending on the level of trust afforded to others. Where trust does exist between individuals in relationship, its strength is partly driven by the perceived integrity of the other party—and within the Spanish language context, the level of integration or wholeness of an individual. The bond strength of the collectivist, in-group relationships defined by the culture or society, appeared in this research to be more significant to the city dwellers than individually defined relationships. This conforms to the description of collectivism given by Wright (1998), where individuals within the society see themselves as being interconnected with other group members, placing a high value on group harmony and solidarity This may be the case even when personal interests are endangered: "When personal goals conflict with group norms, collectivists tend to conform to group norms" (para. 3).

In terms of the impact this may have on ethical decision-making, contrasts are presented by Blum (1988) between the impartialist, Kantian, or neo-Kantian positions of ethicists such as Kohlberg and Carol Gilligan. Gilligan, Blum argued, saw that "care and responsibility within personal relationships constitute an important element of morality itself, genuinely distinct from impartiality" (p. 473). Gilligan's conceptualisation of the moral self is as "radically situated and particularised . . . defined by its historical connections and relationships" (p. 474). The relational context and contrast with the deontological Kantian position is given by Blom as follows:

> [Gilligan] rejects the contrasting metaphor in Kohlberg, drawn from Kant, in which morality is ultimately a matter of the individual rational being legislating for himself and obeying laws or principles generated solely from within himself (i.e., from within his own reason). Gilligan portrays the moral agent as approaching the world of action bound by ties and relationships (friend, colleague, parent, child) which confront her as, at least to some extent, givens. These relationships, while subject to change, are not wholly of the agent's own making and thus cannot be pictured on a totally voluntarist or contractual model. In contrast to Kohlberg's conception, the moral agent is not conceived of as radically autonomous (though this is not to deny that there exists a less individualistic, less foundational, and less morality-generating sense of autonomy which does accord with Gilligan's conception of moral agency) . . . . For Gilligan . . . morality necessarily involves an intertwining of emotion, cognition, and action, not readily separable. Knowing what to do involves knowing others and being connected in ways involving both emotion and cognition. (pp. 475–476)

The issues of ethical decision-making, relationships, culture, or worldview, therefore, coalesce to provide the highly situated context for action that is deemed by an individual to be the right thing to do. The strength of each facet of the context will vary, including the level of inculcation of the culture or worldview, and the strength of the relationship bond.

In-groups and trust in collectivist cultures

Triandis, Bontempo, Villareal, Asai, & Lucca (1988) commented on the strength of relationship bonds and the resultant behaviour of individuals towards those in in-groups and out-groups: a distinguishing feature of collectivist cultures. Their comments regarding in-groups in collectivist cultures were particularly pertinent to the Bolivian culture:

> In collectivist cultures people share and show harmony within ingroups, but the total society may be characterized by much disharmony and nonsharing, because so many interpersonal relationships are individual—outgroup relationships. For instance, if the ingroup is defined as "family and friends and other people concerned with my welfare" (Triandis, 1972), then most relationships with merchants, policemen, government bureaucrats, and so on are outgroup relationships. (pp. 325–326)

The level of trust expressed to those in one's in-group has been linked to collectivist cultures, where it has been seen as being high compared with individualistic cultures (Huff & Kelley, 2003). Huff and Kelley (1999) explained the collectivism-trust phenomenon in terms of the relationship of individuals to in-groups and out-groups in that they, "use avoidance behaviours, and compete with, manipulate, and exploit out-groups more extensively than individualists" (p. 83).

O'Toole (2008) wrote in a personal email from China:

> With good *guanxi* almost anything is possible and without it everything becomes difficult. The stranger does not really exist. In personal terms this means that people spend much time and energy establishing relationships that will further their plans and ambitions and in wider terms it means that levels of public courtesy seem very low by our standards. Walled and gated communities are normal here but the windows inside the wall are rarely barred. Only free-standing homes seem to have window bars and I suspect that the doors within traditional walled villages did not have locks . . . . We trust because we feel that we must. (para. 2)

The situations described by Huff and Kelley (1999) and O'Toole (2008) were very similar to those found in Cochabamba, where the element of trust was something reserved for the very closest of relationships. While walled and gated communities exist in the city, most houses are in the suburbs, and most have high walls with barbed wire and barred windows, and many neighbourhoods have security guards.

Fictive relationships within collectivities

The concept of fictive relationships has its origins in the early history of the Catholic Church and "designates the particular complex relationships set up between individuals primarily, though not always, through participation in the ritual of Catholic baptism" (Mintz & Wolf, 1950, p. 341). This rite, introduced to Latin America by the Spanish Conquistadors, is solemnly sworn in the presence of God and establishes three sets of relationships: Child and parents, child and *compadres* [godparents, also *padrino*—a term also referring to 'patron'], and parents and the child's *compadres*.

These relationships were very strong, and it was understood that one would never *tutear* a *compadre*—that is, use the second person pronoun and associated verbs in their familiar forms. According to Albro (2001), these relationships involve a lifelong commitment that is ritually consecrated in the church. *Compadres* were seen as the spiritual fathers of one's children and carried a great deal of moral authority.

> An indication of the padrino's authority is that it is he who pays the fee and signs the baptismal registry kept in the church archive. He has the right, as someone put it, to morally castigate (*chicotear*, "to whip") a godchild gone astray with an

absolutism even surpassing that expected of the biological father. (Albro, 2001, p. 145)

Traditionally, these fictive relatives are chosen with great care, with the intention that the godparents would be people they wish their child could emulate (Mintz & Wolf, 1950). The ritualised fictive kinships, however, have been used over the centuries to establish trust relationships with others and particularly with those, where possible, of a higher social class. Based on obligations of fictive relationship, the *padrino*, traditionally, was expected to meet expectations of largesse (*noblesse oblige*) and sponsor fiestas and other events involving their *ahijados* [godchildren] and the various rituals marking the godchild's growth to Catholic personhood.

While this form of the *compadrazgo* institution, which Albro (2001) describes as "genuine ritual *compadres*" (p. 148), has existed for centuries in the country, Albro claims that over the past forty years, the normative ideal has been giving way to a different form of relationship. This he saw as "a newer, debased, form of ritual kinship, now depicted as a purely strategic act" (p. 148), which, he claimed, ethnographers also have noticed in Bolivia. This "commercialisation" of relationships has led them to be considered more in terms of strategic expedients where the relationship is occasion specific and short lived: "Typical examples would be [funding] a fiesta for the purchase of a new taxi, or [funding] a party to bless a new TV (events entirely outside the scope of the Church)" (p. 150). These obligation structures would appear to have been partly responsible for the evolution of these contrived kinships to what has been seen as their devaluing due to "inflation" (Albro, 2001), to an economic rationalism involving the future economic success of the family and the business. Albro relates his experiences with fiestas in Quillacollo (now a satellite suburb fifteen kilometres from the centre of Cochabamba and from which several of the participants in this research came) to illustrate this type of kinship relationship. At these, Albro observed that individuals often would be invited to be *padrino de aro* [patron of the drink], *padrino de comida* [patron of the food] or even *padrino del video* [patron of the video recording]. The changes to which he points will have influenced in some way most of the participants in this research.

In the city and in the *barrios periféricos* [outlying suburbs], these obligations have replaced the indigenous concept of *ayne* (or *ayni*), where favours (usually labour at planting or harvest time in the *campo*) were repaid in kind. In the cities, the repayment often has either been monetised or involves reciprocal *compadrazgo* relationships. The ephemeral nature of the relationship is illustrated by Albro (2001) as follows:

And so, when a fiesta padrino receives deferential treatment from his host, he still might retort, "But it's just ayni!" [that is, something to be paid back] . . . . Families often kept written lists, so that when fictive kinship is sought, someone wearily responds, "Okay, okay. Just sign me up. Sign me up!" (p. 152)

Apart from the evolving nature of the concept, these fictive relationships, as stated earlier, provide the means by which the Bolivian collectivities can form trust relationships outside of the nuclear family. These relationships, having a religious history and force, at least originally, and now enforcement based on mutual obligation, provide an essential framework within the society. The trust implied in these relationships may vary in strength depending on their nature—traditional and religious, modern and commercial, or political—and can extend, as noted by a participant in this research, beyond the quid pro quo interactions of *ayne*-like interchanges to lending money based on trust rather than commercial interests.

The levels of trust implicit in fictive relationships have led, as Albro (2001) has noted, to a situation where politicians at different levels eschew fictive relationships in favour of friendships. The reason Albro gives for this was that friendships may easily be broken and supposed friends may be betrayed, but that it was a much more serious undertaking with *padrinos*. At the same time, however, relationships in enacted governance, by politicians and other leaders, were theoretically bound by laws and regulations generated by the government system of Hispanic origin and in the *campo* by the set relationships within community government and where a different set of relationships exists.

Animistic cultures, fear and power

The third avoidance-pursuit pair is that which contrasts fear, anxiety or dread, and power, powers, or influence. In terms of a different religious perspective, Blaschke (2001) and Hegeman (2006), who had worked with animistic people groups in West Africa, claimed that the cultures of these groups are led by what is termed in this research the fear-power avoidance-pursuit pair. Apart from fearing the physical pain and suffering that may pertain to living in an African "bush" setting, the people in these groups experience a very substantial fear of the supernatural: fear of spirit beings, fear of their ancestors and a fear of curses (Blaschke, 2001). For these people, spiritual beings—gods, spirits of ancestors, spirits inhabiting natural phenomena, demons, etc.—exist in an unseen or rarely seen form as powers that may benefit or harm them. In the anthropomorphised forms in which these powers are understood by the community, they may be angered, placated, or turned to in particular times of need (Barth, 1988). In order to coexist with these powers, human beings must learn to "live quietly" or appease them (Muller, 2000).

Muller (2000) added to this by saying:

> [The West African] needs to live at peace with the powers around him, and often
> man lives in fear. This fear is based on a number of different things. First, man
> fears man. Tribal wars are endemic, with captives becoming slaves or,

sometimes, a meal for cannibals. Whenever tribes encounter people from outside of their own group, they approached them with suspicion and fear. Secondly, these people fear the supernatural. All around them events are taking place that can only be explained by the supernatural. Much like the ancient civilizations before Christ, they have developed spiritual explanations for how things work in this world. If crops fail, then specific gods or demons are responsible. If sickness comes, then other gods or demons are responsible. If a tribe fails in battle, it is because of the activity of a god or demon. Sickness is often viewed as a god reaping revenge. Everything in life, even romance, is somehow attributed to the activities of gods or demons.

The struggle that these people face is simply one of needing power. Using their voodoo, charms and other methods, they seek to gain control over other people and over the controlling powers of the universe. The paradigm that these people live in is one of fear versus power. (p. 42)

Much of life for people holding these beliefs is therefore dedicated to dealing with these fears. As Muller (2006a) explained:

In most fear-power worldviews the main way of dealing with a power is to establish rules to protect the unwary from harm and procedures to appease those powers that are offended. These rules and procedures are generally referred to as taboos. Taboos come in the form of things like special people, forbidden or unclean foods, sacred objects, special acts or rituals, and special names. Appeasements are usually made in the form of sacrifice or dedication to the invisible powers. In order to deal with these powers, rituals are established which people believe will affect the powers around them. Rituals are performed on certain calendar dates, at certain times in someone's life (rites of passage), or in a time of crisis. In order to appease the powers of the universe, systems of appeasement are worked out. They vary from place to place. Some civilizations offer incense while some offer a chicken or even their children as sacrifices. However it is done, a system of appeasement based on fear is the norm for their worldview. (p. 177)

Those with a secular worldview see all power as having its source within the physical world, but those with "primal" worldviews (Burnett, 1988) not only see power evident in the physical world but believe its source to be in the spiritual realm (Burnett, 1988). In fear-power cultures, then, the spiritual leaders of the community—shamans or priests—hold positions of prestige and power as they control the rituals and the interface between the physical and spiritual worlds. These individuals, therefore, can have a very formidable hold over other community members (Muller, 2000).

David Burnett (2002) claimed that the major religions had so penetrated the world that only approximately three per cent of the world's population may now be classified as holding solely to their "traditional worldview" of an animistic religion. Burnett did add the caveat, however, that many people in cultures that have historically practised animism have not converted totally to a new religion; instead, they continue to practise a syncretistic religion. This would certainly be true of the Bolivian animistic cultures, where most would claim to be either Catholic or Evangelical, but sacrifices are still made by many to *Pachamama*—Earth Mother—either on a regular basis or in times of great need. In UNESCO's report on Bolivian Culture, Baptista Gumucio (1978) stated that:

> The Spaniards were unable to suppress the native languages, communal rites, dances, music, clothing and festivals which, by a process of religious fusion or syncretism, finally reappeared in the Catholic festivals in honour of the saints, under a more or less superficial varnish of Christianity. (p. 16)

Apart from the direct references to the metaphysical, within an Aymara context in the *campo*, rather than speaking of fear and power, Thomas (2003) used the terms void and spirit.

> The categories of spirit and void describe personal and social awareness of what affirms and what negates life in the Aymara context. While persons exert tremendous effort to obtain what affirms life and to control or avoid what threatens life, these categories are finally perceived to be beyond personal control. The common perspectives of fate, luck, and chance emphasize the perceived otherness of the two categories. (p. 211)

> Void references the threat of the impinging reality of the outside world on the self when its personal and cultural projections of the outside world fail to fit the reality. The self desperately struggles to solve the tensions and to rebuild a more adequate projection of the world in which it lives. (p. 40)

The seeking of spirit and the avoidance of void in this model gives an additional insight into the thinking of the *campesinos,* but because Bolivians lie on a continuum between *campesino* and *ciudadano* [citizen, city dweller], apart from the void-spirit and fear-power constructions seen in the *campo*, the concept of power in Bolivia is also seen to be evident in the city cultures. Within the cities, the gaining and use, or misuse, of power and influence has been a leitmotif of Bolivian politics at least since independence (Tapia, 2002). This has been evident in the use of coups, often violent, to gain control of the country, but also in the very strong concept of the use of influence (*muñeca*) in all levels of the Bolivian society.

Fear in the cities also takes a different form. While there may be levels of fear similar to those in the *campo* with reference to the spiritual world, as seen in the syncretistic practices or rituals and the use of burnt offerings, more pressing concerns usually pertain to the economic and political situation. In particular, at the time of this research, those living in the cities reflected Muller's (2006) observation regarding fear-led cultures in Africa in that the first thing that was feared was other people. In Cochabamba, the citizens were particularly afraid of the possibility of politically inspired violence. Garcela Tapia, an Argentine mediator, was quoted in the Bolivian newspaper, *Los Tiempos* (2008), as saying regarding the time when the Phase I data were being collected that the country showed civil war indicators similar to what she had seen in Kosovo and Croatia. Historically, this situation has strong antecedents that link the indigenous cultures of the region, the Spanish conquest and the social inequalities that have been poorly managed by generations of political leaders. Each of these categories implies a different context for the development and maintenance of worldviews.

Worldviews and the avoidance-pursuit pairs

The literature surrounding worldviews indicates the development of the conceptualisation of worldviews from the apparent first use of the term (*Weltanschauung*) by Immanuel Kant (Muller, 2006), then Hegel, through other European—particularly German—philosophical traditions of the last century, to its use by anthropologists, sociologists and missiologists working within a cross-cultural context. The power of the valuated hierarchy for individuals, or leaders, of the guilt-innocence, shame-honour and fear-power avoidance-pursuit pairs acting on ethical decision-making processes arises from their location within our filtering, valuing and directing, culturally-embedded worldviews.

Defining the term 'worldview' as used in this research

The worldview concept has been defined in many ways, at least some, if not all of which may be, effectively, worldview-dependent definitions. The German word from which the term worldview was calqued, *Weltanschauung,* is a specifically German notion that, according to Freud (1932) would be difficult to translate into another language. Rather than translate the word in its fullest German context, the literalist "world view" translation has been introduced into English as a specific term requiring definition.

In a general sense, worldviews have been seen as the set of presuppositions (or assumptions) that we hold (consciously or subconsciously) about the fundamental makeup of our world we experience (Sire, 2004).   Indeed, while the word *Weltanschauung* has been translated as worldview, *Schauung* denotes intuition. These presuppositions, assumptions and intuitions provide for us a conceptual model of the world (Walsh & Middleton, 1984) based on our basic perceptions and understandings of the world (Lynch, 2002). According to Flew (1984) this includes the moods, perceptions, attitudes, and states of human consciousness as frameworks of reality. In terms of cognition, Jenkins (1979) wrote that an individual's worldview was their cognitive culture: "the mental organization in each individual's mind of how the world works." Given these definitions, worldviews can be seen to play an important role in decision-making processes.

Anthropologist, Michael Kearney (1984) described worldviews as not just our perception of reality, but the *way* we look at reality—thus affecting our ranking of cultural values through our considerations of relationships:

> It [worldview] consists of basic assumptions and images that provide a more or less coherent, though not necessarily accurate, way of thinking about the world. A world view comprises itself of Self and of all that is recognised as notSelf, plus ideas about relationships between them, as well as other ideas. (p. 41)

Apart from rationalistic perspectives, the concept of worldview identified with the Self and relationship also implies a profound influence on affect and therefore is significant in terms of the affective domain including feelings of guilt, shame and fear. The active influence of worldview is seen in Olthuis (1985) as a channel for the ultimate beliefs which give direction and meaning to life and the set of hinges on which our everyday thinking and doing turn.

Worldviews provide all leaders, Bolivian or otherwise, with an intellectual framework by which they can understand and interpret the cosmos and life (Orr, 1893; Schelling quoted in Copleston, 1994). They include the set of pretheoretical assumptions and presuppositions that all human beings have—that shape the meaning of life (Cunningham, 1987) and help us to cope with the inconsistencies, non-sequiturs and incongruencies that pertain to the "riddle of existence" (Dilthey, quoted by Plantinga, 1980). They are not only a vision *of* life, but also a vision *for* life (Walsh & Middleton, 1984) that helps us to interpret the world and function purposefully in it.

A worldview's usefulness in providing answers to life's questions means that worldviews provide us with a horizon, a set of standards, or ethical bases, by which all things may be measured (Nietzsche, 1980), enabling us to determine what is important and what is not (Walsh & Middleton, 1984). In other words, our worldviews guide our valuation—both of objects outside the Self and of the constructs within our worldviews, including values and virtues and the avoidance-pursuit pairs. This makes them powerful entities in terms of their behaviour orienting or normative role (Peterson, 2001), but adds to their complexity.

The integrative and interpretative framework provided by our worldviews gives us the standard by which reality is managed and pursued and by which order and disorder are judged (Olthius, 1985), with the implied effect on decision-making. Within this conceptualisation, we can see why Orr (1893) would have believed that worldviews were founded on some particular philosophy or theology, and Geisler and Watkins (1984) commented that they include how one sees the world in relation to God (Muller, 2006). In this regard, it is interesting to note that, as Hegeman (2006b) has observed, the different avoidance-pursuit pairs may originate in cultures with particular religious perceptions: guilt-innocence from monotheistic cultures, shame-honour from cultures that have some degree of deification of a human being and fear-power from animistic cultures. The avoidance-pursuit pairs would therefore be used in this context to make sense of the structures of cultures, given their particular religious orientation.

For the purposes of this research and the identified avoidance-pursuit pairs, Audi's (1999) comment was pertinent: "A worldview constitutes an overall perspective on life that sums up what we know about the world, how we evaluate it emotionally, and how we respond to it" (p. 236). This definition includes a sensory engagement with our environment (input), the evaluating and structuring of information (processing), the role of the affective domain and, finally, the function of worldview as a determinant of action (output) or decision-making.

This research has sought to make links between the avoidance-pursuit pairs and their worldview origins, but while the descriptions, analogies and metaphors relating to the worldview concept given above are useful, they do not include indications of the source of our worldviews.

The origin and development of worldviews

Wittgenstein (1969) believed that many of the beliefs we have about the world arise from our "inherited background" and are "swallowed down" or, to use an expression of Claudel quoted by Bourdieu (1980), "*connaître, c'est naître avec*" (p. 67). This is similar to Kant's view of worldview construction, which, according to Wolters (n.d.), includes the thought that worldview development begins at least at birth and is initially constructed through our sensory perception, then continues to be constructed out of our lifeworld experiences and cognition. As Naugle (2002) expressed Dilthey's conceptualisation: a *Lebenswelt* [lifeworld] begets a *Weltanschauung* [worldview]. It is this process that gives rise to the different worldviews seen in the Bolivian cultures in this research—where two different lifeworlds have begotten two different worldviews— for as Sarason (1984) wrote regarding the growth of worldviews and the socialisation process:

> . . . from the moment of birth, in ways direct and indirect, purposeful and unwitting, we absorb a view of ourselves and the world. It is too easy to overlook the obvious fact that in practice the major purpose of socialization is to maximize continuity between generations, and the effectiveness of the process resides less in the conscious purposes of parents than in the myriad indirect ways in which we come to acquire our world view. (p. 477)

The early formation of the Bolivian leaders in different subcultures in Bolivia must reflect this worldview development out of the dynamics of human experience (Naugle, 2002) and reflection on the world in general and the human *Dasein* (Heidegger, 1982) in particular. According to Heidegger, this may occur explicitly and consciously in individuals or by appropriating an already prevalent worldview, formed from the cultural worldview or from a natural worldview. Certainly, they are at least partly environmentally determined, as well as by people group, race, class, and the developmental stage of the culture (Heidegger, 1982). Importantly, in this sense, the locus of our personhood is conceptually embedded within our worldviews as our perceiving selves exist, in a sense, inside our worldview. This means that there are as many different worldviews as there are human beings, even within the same cultural group (Sue, 1981) and these differences are not always insignificant:

> Millennial global politics, as recent events have all too starkly reminded us, bear witness to the huge differences between perspectives and dispositions at the cultural and religious levels. We may all operate within the same Kantian Categories—even the same Wittgensteinian language games—but the worldviews we construct can still be radically different. (Stables, 2002, p. 3)

As our worldviews emerge in part as a result of the socialisation process (Sarason, 1984; Lynch, 2002), they do so somewhat from pragmatic necessity: the necessity of making sense of the world around us and the necessity of having some understanding of our place and purpose in it. However, despite this, our worldviews may not be explicitly developed into a conscious and systematic conception of life nor codified into a creedal form (Olthius, 1985). It is unlikely, therefore, that Bolivian leaders recognise the full import of their worldview formation process, although they are able to identify themselves as belonging to a very specific subculture and are able to identify their significant subculture definers.

The location of worldviews

Even though our worldviews may not be articulated fully and may be so internalised that they go largely unquestioned (Olthius, 1985), Dilthey believed that they were fundamentally intuitions that were "grounded in the architecture of the mind" (Naugle, 2002, p. 88). Added to this conception within cognition is the effect of the affective domain and the avoidance-pursuit pairs that are central to this study. Worldviews therefore, appear to be all-embracing in terms of our personhood, not only giving outward-looking perspectives as from the standing-in-the-middle-of-life (Naugle, 2002), but giving everyone, in all cultures and including leaders, a framework or set of fundamental beliefs through which we interact with our environment, and view it and our calling and future in it (Olthius, 1985). Perhaps conceptually, this begs the question, do we inhabit our worldviews or are we inhabited by them? As Sarason (1984) noted, as a result of the socialisation processes through which we pass, each of us both possesses and is possessed by a worldview.

> Briefly put, the limitation is that each of us possesses a world view much of which, by virtue of the socialization process, we never have to articulate and therefore do not have reason to challenge. More accurately, we are possessed

by our world view as much as we possess it. When we set our minds to it, we
can begin to fathom heretofore unexamined axioms in our world view, but we
can never unimprison ourselves, except in small measure, from our world view.
(p. 477)

This would indicate that the worldview structures of Bolivian leaders should be
reasonably stable and not subject to change on the basis of whim or the result of a
moment of rationalisation. Such stability in worldview structure is useful in terms of the
worldview analysis of the responses given in the research participant interviews.

Worldviews and culture

From the researcher's observations within the Bolivian community, the Bolivian
leaders generally come from relatively well-defined subcultures and therefore have
worldviews that reflect their cultural heritages. As cultural entities, worldviews are
dependent on, and subordinate to, cultures (Nietzsche, 1980) and express themselves
differently in "cultural" articulations such as in the arts because they provide, as Hegel
claimed, the criteria for all thinking and define what is good, true and beautiful (Naugle,
2002). Cultural distinctives and differentiation are important, though there exist multiple
sources of variation within a culture—including shared cultural experiences, unique
experiences and human universality (Lynch, 2002). It is the cultural distinctives that set
a culture apart from other cultures and give shared and personal meaning to its
members. Many of these distinctives may not be seen as they involve internalised
beliefs and philosophical ideas of being (Jezewski & Sotnik, 2001), but they are given
communicative expression in the arts, as mentioned, but also in religion and religious
practices, in the rites and rituals of the culture and in the myths and legends through
which much of the cultural history of the people is expressed. Generally, commonalities
can be identified among people who share a geographic location, language, and
historic period, and will be seen to be organised around particular themes with less
variability within the culture than between cultures (Au, 1999). These factors have
appeared to the researcher to be evident in the different Bolivian subcultures.

Culturally based components of worldview that were identified by Brislin (1980) and
cited by Mojab (2006) involved socialisation, intergenerational transmission of ideas,
internalisation of values based on childhood experiences, consistent patterns of
practices and concepts, patterns that are maintained even when maladaptive, and
feelings of confusion or helplessness when the patterns are changed. Within the
context of this research, these "patterns" will have been under considerable pressure
to change for those leaders who have come to the city to work after having been
brought up in so-called third-world, rural villages[13]. In the cities, they find different

---

[13] In the country areas villages in the English sense may exist but traditionally these were
"communities" that may have included a small nucleus of houses. The development of more

practices, a different first language and a different set of values.

Worldviews and axiology

Begley (1999) claimed that rather than "retreating into managerialism" (p. 12), the study of the philosophical bases for values was important—though to claim any activity, including management, as being value neutral is not defensible. It is worth noting, however, that the term "value" is used in different ways. As Beck (1999) wrote:

> The term values has two connected but different meanings. In one sense, values are the things we pursue and consider important in life, the things we *value*. However, in the context of educational philosophy and theory the focus is normally on a narrower category of values, namely the things that are *worthy* of valuing, the things that are *valuable*. This is what we are talking about when we say schooling should have a basis in values or students should be taught values: we do not mean just any values but rather a set of *sound* values. (pp. 223–224)

The placing of a value on things as being worthy of being valued and on those things we believe to be worth pursuing takes place within the framework of an individual's worldview. The relationship between worldviews and *values* is important. Charles Kraft (1979) wrote of worldviews as "the central specialization of conceptions of reality to which members of [a] culture assent (largely unconsciously) and from which stems their value system" (p. 53). The set of values is not independent of the culture of the individual (Begley & Johansson, 2003), although, as Begley also noted, "It is likely that individuals may also possess at least a few distinctly personal values" (p. 2). The internalisation of values based on childhood experiences Mojab (2006) within worldviews provides the initial valuation of the avoidance-pursuit pairs that will begin to play a role in the individual's decision-making.

Decision-making by leaders necessarily involves choices between options and a valuation or prioritisation of possible action paths. The use of the term *value* in this study is not synonymous with the concepts of *values,* nor *virtues,* nor "the beliefs about how to behave and what goals are important to achieve . . ." (Sarros & Santora, 2001, p. 3). While perhaps linked to this perception of *values* as an implicit or explicit conception "of the desirable which influences the selection from available modes, means, and ends of action" (Parsons & Shills, 1962, p. 395), the term *value* is used here also to refer to the priority given in an individual's worldview to the avoidance-pursuit pair components by an individual or by a culture.

---

structured concentrations of populations into towns and villages was introduced by the Spanish in order to facilitate governance and evenagelisation (Thomas, 2010a).

Values, as worldview components, help us to understand as well as to compare and contrast other cultures—be they from the Bolivian country and city settings in this research, or on a broader scale. Not only are these values held and expressed in behaviours such as decision-making, but, as Hegeman (2006a) suggested, they form part of a system in which one's ethical and ideological values exist, are ordered and are prioritised. In this research, a set of espoused values of the participants was evident in the data, and underlying, culturally inculcated valuations of the avoidance-pursuit pairs were either elicited or inferred, and the importance of relationships is evident in both schemas. The espoused values of the participants were, however, not necessarily controlling values. Behind comments such as that something is not considered to be wrong in the culture unless the individual is caught, lies a dualistic morality. An example of this would be the actions of some young people quoted by participants who appeared to think that being found drunk in a distant city was not considered to be a problem, but being found drunk by family members would bring shame and disgrace. In this case, relationships, acting through the shame and honour pair components, appear to mediate between the espoused and controlling value sets of culture members.

Values, in both senses of the word, being integrated into worldviews, are strongly culturally dependent. Begley (1999) proposed a model of the concentric spheres of influence that affect values and decision-making. He posited nested spheres that defined the morphogenetics of value dimensions. These ranged from cultural, to sub-cultural, to organisational, to group levels of influence and finally the individual. Begley and Johansson (2003) developed this concept as "arenas of valuation" (p. 9) that they suggested were representative of the multiple domains and functions of administration as concentric circles.

Of the cultural level of these circles, Schwartz (2006) concluded that the emphasis of values could be "the most central feature of culture" (p. 139) that "shape and justify individual and group beliefs, actions and goals" (p. 139), promoting coherence in the culture. Values are accumulated formatively from the culture so that people may appear to hold the same values even though they may have arrived at them by different means (Begley & Johansson, 2003). Begley and Johansson also conceded, however, that individuals within a culture will probably have some different values. This concurs with the lifeworld formation of worldviews for the individual discussed earlier.

At the centre of the spheres is the self, highlighting the unique influence potential an individual leader has in an organisation. In terms of this research, the second level, Group, may be seen as the in-group of the individual. The group has significant influence, but less influence than the Profession, and so on till the Transcendental level is reached. The final level, Transcendental, Begley and Johansson (2003) proposed as being important but overlooked in much of the leadership and administration literature. These arenas are all evident in this research context and provide the setting into which decision-making operates while being mediated by the influence of the avoidance-pursuit pairs.

The elevation within an individual's worldview of the status of an avoidance-pursuit pair to have the highest value in the matrix may therefore be indicative of the strength and consistency of that pair within a culture. Following Kilmann (1981), Bilsky and Koch (2003) stated that in order to arrive at a useful conceptualisation of values, and presumably to an individual's valuations, it is necessary to address a specific behaviour and the same is presumed to be true for the determination of the valuation of an avoidance-pursuit pair component. The strength of the value placed on these is assumed in this research to be acquired within a culture in a similar manner to other values. This acquisition, according to McClelland, Koester and Weinberger (1989) is "usually activated by explicit, often social, incentives such as rewards, prompts, expectations, or demands" (p. 693). Gudykunst and Nishda (2000) also noted the importance of the socialisation process in value acquisition but added that the process also works in the other direction: "Cultural values provide broad guidelines about what are acceptable means for achieving end-states in different situations, and influence cultural norms and rules" (p. 2). Given the relational bonding in collectivist cultures, one might expect that this might be more the case in those cultures, rather than in cultures based on individualism.

An important connection with this study involving participants from a collectivist culture is seen in the work of Schwartz (1994, 2006), who isolated values at a cultural level that he claimed were associated with the Individualism-Collectivity cultural distinctions. He further suggested that what he termed conservatism was related to collectivism and therefore relates to the collectivism found in the Bolivian subcultures (House et al., 2004). By conservatism, Schwartz (1994) meant culture-level value types that focus on "those values likely to be important in societies based on close-knit harmonious relations, in which the interests of the person are not viewed as distinct from those of the group" (p. 101).

Being qualitative in nature, this research undertaken in Bolivia involved the examination of participant responses very much at an individual level. It is from the examination of these responses that patterns pertaining to general cultural patterns, including those such as shame and honour that are linked with relationships in a collectivist culture, may be perceived. A study by Slater (2006) of students from Texas and Mexico City found cultural differences in values that suggest a link to the avoidance-pursuit pairs: "The educational leader has a different task in each country. The U.S. educational leader takes action to give others a sense of mastery, while the Mexican educational leader trusts people to give them a sense of pride in past accomplishments and hope in the future" (p. 168). This data summary points to a Mexican, and therefore to at least some extent, Latin American inclination towards the shame-honour avoidance-pursuit pair.

The essential feature of the function of the avoidance-pursuit pairs in this research is the assumption that one of the avoidance-pursuit pairs will have a value attributed to it that is higher than that given to the others. In the production of a system of values in our *Weltanschauung* that then leads to acting according to our understanding of "the correct thing to do," the importance of the ordering or valuation of the avoidance-pursuit pairs was stressed by Hegeman (2006), who wrote:

> A value system is in essence the ordering and prioritization of the ethical and ideological values that an individual or society holds. While two individuals or groups may share a set of common values, they may differ in their determination of which values in that set have precedence over others. The two individuals or groups are said to have different value systems, even though they may have many values in common, if their prioritization of values differs, or if there are different exceptions they attach to these values. Groups and individuals whose differing value systems have many values in common may still wind up in conflict, ideological or physical, with each other, because of the differences in their value systems. People with differing value systems will thus disagree on the rightness or wrongness of certain actions, both in the abstract and in specific circumstances. In essence, a value system (if sufficiently well-defined) is a formalization of a moral code. (p. 47)

The priority given to any one pair, or pair component, will vary from one culture to another as well as from one individual to another, as mentioned above by Gudykunst and Nishda (2000). It may be expected that participants' different work contexts will also influence their personal value systems. As many of the participants in this research are educational leaders, some consideration should be given to the general conceptualisation of values in educational leadership, as it is within the context of education that considerable effort is expended in the acculturation of the next generation of citizens in a culture.

Values and educational leadership

Much has been written regarding the role of values in general in leadership (Starratt, 2005; Starratt, 2004; Begley & Johansson, 2003; House et al., 2004; Begley & Hodgkinson, 1999; Sergiovanni, 1992). With regard to the centrality of values for educational leaders, Willower (1992) wrote: "Because a significant portion of the practice in educational administration requires rejecting some courses of action in favour of a preferred one, values are generally acknowledged to be central to the field" (p. 369).

In a study of school administrators in Canada and Sweden, Begley and Hodgkinson (1999) found that rather than administration being a value-neutral exercise, they found that administrators were responsive to consensus and consequentialist values rather than relying on personal preferences as a guide to their professional actions. Despite this, as Begley and Johansson (2003) have pointed out, "Some respected scholars of school leadership working in the empiricist tradition still dismiss values and ethics as concepts too abstract and resistant to inquiry to be of any practical use to school administrators" (p. xvii). If, as Biggart and Hamilton (1987) claimed, "leadership is embedded in social and cultural beliefs and values, [and] cannot be fully understood apart from the context in which it exists" (p. 437). Begley (2005) described the ethics in educational administration as being isomorphic across cultures: "By isomorphic is meant social conditions or value postures appearing to share the same shape or meaning from country to country, but actually structured of quite different elements" (p. 1).

While it might be expected that values such as care for students and the importance of school as an institution might be held by school principals in both the city and the country in Bolivia, and also in the West, this research claims that within the Bolivian contexts, the origins and outworking of these values do depend on "different elements." This begs the question: if this is the case, how is it manifested in terms of the avoidance-pursuit pairs within the Bolivian cultural contexts? Starratt (2005) described three foundational virtues in school leadership that may be found at least within Western cultural contexts: integrity, authenticity and presence. While these may also apply in a Bolivian context, one may suppose that there could be differences in their relative importance or in different definitions that may be given to them within a different culture.

Writing from a Latin American (Colombian) perspective, Ogliastri (1998) wrote of the significance of a personal code of ethics for leaders, saying that it is the beginning of a definition of personal integrity. This was said to be important in order to be able to "make people feel that what the company is doing is morally and socially correct" (p. 32–33). Of course, this implies, though not stated by Ogliastri, a particular perception by the community of what may be considered to be morally and socially correct. So, while leaders may be "perceived as having integrity if they are 'genuine' and 'authentic'; that is to say that they tell the truth and keep their word" (p. 33), the perception of others will depend on their ethical framework. Ogliastri (1998) went on to indicate some of the ethical complexity by noting that: "An exemplary outstanding Colombian leader is also guided by just moral and social values; and, is able to make others believe in his/her sincerity; sense of justice; and consistency in word and deed" (p. 33). Ogliastri did not define what he meant by "morally correct", but presumably, such a determination falls within a normative perspective on the ethical framework determined by the culture. An ability to observe another culture objectively and from a useful interpretive framework, such as that provided by the avoidance-pursuit pairs, can help us to see more clearly why those in other cultures speak and act the way they do. While the deontological imperative to do the right thing may be similar in the two subcultures studied in this research, the definition of what constitutes the right thing to do may be quite different. The normative approach that is naturally taken to cultural differences is understandable in terms of the sociological construction of cultures and what it means to belong to a group, but it is unhelpful when it impedes a more comprehensive understanding of others. The question of ethics in a more general sense may therefore be addressed.

Ethics and cultures

Ethical considerations are one part of the values and valuation processes (Begley, 2005). As what may be considered to be "the correct thing to do" depends to a large extent on the individual's alignment with one of the avoidance-pursuit pairs, ethics must be considered in this research project. While definitions of morality and ethics vary, moral perspectives may be seen as considerations of *what* actions or attitudes are obligatory or virtuous, whereas ethics considers *why* actions or attitudes are morally right or wrong (Edwards, 1985). Starratt (2004) defined ethics as "the study of what constitutes a moral life; an ethics is a summary, a systematic statement of what is necessary to live a moral life. Morality is the living, the acting out of ethical beliefs and commitments" (p. 5). An extension of this definition was given by Duignan et al. (2003): "Ethics is not about my belief that X is good and Y is bad. Ethics begins when we start giving reasons for our views about X and Y . . . . Ethics can be viewed as a way we do our systematic thinking about values and their application to real situations" (pp. 80, 88). The determination of the "correct thing done" falls within the moral category and acting on that determination or conviction, is an essential component in the decision-making process. This research reflects some of the conscious or unconscious ethical reasoning processes by examining moral decision-making.

The importance of both the cognitive and affective domains in ethics was spelled out by Rawls, regarded by some to be perhaps the most influential ethicist of the twentieth century (Jagger, 2000). Rawls believed that the affective domain was not mindless but was both intelligent and discriminating, ascribing both complexity and ethical centrality to particular emotions such as shame, guilt and love (Freeman, 2003, p. 497). In the research project of the SOLR group (Duignan et al., 2003), the statement was made that, "They [feelings] can easily prejudice our judgment, but they can also be a good, almost instinctive guide to right and wrong" (p. 91).

Kohlberg's (1969) reasoning regarding ethics was that while different cultures may have different beliefs regarding specific behaviours—one may promote a behaviour while in another it may be taboo—the moral reasoning behind the thinking in each culture would be the same for individuals at the same stage of moral development in each culture (Crain, 1985). Kohlberg tested his theory in studies across a number of cultures and found that his proposed sequence of development appeared to hold true (Crain, 1985). Shweder, Mahapatra and Miller (1987), however, using their "social communications" model of moral development, found that there were significant differences in moral development between cultures in the United States and in India.

In order to elicit accurate information regarding the complex ethical beliefs that community members hold, Edwards (1985) claimed that a cognitive-development research methodology would be most useful. Edwards also claimed that, unlike the assertions of descriptive relativism, research had shown that people from different cultures can "quite easily" understand each other's ethical discourse. Despite this assertion, the process would appear to be more complex across cultures than Edwards conceded.

Ethical decision-making across cultures

While this research is not a comparative study between Western and Latin approaches, it is interesting to see the perspective of recent writers on ethical educational administration, such as Starratt. Starratt (2004, 2005) proposed that leaders, specifically educational leaders, should operate across five ethical dimensions: as a human being; as a citizen-public servant; as an educator; as an educational leader; and as a leader—specifically a leader who employs a transformational ethic. Leadership across these dimensions should be based on what Starratt termed the three foundational virtues of educational leadership: responsibility, authenticity and presence. All of the dimensions may have application within a Bolivian cultural context, and possibly across all cultures, but the outworking of the virtues may be highly culturally contextualised. Within a Bolivian context, this could be influenced by the importance of relationships in the culture and the concept of honour or face. It would therefore be likely that Bolivian leaders would show a concern for being seen to be responsible, being seen to be authentic, and the concept of presence takes on a different colour when account is taken of the importance of interpersonal relationships and the distinctions that are made between different types of relationships.

The difficulty encountered when trying to examine ethics across cultures was seen by Srnka (2004), who sought to determine the role of culture in the ethical decision-making of marketers. In doing so, she noted that "it was disappointing that no study could be identified, which *simultaneously* investigated the impact of the *various cultural dimensions*" (p. 14). According to Srnka (2004), these levels of moral awareness in decision-making processes influenced ethical frameworks through different levels of culture that she identified as:

> • *supraculture* shared by nations with similar economic systems and development, ethnicity, religion, etc.
>
> • *macroculture* shared by people of the same nationality, origin or country of residence
>
> • *mesoculture* shared by groups or communities, e.g., a professional group or industry, within a macroculture
>
> • *microculture* shared by the smallest social collectivities, e.g., the organization, family or clan (p. 3)

Each of these levels, and the significance of the different relationships that exist in each, is considered in this study of participants in Bolivia (supracultural), rural and urban communities (macrocultural), work contexts (mesocultural) and families and extended families (microcultural). The evidence of the Srnka (2004) study indicated that the broader cultural environments had a dominant influence on the affective part of moral reasoning processes, whereas the "closer environment" influenced the part of ethical decision-making related to specific behaviours.

Aurolyn Luykx (1999), who spent some years in Bolivia, described the influence of the supracultural factors relating to government influence on rural culture in Bolivia in her book *The Citizen Factory*. Luykx's research indicated that one of the key enculturation media used by Bolivian governments was the *Normal*, or Teachers College. Luykx claimed that young adults, very often from the country, entered the *Normales* where there was a substantial effort to enculturate them with the values of the government and the *Mestizo* societies in the cities. As a number of the participants in this research are educators, it might be expected that this may be one of the processes that affected the integrity of the rural cultural origins of the participants. The contentions of Luykx (1999), however, were not supported by the participants in this research, nor by the findings of Regalsky and Laurie (2007). In this context, Regalsky and Laurie also quoted Arnold and Yapita (2000) regarding the role played by schools in the enculturation process:

> They describe a ceremony in a small indigenous rural community during Independence Day celebrations which they see as signalling the ambiguity of the school. They pick out 'the curious combinations of opposed toponyms for the ritual sites honoured within the schoolyard (the national flagpole and the platform)' where both indigenous rituals and official nation state activities are practised. They argue that the position of the teachers in this setting is ambiguous, 'they seem to operate not only as functionaries of the bureaucracy of the Nation, based on [written] paper, but also as a vital part of the production

of communal lands' (p. 145; our translation). Teachers provide a point of entry for state power relations but at the same time the school space is appropriated for indigenous rituals which are crucial to the social reproduction of cultural values, norms and forms of collective decision-making which potentially question homogenizing constructions of the hispanicizing nation state.

The structuring of a mediating sector between community and school is also influenced by the professionalization strategies of some peasant families. A number of peasant children enter *Normales Superiores* [teacher training colleges] upon graduation; however, they pass from the category of *indios* to that of *cholos* or *mestizo*. In this way, state education has reinforced a group of political and cultural brokers in the heart of Andean communities for more than three decades. Luykx (1999) refers to this production of a great number of teachers from peasant communities as 'the citizen factory'. (p. 238)

This research in Cochabamba did not support the suggestion by Aurolyn Luykx's research that the *Normal*, or Teachers College, was one of the key enculturation media used by Bolivian governments, and therefore one that would have a significant effect on ethical considerations. This, however, may have been due to the limited number of school leaders from the *campo* who were interviewed. Luykx lived for some time with teachers in training in the *campo* and had useful insights into the thinking and actions of rural teachers. Many teachers, however, move between the country and the city, and this affects the way they think and act.

The cultural origins of much of, if not all of, an individual's ethics and morality must produce a culturally influenced behaviour. Fritzsche and Becker (1984) noted that "little effort has been made to try to link ethical theory to management behaviour" (p. 166) but that such a connection would appear to be useful for society. They surveyed managers—presumably in the USA—and found that the most common basis for ethical decision-making was based on rule (the rules say so) or act (for the greatest social or personal good) utilitarian theories. A number of other studies have highlighted differences between the moral reasoning used by different cultures and have included: between the USA and Japan, Korea and Taiwan (Friztsche et al., 1995); between Japan, Canada and the USA (Abramson, Keating, & Lane, 1996); Mexico and the USA (Husted et al., 1996); Singapore and the USA (Swinneyard, Rinne, & Kau, 1990); and Ireland and Lebanon (Rawwas, Patzer, & Vitell, 1994).

Edwards (1985) argued that research has suggested that children in all cultures look for clues derived from their culture to construct their notions of what is morally desirable or obligatory. Between different cultures, therefore, individuals may have the same moral obligation or virtue, but the ethical reasoning passed on to the children may be different. This, she wrote, included "the *affect* motivating obedience (empathy, guilt, shame and so on)" (p. 334), which is particularly pertinent to this research.

Regarding this educational or enculturation process, she wrote: "Sanctions are highlighted by use of "power-assertive" techniques, such as physical punishment and frightening threats. Affects are highlighted by use of guilt- or shame-producing techniques, such as love withdrawal, ridicule, shaming, and so on" (p. 334). The specific positive and negative forces that are used to shape morality in the young will vary from culture to culture.

The decision-making of leaders, which takes cultural norms into account and considers the affective impact on others, while complex, does not produce the most troublesome cases for leaders. Apart from the behavioural and general, personal outcomes, a difficult facet of the decision-making process is the fact that moral dilemmas are involved in a significant proportion of the decisions to be made.

Dilemma analysis

Obviously, not all of the decisions that are made by leaders are a simple matter of choice between positive and negative potential outcomes. Many decisions involve moral dilemmas, and these are defined in this research as the necessity of choosing between the better of two moral choices or the lesser of two immoral choices. Making these decisions requires a deference to values that are subtly differentiated from options that must be designated as inferior in order for the decision to be made. The ubiquitous nature of moral dilemmas in the lives of leaders was noted by Foster (1986):

> Each decision carries moral, rather than just technical implications. This realization distinguishes the administrator from the technocrat. Each administrative decision carries with it a restructuring of a human life; this is why administration at its heart is the resolution of moral dilemmas. (p. 33)

In urban Bolivia the network of relationships—familial, fictive, friendship, acquaintance and organisational—and the hierarchy of the class structure is so strong within the culture that often they outweigh the effect of the professional ethics, legal issues, policies and the other filters posited by Cranston, Ehrich and Kimber (2004), even though these are seen to have relevance. In an individualistic society, such as Australia, Cranston, Ehrich and Kimber found that school principals experienced a sense of isolation and liked to be able to share a dilemma problem with trusted friends. The effect of these "significant others" would appear to be much, much less than in Bolivia, where very often these play a very powerful, though often hidden, role in determining the outcome of the decision. The research work of Cranston, Ehrich and Kimber (2004) saw, however, the importance of the more general implications of ethical dilemma decisions because of the difficulties they presented to school principals as they were forced to decide between what was best for the individual, the school population, the school as an organisation and the wider community.

The implications of the decisions made in urban Bolivia, as elsewhere, are certainly considered carefully. The consequences that are most important are those affecting the organisation member about whom the decision is being made (will this decision bring the member shame or honour?) and how the decision-making person or group (and, indeed each individual in the group) feels that the results of the decision will impact on *them* and how *they* will be seen by others (bringing shame, honour and reducing or increasing respect). At a more personal level, an important consideration is whether the decision that is made is appropriate given the social status of the parties involved. Finally, decisions are made that will bring peace of mind to the decision maker—a sense of finality and that all within their social network is in order.

It should not be assumed, however, that the perspectives of Bolivian leaders with regard to their negotiation of the moral dilemmas surrounding the decisions they must make are either different or the same as those of Western leaders. A consideration of these deliberations of leaders in other cultures must also include a consideration of the perspectival issues involved. This implies a degree of cultural relativism.

The issue of cultural relativism

This research involves not only the examination of the frameworks for decision-making by leaders in other cultures, but also involves sub-cultural differences in terms of the ranking of the avoidance-pursuit pairs and, therefore, the ethical or value frameworks within Bolivian subcultures. Pojman (2002) described ethics as "the systematic endeavour to understand moral concepts and justify moral principles and theories" (p. 1) and said that it was concerned with normative values within cultures. The linking of morality and culture was made by Jurgen Habermas (1992), who felt that morality was subject to reason but that "Aristotle was right in his opinion that the moral intuitions which theory clarifies must have been acquired elsewhere, in more or less successful *socialization* [italics added by Habermas] processes" (p. 168). The perspective of Ruth Benedict was seen in her statement: "Morality differs in every society, and is a convenient term for socially approved habits" (Mead, 1959, p. 276).

In the research context of the valuated avoidance-pursuit pairs, these principles and theories do not conform to a universal moral absolutism but, rather, carry features of both moral objectivism—moral principles that may have universal validity but many or even all may be overridden in different circumstances (Pojman, 2002)—and conventionalism, where the moral principles depend on social choice or interpersonal agreement. Pojman (2002) quoted Benedict, referring to the human tendency to believe something to be good when it was merely something that was habitual, and concluded that morality was "dependent on the varying histories and environments of different cultures" (p. 33). Conventionalism, according to Pojman (2002) therefore appeared to be "an enlightened response to the sin of ethnocentricity, and it seems to entail or strongly imply an attitude of tolerance towards other cultures" (p. 42).

Others might make the point that there are universal principles (Chomsky, 2007), basing their religious stance on observed habituation. Fried (1978), however, observed that in the moral theory of many major traditions in the West, as well as in "ordinary moral understanding" (p. 7), there are things such as harming the innocent, lying, enslavement and degradation that might be seen, in particular cases, to be necessary for the greater good. This argument from an objectivist stance is conditioned by the stated Western moral theory context. However, any attempt to generate a universal ethical base may be driven by the economic rationalist concerns of globalisation or some other ideological forces and may ignore a culture-specific subjectivism. As Nigel Dower (1998) noted, this does not necessarily refer to a genuinely universalist perspective, "but is in fact a projection of the values of the power that uses them, and indeed may be a mask for the pursuit of interested objectives" (p. 32). Dower (1998) also concluded that the concepts of a global ethic and ethical relativism are mutually exclusive. In the consideration of ethically informed decision-making in this research, the differences between cultures—a form of cultural relativism—are seen not so much in the differences in ethical thinking that may or may not be found in cultures, but are based on the emergence of different valuations in different cultures of the avoidance-pursuit pairs. This, in turn, leads to a contrasting of moral actions.

The statement by Fried (1978) above presumes a universal definition of what a "moral" or "decent" person may be and, in fact, reflects a Western, dare one say, North American, naivety and ethnocentricity. While stating that there could be some "universals" to be identified by anthropologists, Herskovits (1972) believed that evaluations are relative as they arise from a particular cultural background. If ethical norms are considered to be binding only within a specific culture, then one would expect the values and disvalues, in terms of the intrinsic and extrinsic value sets, to vary across distinct cultures. Within cultures, then, the perception of correctness of decisions that are made "lies in a moral perception and not in some abstract, general rule" (Pojman, 2002, p. 252). Cultures, as collectivities where individuals are enculturated and bonded, provide the framework for what David Hume referred to as "conventions" or "shared intentions" (Baier, 1997). Baier claimed that these "mental commons" are not merely at a cognitive level but inform "common intention." The importance of this was underlined by David Hume (1997) when we wrote: "The mutual dependence of men is so great in all societies that scarcely any human activity is complete in itself, or is performed without some reference to the actions of others" (p. 15).

The adherence to a valuated, avoidance-pursuit pair and the decisions and actions that this will produce, to some extent, echoes Kantian deontology. The members of a culture believe intuitively that they are duty-bound to act as an unconditional imperative in a manner indicated by cultural norms and guided by the avoidance-pursuit pair of highest value in their community. The decision to act in this case "lies in a moral perception and not in some abstract, general rule" (Pojman, 2002, p. 252). As Pojman also pointed out, however, "deontological systems have some serious disadvantages. First, it is difficult to see how any argument can take place with an intuitionist. Either you both have the same intuition about [something], or you don't, and that is all there is to it" (p. 252). The evidence in the daily media would appear to support this view, particularly as Eastern and Western cultures endeavour to communicate with and understand each other.

This poses a significant problem in the study of ethics cross-culturally, such as in this research, because, apart from moral differences, what may be perceived as being ethical in one culture may be considered to be highly unethical in another (Rubenstein, 2003). In cultures that have value systems that are primarily deontologically based rather than consequentially based, it may be considered "wrong" to lie, but if lying is initiated in order to preserve family or tribal *honour*, then lying would be seen as a duty or imperative (Muller, 2006). It could also be noted here that lying to cover *guilt* is very common in Western cultures, though it would not be seen as a cultural imperative.

In a study of managers in Nigeria, Sokoya (2005) wrote that while there was an acknowledgement that: "The ethical-moral mode of valuation is represented by a 'right' scale suggesting an evaluative framework guided by ethical consideration, influencing behaviour towards actions that are judged right and away from those that are judged wrong" (p. 228), no definition of what may constitute "right" was considered apart from the observation that in Nigeria Western ideas are often seen as being right. A significant finding in relation to this Bolivian research was that: "there is a definite indication that there are probable cultural explanations for the personal value orientations of Nigerian managers, which in turn may affect management practice in the country" (p. 234).

It would be expected that the ethical considerations directed by the avoidance-pursuit pairs would, at the level of the personal, affective domain, provoke a consequentialist ethic in that they involve the avoidance of unpleasant consequences or the active pursuit of egocentric goals. However, as mentioned, at a cultural level, the avoidance-pursuit pairs appear to be directed towards a Kantian deontology with decisions foreshadowed by a culturally defined categorical imperative.

For the purposes of this research, there may well exist ethical, universal verities, but they are not the focus of the research. Returning to the definition of Edwards (1986), morality considers *what* actions or attitudes are deemed to be virtuous, whereas ethics considers *why* these may be morally right or wrong. This is perhaps illustrated by Heine and Norenzayan (2006) who referred to work by Nisbet and Cohen

(1996), stating that "people participating in cultures of honour are not more aggressive than other peoples across all situations; rather, their aggression emerges specifically in situations in which their honour has been slighted" (p. 245). There is a difference between understanding the "correct thing to do" in a general, universal sense and a moral obligation to a particular course of action.

The cultural relativism inherent in this research, then, is positioned at the convergence of possible ethical universalities, culturally influenced ethical frameworks, and sub-culturally determined moral obligations. The difference between this conceptualisation and that described by Benedict (1934) or Herskovits (1972) is that it provides a theoretical explanation for the differences in the perception of what constitutes ethical behaviour in different cultures. The constructs of ethical behaviour, then, could be universal, but it may be the valuation of the avoidance-pursuit pairs that will determine the acted outcomes of the decision-making process within specific cultural settings. "Thus, in the West we debate ethics by trying to determine if things are right or wrong. In the East, they debate ethics by trying to determine if things are honourable or shameful" (Muller, 2006, p. 189).

The undertaking of this study in Bolivia assumed that if our worldview comes from our lifeworld, as Dilthey suggested (Naugle, 2002), then it would be expected that for any individual, there would be as follows—the first two requiring examination using ethnological methodologies and the last three using ethnographies.

(a)   some universal ethical perspectives on moral behaviour that arise from a shared-earth lifeworld,

(b)   some penuniversal[14] ethics flowing from early history commonalities,

(c)   some perspectival ethics flowing from a shared culture,

(d)   some perspectival ethics flowing from a shared subculture, and

(e)   some particularist ethics flowing from the individual's lifeworld.

The list of perspectives above is not to suggest the primacy of a Nietzschean moral relativism as a normative framework for ethical thought and moral conduct, nor an Aristotelian universal-particular, is-ought or fact-value dichotomy (Carr, 2000). Rather, it indicates an observationist, phenomenological approach to the issues from both ethnographic and ethnological perspectives.

Pecorino (2000) defined two important terms relating to cultural relativism and to this study, which is based on a descriptive ethical relativism by contrasting it with

---

[14] The term *penuniversal* is used here to indicate those ethical constructions that are *almost* universal. Such would be the case, for example, with an understanding that treachery is morally reprehensible. While the majority of cultures would concur, the Sawi of New Guinea would not hold this view (Richardson, 2007).

normative ethical relativism. Descriptive ethical relativism he defined as a simple recognition that different cultures will vary in their mores, customs and ethical principles. Normative ethical relativism, however, claims that there is no such thing as a universal moral principle and that nothing can be claimed to be universally right or universally wrong, that all moral considerations always have been, and always will be, relative. In this specific piece of research, the existence of universally valid moral principles was not considered. The descriptive ethical relativism on which it was based gave the freedom to observe, somewhat objectively, the value structures of leaders within other cultures in terms of the ranking they give to the avoidance-pursuit pairs.

Leadership in another culture

Generally, at an international level, research into leadership has been driven historically by an economic rationalist desire to find effective human resource management models (Owens, 1991). More recently, the human relations side of leadership has risen to the fore as researchers investigated transactional (Holander, 1978; Burns, 1985) and transformational (Bass, 1985; Hoover, Petrosko & Schulz, 1991; Silins, 1992) models as well as many other forms from the temporal to the transcendental (Sanders, Hopkins, & Geroy, 2003). At the same time, systems approaches (Owens, 1991) have gained popularity as well as the corporate nature of organisations and the importance of organisational learning (Evers, 1991; Argyris, 1982; Argyris & Schon, 1984). Each of these perspectives on leadership and effectiveness has been sourced in the particular value orientations of the researchers, international companies, and the cultures from which the researchers have come.

Hallinger and Leithwood (1996), commenting from an educational leadership background, said that there was a scarcity of knowledge regarding the cultural foundations of educational administration, and that the material published on this theme was based within a Western context. "Exceptions to this characterization generally appear outside the educational literature in the field of private sector management. Even there they remain surprisingly scarce and mostly concern issues of training and socializing managers in cross-cultural settings" (p. 101).

Biggart and Hamilton (1987) noted that leadership is embedded within cultural belief systems and therefore must be viewed from within that worldview context. The cultural distinctives that differentiate one category of people from another (Hofstede, 1995) are so broad that they also may be found in leadership styles (Jung, Bass, & Sosik, 1995). Jung and Avolio (1999) found that, for example, the effects on followers of transactional and transformational leadership styles did not generalise across Caucasian and Asian cultures. They concluded that "future leadership research should be based on a broader theoretical framework that includes both the type of cultural contingencies examined here and a broader range of tasks and cultural value orientations" (p. 217). This research examined some of the cultural contingencies and cultural value orientations within Bolivian cultural contexts.

Bolivian leadership

Some understanding of what is meant by the term "leader" within a Bolivian context is important. The Spanish word for leader (*líder*) is a relatively recent addition to the language (Prieto, 1960), having been calqued from the English word. The word has gained wide acceptance though there are many words in Spanish that are used in leadership settings and all have their own connotations and contexts. Prieto (1960) illustrated the difficulties encountered in attempting to study this construct across cultures: "In the leader one draws together a series of qualities related to the socialization of giving direction that one cannot express in denoted Spanish words, charged by use in a different context and at times with opposite meaning to that signified by the word leader" (p. 13).

Other Latins have variously seen leadership as being something that draws people together within a society to have common distant goals (Ocampo Flórez, 1999) or as someone who has dominion over a group (Tapia, 2002). Tapia, in his book dedicated to Che Guavarra—who was killed in Bolivia and is still regarded by many Bolivians as a hero—spoke of imposed leaders, natural leaders and true leaders. In his work, he demonstrated the influence of Communism (particularly through Russia and Cuba, where many Bolivian leaders undertook tertiary study on generous scholarships), and Socialism that has been so much a part of the politics for the last century and which received considerable momentum from the Liberation Theology movement in Latin America, including Bolivia.

Tapia (2002) also wrote strongly against the practice of *caudillerismo*, a term in Latin America for a form of authority but which usually has negative connotations. *Caudillos* have been very common in Latin America and Bolivia, and their effect on the concept of leadership has been significant. A *caudillo* is often seen as a military chief (Ferguson, 2003) or one who takes to himself or herself all authority, monopolising control and removing all competition. At the same time, *caudillos* traditionally seem to avoid doing very much that is constructive—though they are known for their speech-making (Tapia). Tapia contrasted this form of domination with an "accommodating" leader who has "the golden keys to many hearts" (p. 33) and serves his or her people.

Leadership in rural Bolivia

Within country areas, particularly in the southern highlands and valleys of Bolivia, the rural people of the Quechua and Aymara communities have long-established *ayllus*. These are groups of villages that function as communities brought together by kinship ties under an ancient system that predates the Incas (Oxfam America, 2005). These communities are led by a variety of leaders, both male and female, called *malkus* or *mama t'hallas*. Another form of leadership at the village level is the *jilacata*. This person, whose title originally meant brother or son of the creator in Aymara, is a political and often religious leader of a village. Villagers take turns in this role and each male in the village would be expected to take on the role of *jilacata* at least once during their adult life (Machicado, 2009).

These men and women lead dialogue and local committees, supervise agriculture, housing construction, and water distribution (Oxfam America, 2005). This type of structure is similar to what Sandóval (1998) referred to when he wrote of "strong" cultural identities that make it possible to consolidate grassroots organisations that are patterned on norms socially accepted by the community and also to mobilise the community on the basis of that identity. It is within these lifeworld settings that the worldviews and avoidance-pursuit pair orientations of the leaders in rural Bolivia have been formed.

When these people from the country move to the city, they must learn Spanish, if they do not already have it, and must accommodate themselves to very different networks of relationships and lifeworlds. Many of the clan and kin relationships will have disappeared due to the physical separation, and re-acculturation must take place. Having said this, the ideal structures within the cities include strong dialogue-based problem-solving systems. Writing regarding leadership within city *mestizo* [mixed race] societies, Rey (1995) said that group members need to have a level of intellectual maturity and be willing to work together in an integrated fashion. He stressed the importance for leaders of communication, authentic participation of followers, cooperation, moral authority, emotional stability, dialogue, popularity, and the meeting of the needs of the community being led.

The national elections in 2005 saw, for the first time, a member of an indigenous group, Evo Morales, elected to the Bolivian presidency. The presidency of Morales has been marked at times by considerable unrest as his government has attempted to redefine the country in terms of its political power base—mostly from the rural communities—rejecting foreign influence where possible, and writing a new constitution. The intent of the government is to restore a form of indigenous culture as the national culture. Key to the government's attempts to re-acculturate the country is the use of the education system through the promulgation of a new education law to be implemented by educational leaders across the country. These changes have become of considerable importance for the leaders who participated in this research and while concerns come from a number of directions, those participants who were educational leaders would have been charged with promoting the cultural change through their schools.

Bolivian education

The system within which educational leaders in Bolivia endeavour to function and make ethical decisions is one fraught with difficulties. Despite the fact that education has been described by the Bolivian government as the highest function of the state (*Ministerio de Educación*, 1994), as Healy (1994) observed last century: "For years, Bolivia's presidents have thrown up their hands in despair at the condition of the country's schools, wondering what, if anything, could be done to bring the educational system into the twentieth century" (p. 32).

The integration of effective educational leadership and the making of moral or ethical decisions within these conditions has also been hampered by perceived incompetence and corruption. Problems in schools "are often attributed to ignorance, incompetence, or malevolence on the part of those responsible for educational governance" (Plank & Boyd, 1990, p. 4587). Plank and Boyd add that, because of this, reform is demanded "in the hope that new institutions will place braver, wiser, and nobler persons in charge of children's schooling" (p. 4587).

In the late 1980s, an education reform program (Contreras & Talavera Simoni, 2003) was planned to try to overcome some of these obstacles, and this has affected the decision-making processes of school leaders. The reform was designed to force schools to leave behind the traditional educational models that had been in vogue for over a century (Contreras & Talavera Simoni). This old model had involved an almost exclusive use of rote learning and memorisation, highly structured classrooms and a highly structured bureaucracy (Pachón, 1995). Under the new model, the centralised educational bureaucracy was devolved to allow considerably more decision-making at the school level (*Ministerio de Educación*, 1994), thus forcing school principals to make decisions pertinent to their school.

The current government, under an indigenous president, has moved to "*decolonizar*" [decolonise] schooling, or move schooling further away from its Spanish conquest roots (*Los Tiempos*, 2006). At the same time, due to the media and the interchange of people studying in other countries, the effects of globalisation are still being felt on the leadership of schools (Tiznado, 2001) as school leaders, particularly of private schools, endeavour to gain an advantage for economic and prestige reasons.

For the new generation of educational leaders, educational leadership theory is largely sourced in the Western world, particularly in the United States. An example of this is typified in an article by Bolívar (2001) on educational leadership and school restructuring in Latin America, where less than twenty per cent of the bibliographic references are from Latin authors, and many of these have relied heavily on North American thinking and models. (Another example of this is seen in Antonio Bolívar's (2001) article *Liderazgo educativo y reestructuración escolar* [Educational leadership and school restructuring].) Despite this theory orientation to Western models, considerable research has been carried out in the other direction. Further insights into the functioning of leadership in Latin American societies, therefore, may be gained by examining research that has been conducted by North American and European researchers into leadership in different cultural contexts, including Bolivia, or at least Latin America. Two sets of research studies that have been most notable in this area have been those conducted by the GLOBE Project and by Geert Hofstede.

Cross-cultural leadership research

i. The GLOBE Project

The most far-reaching research into international leadership that has examined cultural differences in leadership conceptualisations has been that undertaken by Robert House's GLOBE Project (House et al., 2004). This meta-analysis by one hundred and seventy "country co-ordinators" examined leadership characteristics across 17,300 middle managers in sixty-two of the world's cultures. For the purposes of their research, leadership was defined as "the ability of an individual to influence, motivate, and enable others to contribute toward to effectiveness and success of the organizations of which they are members" (House et al., 2004, p. 15). Using this general definition that appears to be based on a Western construction of the leadership concept, the study sought to assess nine dimensions of societal and organisational cultures and to attempt to determine the effectiveness of behaviours exhibited by leaders on the performance and attitudes of subordinates (Grove, 2005). The dimensions studied have significance for this research in that they are differentiated culturally, and all of them influence decision-making. The dimensions identified by the GLOBE Project were: Power Distance, Uncertainty Avoidance, Humane Orientation, Institutional Collectivism, In-Group Collectivism, Assertiveness, Gender Egalitarianism, Future Orientation and Performance Orientation.

The GLOBE Project results indicated the emergence of six dimensions of leadership that were thought to be universal: Charismatic/value-based, team-oriented, self-protective, participative, humane-oriented and autonomous (Grove, 2005). The strength of each of these, however, varied from culture to culture (House et al., 2004), giving rise to a theory of both culturally independent and dependent leadership characteristics that contribute to culturally endorsed Implicit Leadership Theories (Den Hartog et al., 1999). The results of the analysis of the GLOBE Project data by Den Hartog et al. (1999) elicited factors that were thought to facilitate or inhibit excellence in leaders and indicated a considerable variation between cultures. This was particularly so for such culturally contingent attributes as Intra-group conflict avoider, Subdued, Cunning and Sensitive. In this research relating to the ranking of avoidance-pursuit pairs, the GLOBE Project results indicate the variation between cultures across a range of variables that are closely linked with relationships, as do the findings of Geert Hofstede's research.

ii. Geert Hofstede

The series of studies across cultures undertaken by Geert Hofstede has analysed data from 117,000 managers in fifty-three countries from 1967 till the conducting of this Bolivian research. The primary cultural dimensions relating to leadership that Hofstede (2006) has identified are Power Distance (PDI), Individualism (IDV), Masculinity (MAS), Uncertainty Avoidance (UAI) and Long-Term Orientation. His research indicated that these dimensions have different strengths in different cultures and as with the GLOBE Project results, the results of the Hofstede studies may be seen in the context of the avoidance-pursuit pairs matrix. Hofstede's analysis of the results from Peru, the closest country culturally to Bolivia, showed that the values for four of his cultural dimensions, Power Distance, Individualism, Masculinity and Uncertainty Avoidance was very close to that of the average for all of Latin America (Hofstede, 2006).

> Peru's highest Hofstede Dimension is Uncertainty Avoidance (UAI) is 87, indicating the society's low level of tolerance for uncertainty. In an effort to minimize or reduce this level of uncertainty, strict rules, laws, policies, and regulations are adopted and implemented. The ultimate goal of this population is to control everything in order to eliminate or avoid the unexpected. As a result of this high Uncertainty Avoidance characteristic, the society does not readily accept change and is very risk averse.
>
> Peru has a low Individualism (IDV) ranking (11), as do all other Latin countries (average 21). The score on this Dimension indicates the society is Collectivist as compared to Individualist. This is manifest in a close long-term commitment to the member 'group', be that a family, extended family, or extended relationships. Loyalty in a collectivist culture is paramount, and over-rides most other societal rules and regulations. The society fosters strong relationships where everyone takes responsibility for fellow members of their group. (paras. 2–3)

In a table of country comparison of index scores taken from work by Hofstede,

Schwartz, Trompenaars and Inglehart, Basabe and Ros (2005) showed that Bolivia scored very low on individualism along with several other Latin American countries. Not all researchers have agreed with Hofstede's methods or findings, however. Slater et al. (2006), for example, have argued that Hofstede's dimensions may not necessarily carry the same meaning in different cultural settings. Presumably, there will always be difficulties in this regard due to a possible lack of accurate dynamic equivalence in translation, as well as the already mentioned conceptual and metric equivalence (Heck, 1996) issues. Shalom Schwartz's (1994) surveys of worldwide values among primary school teachers and students found seven culture-level dimensions that he claimed were "quite different" from Hofstede's. McSweeney (2004), who has been critical of Hofstede's work, wrote:

> Even if it is crudely supposed that a national culture is somehow composed of separately identifiable independent dimensions, why should we accept that Hofstede successfully identified even the "dominant" dimensions? Questionnaire answers are not neutral 'windows' through which national cultures can be perceived. (p. 19)

Along with many other criticisms, McSweeney (2004) quoted Robinson (1983) as stating that Hofstede's dimensions are a 'hodgepodge' of items of which few were relate to the intended construct. However, it is interesting to see that Hofstede's (1984) model posits shared, societal norms at the centre. These have their origin in environmental factors and their outworking in social institutions and structures including the family, systems of education, politics and legislation. The model forms a system whereby, "These institutions, once they have become facts, reinforce the societal norms and the ecological conditions that led to them" (p. 22). It is interesting to note that while this conceptualisation emphasises the centrality of societal norms in terms of the values systems of major groups within a population, it includes "Religion" as primarily consequential rather than influential of both Origins and Societal Norms. Although evidence for this may exist in the explanations of variance in their studies, these were studies of commercial enterprises that generally did not take into consideration spiritual, ontological or existential questions. The literature surrounding the affective domain pairs, particularly that of Muller (2006a), would suggest a more dominant role for religion.

The cultural variations that exist are significant for this research and also may be extrapolated to considerations of world events. For example, the importance of a consideration of cross-cultural differences in decision-making was highlighted in a study of airline accident rates. This showed (Phillips, 1994) that in cultures identified by Hofstede (and also by the GLOBE Project) as being collectivist in nature, airline accident rates were three times more frequent per head of population than in individualistic societies. One possible reason that was given for this was that in collectivist and high power-distance cultures, there is less openness and questioning. This would appear to imply the importance of relationships, to the avoidance of shame at all costs and the promotion of honour. As "Latin cultures also share a lower capacity for openness, trust, and the rational expression of feelings" (Bass, 1990, p. 764), one would expect this to be the case in Bolivia as well. Bolivia, however, has a remarkably good record in terms of aircraft safety. This would point to a different conceptualisation of collectivism within a Latin American context, as discussed earlier.

While cultural differences exist, various theories may be used to better understand the differences with a degree of objectivity. One useful theory central to the work of both House and Hofstede, and which has significance for this research, is the concept of a Value-Belief Theory.

Conclusion

The literature surrounding this research points to the existence and importance of worldviews. These arise from, and are shaped by, our culture and our experienced lifeworld and will therefore differ between cultures and between individuals within cultures. Within these worldviews, the literature suggests the existence of a matrix of avoidance-pursuit pairs: guilt-innocence, shame-honour, and fear-power. These are said to be ranked by cultures and individuals, and while the ranking may vary over time or circumstances, there is a culturally driven tendency for one avoidance-pursuit pair to hold the highest value within the matrix.

The orientation of an individual or a culture to an ethical framework, the literature suggests, is at least in part determined by the avoidance-pursuit pair having the highest value. The alignment of the decision-making process for an individual to this avoidance-pursuit pair will determine, in deontological fashion, his or her perception of the "correct thing to do" in a given circumstance. An implication of this is that in the examination of the ethical decision-making of leaders, it is important to study the influence of culture on worldview formation and its production of a hierarchical valuation of the avoidance-pursuit pairs.

The variation in ethical frameworks between cultures and individuals would seem to indicate a form of cultural relativist ethics, and in this research, the use of culturally relative moral obligation structures is argued. While an individual may know that, according to some universal principle, a certain action may be considered ethically to be "wrong," they may persist with that action because it is the moral "correct thing to do" within their cultural setting and mores.

The adherence, conscious or unconscious, of an individual to a specific course of action that may be considered by them to be ethical or moral depends on the strength, therefore, of their culturally imbued avoidance of guilt, shame or fear and their desire to be seen to be innocent, honoured or powerful. While there is a great deal of literature in psychology on the subject of guilt, there is somewhat less on shame, though the field is growing, particularly within a Western-Asian trade and economy milieu.

Finally, the research considered the functioning of the avoidance-pursuit pair matrix in the decision-making of leaders in Bolivia, South America. Consideration is also given to the cross-cultural leadership research undertaken by the GLOBE Project and Geert Hofstede. The leaders to be considered within Bolivia come from various sub-cultural groups that, as indicated from the literature, have different matrix prioritisations. The leaders considered by the GLOBE Project and by Hofstede are from business communities around the world, including South America.

CHAPTER 3

Research Methodology

The research, using interview data, provided information that was based on the participants' interpretations of real and hypothetical events and decisions. The process also provided a vehicle for reflection on the real and possible outcomes of the decisions made. These reflections were set within contexts that involved the social interactions surrounding leadership environments, such as school-principalship, and were contrasted across two different subcultures. A research methodology was therefore required that would permit the collection and analysis of data so that the existence of the avoidance-pursuit pair priorities may be confirmed for the cultures of the participants. Once this had been established, the priorities assigned by participants could be explored in relation to their cultural background. Finally, possible cultural causation for the priorities was explored.

Methodological relationship to the purpose of the study

The methodology that was chosen was one that took into consideration the cultural context of this culturally situated research, including ethnographic (within culture) and ethnological (between cultures) components. This recognises that "we are situated in particular histories, cultures, and ethical traditions, which provide our orientation toward that which we are trying to understand" (Gadamer, quoted in Dostal, 2004, p. 94). The participants in this research have been enculturated in different subculture situations in Bolivia that are neither Australian nor Western, and therefore, a methodology was sought that was able to take into account both the cultural situations of the participants and that of the researcher as an outsider who had lived in the country for some years. During those twelve years of residence and knowing a number of the participants, provided a degree of lifeworld overlap and something of an understanding of the cultures and lifeworlds of the participants. This overlap included the perspectives gained while acting as a board member for eight years in a Bolivian private school, participating on the boards of various other Bolivian institutions, working closely with Bolivian educators to plan and present seminars, workshops and conferences, and visiting many government departments and businesses. Further enculturation of the researcher revolved around relationships that developed over the years. For a range or work-related reasons, these included relationships with Bolivians in all classes within the stratified Bolivian society. An appropriate methodology was therefore one that allowed for the adequate consideration of both etic and emic perspectives—with the responses of the participants being seen from the perspective of an "outsider" but also as one who has lived inside the cultural setting.

The extent and limitations of the study

The scope of this study was limited for practical reasons to leaders in Bolivia. The participants were drawn from two different subculture groups within the Bolivian society as it exists in and around the city of Cochabamba. The distinct subculture groups were those of the city, being mostly Hispanic or *Mestizo* participants, and Quechua participants from villages, mostly in the mountains surrounding the city. The leaders interviewed included the principals of independent and government schools, business leaders, politicians and other community leaders. The leaders were mostly from the city, but a number of them were leaders from country village communities, and some had lived and/or worked in both cultures. The leadership contexts of the participants were as follows:

City	Country
Education	Community
Business	Professional
NGO	Religious
Religious	Education
Professional	
Political	

Another limitation of the study was one involving language. While the researcher is fluent in Spanish, he is not a native, Hispanic Bolivian, and even less a Quechua Bolivian. In order to understand fully the nuances of language embedded in culture, it would be necessary for the research to be conducted by Bolivians and written up in Spanish and Quechua. This was neither possible nor, in one sense, the intent of the research, which gives a partial outsider's descriptive case study perspective on the two subcultures. Where the participants used expressions that were unknown to the interviewer, they were either asked at the time for clarification, or, as this would break the train of the interview, clarification was sought in Spanish and Quechua dictionaries. Where the issue was one of local idiom, particularly where there was a particularly subtle distinction, participants in Phase II or Bolivian friends were asked to explain the term more fully.

Of particular significance to the research was the language issue of the use of "justice" as a pair component. The literature (Muller, 2000, 2006; Hegeman, 2004; Blaschke, 2001) spoke of justice and guilt, but within the Bolivian context, it became apparent in the first interviews that the participants identified the term very strongly with the judicial system (and its failings) and the perceived injustice of *justicia comunitaria* [community justice]. The term *justo* was used to signify righteous, but this was at times seen by the participants to mean fair. Where there was confusion, the term *inocente* [innocent] was used. There remained, however, a degree of apparent disjunction between the intention of the term in the literature and the meaning connoted by the participants.

The theoretical framework for the research

[It should be noted that since the completion of the research, much more thought has gone into the foundations of research from a biblical base. The concept of research as unhiding God and His knowledge is not included here, but rather the framework that was used was one that was fairly "standard" in universities at the time.]

For this research, so heavily embedded in human actions, interactions and culture, a qualitative paradigm was deemed to be the most appropriate. A quantitative approach would not be suitable because "discrete variables and their relationships do not seem to be sufficient to deal with the complex interactions and patterns of human behaviour" (Guba & Lincoln, 1982, p. 81). Phenomenological research is more suited to an exploration of the lived experience of people (Holloway, 1997) and rather than simply quantifying a behaviour such as decision-making, it seeks to have the participants define their *meaning* of the behaviour (McNabb, 2004). The suitability of a qualitative approach for this study of affective domain constructs and decision-making, with links to lifeworlds and cultures, was particularly seen in a reference from Paton (2002), who wrote:

> [Phenomenological approaches] focus on exploring how human beings make sense of experience and transform experience into consciousness, both individually and as shared meaning. This requires methodologically, carefully, and thoroughly capturing and describing how people experience some

phenomenon—how they perceive it, make sense of it, and talk about it with others. To gather such data, one must undertake in-depth interviews with people who have *directly* experienced the phenomenon of interest; that is, they have "lived experience" as opposed to second hand experience. (p. 104)

The investigation surrounding the research question within a Bolivian context was an innovative academic endeavour—because it appeared that so far research focusing on the role of these specific avoidance-pursuit pairs in leadership had not been undertaken cross-culturally. In terms of the international studies to be examined, House (1988), the leader of the largest study and one that was largely quantitative in nature, wrote:

Within the scientific paradigm qualitative research is most effectively used when we have little knowledge about the phenomenon under study. Under these conditions it is necessary to allow the environment to teach us because we do not have an adequate framework, we do not have hypotheses, we do not have a clear idea as to what the critical variables are, and we have little ability to measure them. (p. 258)

The search for significance using a qualitative approach in this situation provided the depth for what Husserl referred to as *Verstehen* (understanding), rather than merely *Erklären* (explanation) (Husén, 1988), as it sought to comprehend the essences of the processes (Van Maanen, 1990) linking culture, worldview and the framing of decisions. A qualitative study was also indicated as the research was situated within the relationships that existed in the context of human institutions such as government, businesses and schools (Dey, 1993) and took into consideration the lifeworlds of the participants and the researcher (Chilcott, 1987). The use of a qualitative methodology was also deemed to be most fitting to get at "the subtleties of how leaders think and how they frame their experience" (Chilcott, 1987, p. 271). Wei-Ting and Gutierrez (2003) referred to Merriam (1998 and 2002) and Rossman and Rallis (2003) when making the statement: "Qualitative research acknowledges that any individual enters a context with a personal perspective that shapes and is shaped by perceptions" (p. 65). It was the personal perspectives of the participants that constituted the data for this study within the framework of an interpretive inquiry.

Theoretical perspective of the research

The theoretical framework indicated the employment of a relational epistemology working through a symbolic interactionist framework to extract the essential meanings of decision-making processes within the individual experiences of the participants through the use of ethnographic, ethnological and descriptive relativist tools. In this sense, the process may be described as being eidetic or descriptive phenomenology, following Husserl's use of the term *Eidos* to mean essences (Smith & McIntyre, 1982), but also eidetic in terms of the cultural content, including systems of ideas and criteria for interpreting experience.

The symbolic interactionist perspective of this research included the conceptualisation of the self as being socially constructed: "selves exist only in relation to other selves" (Mead, 1932, p. 185). Interactionism was particularly pertinent in this research as the determination of what constitutes an ethical decision would be socially situated in terms of the cultural transmission of ethics and morals, and also in terms of the consequences of decisions. Crotty (1998) wrote that symbolic interactionism "deals directly with issues such as language, communication, interrelationships and community . . . symbolic interactionism is all about those basic social interactions whereby we enter into the perceptions, attitudes and values of a community" (pp. 7–8). The interview situations in this research provided the language and other symbolic communication, such as body language, necessary for an understanding of the processes involved. Qualitative research of this interactionist nature was strongly perspectival: the perspectives of the researcher and the participants, using words and other symbols to make sense of situations and perspectives. As Charon (1979) noted: "In a way the best definition of perspective is a conceptual framework which emphasises that perspectives are really interrelated sets of words used to order physical reality" (p. 3).

That having been said, Blumer (1969) argued that there was "no clear formulation of the position of symbolic interactionism" (p. 1), a term for which he took credit, and different theorists have given it different meanings. At times, the term has been used synonymously with the term qualitative (Bogden & Bilken, 1992), but it remains a useful, distinguishing concept for the framing of research. One of the basic postulates of symbolic interactionism is that human beings inhabit a natural and a social world (Cohen, Manion & Morrison, 2000) and as Creswell (2005) noted: "Humans engage with the world and make sense of it based on their historical and social perspective—we are all born into a world of meaning bestowed upon us by our culture" (p. 9).

The conceptualisation of symbolic interactionism as used by Blumer (1969) was based on three premises: (1) that human beings act towards objects based on the meanings that those objects have for them; (2) that the derivation of this meaning is to be found in human social interaction; and (3) these meanings are manipulated and modified through an interpretative process. In this research, the significance of symbolic interactionism may be seen in the assumption that the leaders make decisions that are based on meaningful choices, that the structure available to inform the decision-making process is derived from the lifeworld and cultural contexts of the leaders, and that the process arises from the worldviews of the leaders.

Three informing perspectives for this methodological framework: ethnography, ethnology and descriptive relativism

To use the terms preferred by anthropologists, the research was ethnographic in that it was focused on gleaning and analysing data from participants, specifically from within their cultural setting: a setting in Bolivia with which the researcher was very familiar. At the same time, the research was ethnological in that within it were comparisons between different cultures: comparisons between the different cultures of the participants—Spanish, *Mestizo* or indigenous—and where appropriate, comparisons with relevant segments of the culture-directed perspective of the researcher.

One important consideration regarding decision-making was the perception of universality regarding the response to ethical and moral questions. If lifeworlds give birth to worldviews, as Naugle (2002) suggested that Dilthey had believed, then it may have been expected that for any individual there would be the possibility of adherence to a range of ethical and moral stances with varying degrees of universality and individuality. The literature in the fields of anthropology and sociology would suggest that, given the exceptions illustrated throughout the world, universals may indeed be penuniversal, or almost universal. Brown (1991) suggested that what are often thought to be universal beliefs in this context, in reality, may be considered as such if they are adhered to by ninety-five per cent of cultures. A study of the consistency of so-called universals, or the variation in penuniversals across cultures, is an ethnological pursuit. Ethnographic studies will identify perspectival ethics from shared cultures and subcultures as well as the particularist ethics flowing from an individual's lifeworld.

This research was also informed by a descriptive relativist perspective. Rather than basing this research on a suggestion of the primacy of an Aristotelian universal-particular, is-ought or fact-value dichotomy (Carr, 2000), or a Nietzschean moral relativism as normative frameworks for ethical thought and moral conduct, a relativist stance was followed. This researcher-as-observer approach to the issues was one in which the researcher endeavoured to consider the moral and ethical content of the participants' decision-making with a degree of detachment.

As with the descriptive ethical relativism (Pecorino, 2000) discussed in Chapter 2, Swoyer (2003) noted that cultural descriptive relativism was one of the approaches to considering culturally or ethically different perspectives. While absolutism implies that the observer considers there to be only one, universal ethic that applies to all cultures, the relativistic perspectives imply a recognition of different cultures having different ethical standards or norms. Swoyer claimed that in descriptive relativistic terms, principles in two cultures may be described, though not evaluated, as being right or wrong within those cultural contexts. That is not to say that the researcher held relativistic beliefs at a personal level, but rather that there was a recognition that different cultures see moral issues differently.

In this research, absolutist or normative ethical and moral considerations were, in a sense, irrelevant. The reason for this was that the key issue was the prioritisation of the avoidance-pursuit pairs and their derivation—regardless of the use to which the prioritisation was put. So, while the researcher may have personal, normative opinions regarding the participants' ethical approach to the decisions they make, as much as possible this was bracketed out—being disregarded as immaterial for the research— or discussed with regard to its influence on the data analysis. For example, a western worldview-informed prioritisation may conclude that a particular decision or action may be "wrong" in a particular context where the removal of shame has been seen as a priority. The rightness or wrongness of the decision or action was irrelevant in that the research was limited to examining prioritisation of the related avoidance-pursuit pairs and their cultural antecedents.

Research methodology: case study

The methodology chosen for this research was that of a case study. This methodology was appropriate as the research purpose was to endeavour to locate sources of influence of avoidance-pursuit pair prioritisation in the worldviews and cultures of participants. Case studies are used to investigate "a contemporary phenomenon in depth within its real-life context" (Yin, 2003, p. 18) and may be used to suggest such cause-and-effect relationships (Yin, 2003, p. 5). Case studies are also indicated for the intensive examination of a given phenomenon (LeCompte, Preissle & Tesch, 1993) and to optimise understanding of that phenomenon (Stake, 2005). Stake went on to write that a case study gives "attention to the influence of its social, political, and other contexts" (p. 444)—in this case, the cultures and subcultures of Bolivia. To add to the legitimacy of the argument for the selection of a case study for this research, Lincoln and Guba's (1985) comments on the importance of case studies was noted:

> [Case study reporting is] more adapted to a description of the multiple realities encountered at any given site; because it is adaptable to demonstrate the investigator's interaction with the site and consequent biases that may result (reflexive reporting); because it provides the basis for both individual "naturalistic generalizations" (Stake, 1980) and transferability to other sites (thick description); because it is suited to demonstrating the variety of mutually shaping influences present; and because it can picture the value positions of

investigator, substantive theory, methodological paradigm, and local contextual values. (pp. 41–42)

Cohen, Manion and Morrison (2000, p. 184) noted a number of important advantages of case study use, adapted from Adelman, Kemmis and Jenkins (1980). These included:

- Though difficult to organise, case study data are strongly grounded in reality;
- Case studies allow generalisations—either about an instance or from an instance to a class;
- Case studies recognise the embeddedness of social truths;
- Case studies provide material that may be used for future re-interpretation; and
- The research data from case studies is in a more publicly accessible form than some other kinds.

A modifier is, however, useful in determining the specific nature of this particular research case study, and that was the term, explanatory. This research may be described as being an explanatory case study (Yin, 2003), as it examined cause and effect, and tested a theory (Cohen, Manion & Morrison, 2000) implicit in the connectedness of culture, worldview, decision-making and the theory relating to the prioritisation of the avoidance-pursuit pairs. As Yin (2003) indicated, explanatory case studies attempt to explain the how and why of event occurrence. In doing this, they may also incorporate potential causal pathways in their explanation.

Participants and data gathering strategies in Phase I

The participants interviewed in Phase I of the research were drawn from leaders of institutions, organisations and businesses in the city of Cochabamba and from rural communities around Cochabamba. Participants from Misicuni, Alto Sacaba and Cliza were within two hours drive of the city of Cochabamba. The key informant from a rural community, Yawisla, in the south of the country, was interviewed to gather valuable data for comparison with the data from the Cochabamba region. The towns near Yawisla are able to provide slightly different perspectives in that they have not been as affected by the Spanish conquest as other communities.

The Phase I participants, whose participation in the research was voluntary, were chosen in conjunction with a research assistant living in Cochabamba and others who have ready access to rural communities. Given the limited time that was available in the country to collect data for both of the phases of the research, the sampling of the participants was a sampling of convenience. Prior to the researcher's arrival in Bolivia in April 2008, a list of possible participants related to the selection criteria was drawn up, and a final list was established with the help of the research assistant upon arrival in the country[15]. The criteria for selection were that the participants must hold a leadership role within their community or organisation, they must be willing to participate in the research, they must be available for interviews during April, 2008, and they must be contactable either directly or, for participants from rural areas, through a third person who would have regular access to their community. Contact with the participants was made by the research assistant, and in the first place, was to ascertain their willingness to be involved in the research. As the participant list was largely position-based rather than specific person-based, where a possible participant did not wish to participate, then another person in a similar position—for example, a leader from another community—was contacted.

Participants in the research were offered a remuneration of Bs50 (approximately $A5) per hour for the time taken for the interview. This equates roughly to a day's wages for a labourer in the country and was felt to be an acceptable amount. Most of the participants accepted this offer, thankfully, two businessmen declined the offer, one with the implication that the amount was inconsequential, and the other saying that he was more than willing to give his time in order to have the conversation.

Notes regarding participant selection

The selection of participants and the differences between the sizes of the groups are related to the following:

i. In general, the number of participants from rural areas was lower due to the travel and communication difficulties that were involved. It was easier to contact and maintain contact with leaders within the city than in outlying, rural areas. The choice of rural participants was also limited by the research assistant's network of contacts.

ii. While the majority of educational leaders were women, the majority of those occupying other leadership positions in the city and in the rural areas were men.

iii. The choice of the leaders in educational institutions was made by the research assistant based on the location of the schools (within the central district of the city of Cochabamba—bounded by Huayna Kapak Avenue, Aroma Avenue, Oquendo Avenue and the Rocha River)—and their

---

[15] The research assistant was a part-time teacher who was able to devote time to finding leaders who were willing to participate in the research and to arrange meeting times and places for the interviews. She was not involved in the data gathering or analysis.

willingness and availability for the project. Those from the business community, politics and non-government organisations were representative of significant institutions within the society. The choice was based generally on the institution or category and not specifically on the particular person who happened to be leading it at the time of the interviews. The political leaders were important for the research due to their acquaintance with the decision-making processes at many levels of society, including significant levels of government.

iv. Church leaders and leaders from church-based schools were chosen in order to provide a context for the possible identification of links that might exist relating to religious beliefs, culture and the bases for decision-making.

v. The choice of participants from different religious backgrounds was an important component in the research. While it may be argued that to be Bolivian is to be Catholic, as the country has been, constitutionally, a Roman Catholic country, the number of evangelicals appears to be growing. The approximately equal number of Catholic and Protestant participants was coincidental but arose from the researcher and the research assistant having numerous contacts in the evangelical community. It must be stated, however, that, as four of the participants acknowledged, there are degrees of syncretism to be found in the Christian churches: Catholicism with Animism, Protestantism with Catholicism and Animism. The particular importance of identifying the religious background claimed by participants was that the literature (particularly Muller, 2006) had predicted that the influence of Christianity, with its Judeo-Grecian roots would result in an elevation of the guilt-innocence pair in this research.

vi. The relatively high proportion of educational leaders in the sample was due to the significance of education as a cultural transmitter and of the rural-urban value bases for decision-making. It would be expected that the principals would come from both backgrounds, but, as mentioned, with reference to the assertion of Luykx (1999), those teachers/principals in Bolivia from rural areas may have had their values changed in the teacher training process.

vii. The Key Informants were individuals who were able to review the data for the researcher and provide insights regarding the research. They were selected on the basis of their expertise or their particular insights into the Bolivian culture. The Key Informants included both Bolivians and foreigners. The Bolivians were an academic (sociologist) and a psychologist. Both of these Key Informants had considerable experience in observing and thinking about the actions and reactions of Bolivians and Bolivian culture. In addition to the Bolivians, an additional perspective was obtained from the foreigners who had spent most of their lives in the country but still were able to give more of an etic (outsider's) perspective. As this research was not an ethnography, these insights of foreigners were important as the researcher and most who would read the research are also foreigners.

viii. A number of the participants had met the researcher at some stage during the past eighteen years, and some were well known to the researcher. None of these relationships involves any form of dependency on the researcher, being relations of natural friendship or maintained from an initial relationship as parents of children in the international school, of which the researcher was the last principal in 1995. As all contact with potential participants was made by the research assistant, the possibility of coercion to participate based on a relationship was greatly reduced.

The importance of the participant choices for this research was that these leaders, from education, business and politics, worked in leadership positions where the making of decisions and moral choices is a part of their day-to-day work. During the data collection period, there was no time available for a "prolonged engagement" (Lincoln & Guba, 1985) with the participants or their lifeworlds, but friendships and acquaintance relationships of different strengths had already been developed with a number of the participants. The relationships with the business and political leaders were not as strong as those with some of the school principals, though some had existed for some years. The business leaders included the managers of a number of significant national and international companies, while the politicians included an ex-deputy minister at a federal level, the spouse of a leader at a department (state) level, and a city councillor.

Finally, the interviewees included several "foreigners" within the Bolivian context, including three from North America and one from Sweden. Each of these had had considerable experience in Latin America, particularly in Bolivia, and had worked with leaders or had studied them. These interviews with the foreigners were in order to gain insights into the perceptions of some of those from outside the subcultures in Cochabamba. The particular perspectival nature of the data garnered from these interviewees provided a form of triangulation within the research discussed below.

The total of forty-two participants in Phase I of the research was felt to be adequate in order to obtain the necessary data. Douglas (1985, cited in Maykut & Morehouse, 1994, p. 63) felt that as few as twenty-five participant interviews could be needed, but Sandberg (2000) claimed that even twenty could be sufficient. It was felt that a total of forty-two, very purposively chosen interviewees, should suffice for the purposes of this research in Phase I.

Priming

It should be noted that a number of the participants in this research had lifeworlds that spanned both the *campo* and the city and as such would have been able to be primed within the interview situation, either by particular words used or by memories they had of the different fields of experience. It could have been the case, therefore, that these participants were to some extent primed by references to the different cultures (Oyserman, Sorensen, Reber & Chen, 2009)—either given in the interview or in the imaginings of the participant as they positioned their thinking in readiness to make responses. The participants who had a degree of bi-culturalness, particularly included city school principals who had either lived in the country as children or who had lived in the country during a prescribed country service commitment. The possible effect on priming in these interview situations on the principals, however, was not tested in this research.

For this research, the responses of the participants will, to some degree, be affected by two things relating to foreign influence. The first is the foreign-sourced information, media images and ideas related to their particular position or profession. The second is that, being aware that the researcher is from a foreign, developed country, attempts may have been made consciously or unconsciously by the participants to present views that would reflect well on them as professionals who are advanced or "developed" in their thinking and practice. This could also be the case for the education leaders, as they would be aware that the researcher comes from an educational background in a developed country. The researcher was aware that there could also be a temptation for participants to feel that they needed to denigrate in some way the particular school, controlling government department or bureaucratic context within which they must function in order to show that they understood that the situation in which they worked was not similar to what they had seen or imagined from developed countries.

The Phase I interviews

Apart from the interviews with the three English-speaking participants, the Phase I interviews were conducted in Spanish in the workplaces of the participants or at an agreed meeting place. The interviews were recorded on an MP3 recorder for later analysis and, where necessary, translation and transcription. Although the interviews with the educational leaders were conducted in schools, and much of the time there was considerable background noise from traffic and children playing in physical education classes, the quality of the recordings was adequate in order to listen to and analyse the content. The participants very willingly gave their time and opinions, and where the demands of the interview timetable dictated a strict adherence to an hour, some of them expressed disappointment that they were not able to spend more time talking.

Sections of the interviews in Phase I were strongly directed in that data related to the participants' sub-cultural backgrounds and lifeworlds were essential for this research. In order to determine the ethical components in decision-making processes, participants were encouraged to recount their own stories to a factual and emotional depth with which they felt comfortable. From these narratives, clues were sought regarding the identification of pair components and their prioritisation, as well as values and worldview constructs. Towards the end of each interview, the participants were asked directly to rank the avoidance-pursuit pair components (fear/guilt/shame and honour/justice (or innocence)/power) as they felt those living in the city and those living in the country would rank them.

It should be noted here that in this research, while the possible existence and valuation of the pairs were discussed with the participants, they were presented initially with the pair components for comment. This obviated some of the difficulty that could be encountered with the introduction of a Western, structuralist concept of individuated opposites to some of the participants whose cultural background was one of holistic and animistic dividuation[16]. That said, the Bolivian *campesino* culture has a strong sense of existence, as mentioned previously, of "balanced pair opposites" (Schaedel, 1988, p. 770). In any case, in this research, the valuation of the individual pair components was used to give an indication of the valuation of the axes themselves.

Previous experience with cross-cultural data gathering within a Bolivian context had led to a careful consideration of interviewing style, the settings for the interviews and the questions that could be asked. It had been found that at times Bolivian educational leaders were less willing than Australians in a similar situation, to be honestly reflective and that they considered some of the requested information—such as their perceptions of the general work ethic of teaching staff—was too sensitive to be given other than in an anonymous manner, to someone they may not have fully trusted. This was not found to be the case in this research, where most of the participants volunteered much more information, and at times at a much greater personal depth, than was required. Just the same, it was felt imperative that the interviews be conducted where possible with leaders known to the researcher and in a private and relaxed setting with a guarantee of complete confidentiality in the data recording process. Ensuring that the

---

[16] Bird-David (1999) used the term dividuate to represent "a person constitutive of relationships" (p. 72). In this research the members of collectivist society were defined by interpersonal relationships and those in an animistic society by the relatedness they had with each other, with the supernatural and with elements in the environment.

participants felt at ease with the interview and with future use of the data was essential in order to obtain quality data.

It may be noted here also that the participants had all received some post-High School education (either at university or in a teacher training college) and were therefore familiar with the concept of research. Those who had completed a *Licenciatura* [undergraduate level university degree] would have had to complete some form of research thesis in order to graduate from university.

As mentioned earlier, "administration at its heart is the resolution of moral dilemmas" (Foster, 1986, p. 33), and therefore, it was expected that school administrators and other leaders would be able to report instances of moral dilemma resolution within their own administration. Given the cultural and cross-cultural contexts of the interviews, it was initially thought that there could be a use for hypothetical moral dilemma situations such as those suggested by Kohlberg (1969). The use of hypothetical dilemma situations was not intended to situate the participants on a moral development scale, as Kohlberg had used the discussion of moral dilemmas, but rather to provide an alternative means for gathering data. The theory was that by this means, if they wished, participants would be able to avoid recounting what they perhaps perceived to be potentially sensitive or embarrassing personal accounts, but still provide valuable data. In the actual interview situations, however, the participants very willingly volunteered their own factual, moral dilemma situations and discussed them quite openly, despite the fact that they saw them as being very difficult situations to resolve: "for us it is very hard to face [confront] such situations" (Participant 20). This was particularly the case with the educational leaders for whom many decisions relating to staff, students and parents involve moral dilemmas.

The Phase I data

In Phase I, code numbers (Participant 1, etc.) were used for the identification of all participants and the corresponding audio file names and any transcribed data from these interviews in order to preserve the anonymity of the participants. Any names mentioned by participants in the interviews were not recorded in any transcriptions. The interviews were copied into NVivo 8, and coding tags were placed on audio segments. These tags corresponded to the predetermined and emergent themes for the research. Each of these segments was then either transcribed or notes were made from the data.

Given the distance between the data gathering and the data analysis locations—Bolivia and Australia—while by no means impossible, the ongoing revision of the collected and analysed data with many of the participants was hindered by the

96

associated communication difficulties. Phase II of the research was used to clarify and revise the data through interviews with a subgroup of the Phase I participants.

The Phase II data

The Phase II data were collected one year after the Phase I data, in April, 2009. The participants in this phase of the research were chosen because of their particular knowledge relating to the issues that had been identified in the Phase I data. The participants, and allocated pseudonyms, in this phase were:

> Participant 1 – Educational leader (Reina)
> Participant 7 – Educational leader (Blanca)
> Key Informant 18 – Sociologist (Alberto)
> Participant 36 – Community leader (Eliana)
> Participant 37 – Community leader (Héctor)
> Key Informant 42 – Community leader and medical doctor (Estuardo)

The interviews in this phase were conducted and recorded in the same manner as in Phase I, but were more directed and focused on the clarification and validation of the Phase I data and clarification of surrounding issues that arose from the original data. As there were only six interviews in this stage, and because the interviews were more focused, NVivo 8 was not used, but notes were made directly from the recordings.

In the interviews with the participants, probes were used in order to elicit responses that, combined with the information gained from the literature and the data analysis, would answer these questions:

> 1. What was the participant's cultural, lifeworld and worldview background?
>> Where did they grow up? What languages did they speak?
>> How long have they lived where they are (city or *campo*)?
>> What religious background did they have?
>> How would you describe their beliefs now?
> 2. How did leadership function in the participant's community?
>> How long have they been a leader in your organisation?
>> What sort of leadership did your community have, and how were decisions made?
>> How did leadership work in your culture?
> 3. Who made decisions, what types of decisions were made, and how were they made, in the participant's organisation?
>> Could they think of difficult, moral dilemma situations that you have had to handle? How were these situations handled, and what were the results? Why would this have been the case? How were the results of

these difficult decisions carried out? (The questions in this section were included as it has been the researcher's experience that often in Bolivian institutions, a decision may be made, for example, to fire an employee, but the employee may not be fired, or the issue addressed outside the meeting where the decision was made. The reasons given for this behaviour were of particular interest in this research.)

4. Which of the avoidance-pursuit pair components (guilt, shame, fear, then justice/innocence, honour, power) were the most important in the participant's cultural sub-group? Which would have been thought to be the most important in the other subculture group?

The responses to these questions were intended to identify the cultural and worldview backgrounds of the participants, the decision-making processes in which they are involved and their perception of the importance of the avoidance-pursuit pair components. These were then analysed in order to confirm the participant's specific identification of a prioritisation of the pairs or the pair components, any role these may play in the decision-making process, and potential links from the pair components to cultures and worldviews.

Analysis of the data

In the research process, the researcher must retrospectively make meaning (Chase, 2005) from the vocabulary participants have used to express their realities. This process is intended to provide a warrant for belief and also to be the source of new knowledge. Wellington (2000) expanded on this outline to include: Immersion, reflection, taking apart / analysing, recombining/synthesising, relating and locating, and presenting. In general, the data analysis process used in this research followed a modification of Wellington's stages, with an added stage involving participant consultation in Phase II. This last stage was added to provide verification and a broader knowledge of the themes being analysed, as indicated in the conceptual framework used for the analysis of the data.

The collection and treatment of the data were presented earlier, but a note is added here pertaining to qualifications regarding the particular data set for this research. The data collected in both Phase I and Phase II were transcribed from an audio recording to text or notes taken from the audio files, but this process involved a translation from Spanish to English. In this sense, the data being analysed was not the same as the original data, though there are still strong links to it. This process involved a more complete immersion in the data than mere transcription, as the translation from one language to another will inevitably bring to the surface nuances that will require reflection and also provide connections to the researcher's cultural context. In undertaking the translation, and in order to improve the understanding of the data, at times a paraphrase or literal translation was used, even though the English may have been awkward; in general, a dynamic equivalence (Stine, 2004) was employed. For example, where the common Spanish interrogative, "*¿No?* (No?) was used at the end of sentences, seeking agreement, which was translated in English as "You see?"

It is appreciated that the handling of data in this way may permit the intrusion of error in that dynamic equivalent translations must, inevitably, be shaped by the translator's worldview. The translation of the material by the researcher was of particular importance as there are subtleties of the Bolivian-Spanish idiom, vocabulary and grammar that provide essential data specific to this research that would not be available from an externally translated text. A simple illustration of this may be provided by pronunciation differences within the country. The Bolivian Spanish versions of a simple sentence, such as "My family arrived from Santa Cruz ten years ago," will contain words that are pronounced differently in different regions of the country. A translation by an external translator would not reveal these differences that may be of potential importance in this research in terms of identifying worldview sources in different subcultures, and this enhanced the reflection on the data in both phases of the research.

Reflection on the whole

A reflection on the complete data set, with the already established relationships, enabled a fuller extraction of meaning (Hollway & Jefferson, 2000). Through this process, individual segments of data, the individual participants and the constructions that had arisen from the preceding activities, were seen in relation to each other and in relation to the whole. In turn, this enabled the data to be seen in its Bolivian cultural contexts and located in relation to other cultures in terms of the meta-studies conducted by other researchers.

At this stage of the analysis, three processes were at work: deduction, induction and abduction. Abductive inferences (Yu, 1994, 2006) were drawn from the data and new hypotheses or explanations were advanced, so that while deduction may prove something to be, and induction proposes an operative, abduction "suggests that something may be" (Peirce, 1867/1960, p. 171) and therefore suggested lines for further enquiry.

In order to determine the pair prioritisation and worldview sources that contribute to ethical decision-making, the analysis of the data relating to experience and practice involved, primarily, abductive and inductive processes. The abductive processes also generated further questions for Phase II of the research, which also added to the validity of the research.

Reliability and legitimation of the research

Quality control in the data analysis process in this research was undertaken through the application of the following techniques:

1. Constant comparison. The data were subjected to a process of constant comparison throughout the analysis. The comparisons used were with data provided by participants from the same subculture, by participants from the other subculture, and by participants within the same category as well as between categories.

2. Negative cases. Negative cases, or aberrations, were used to provide a basis for questioning the data further in order to better understand the strength of responses and to suggest reasons for the responses.

3. Qualifying material. Data that qualified the responses of the participants was very important in the research and was considered in detail.

4. Key informants. Analysis conclusions were checked with Key Informants in order for them to provide confirmation or clarification.

5. Phase II. The data analysis from Phase I of the research was able to be verified in the data collected from participants in Phase II of the research.

The reliability of the data collected in this research was also enhanced by the perspectives of the various categories of participants. In particular, the data was not only collected as pertaining to the perspectives of the city and *campesino* participants of their own cultures, but they were also asked to reflect on each other's cultures. In addition, the data collected in this way was checked with the foreign participants, who were able to add an etic perspective. All of these methods resulted in a form of triangulation of the data.

This data collection structure is replicable in a range of circumstances, and the open nature of the research question was also such that the research would lend itself to be repeated in the same or different contexts. A similar investigation may be carried out in any cross-cultural setting in order to observe specific culture and worldview evidence in particular facets of decision-making processes. Due to the case study setting and the specific sampling process used in this research, the external validity of the specific findings of the research may be limited (Wellington, 2000). It is hypothesised, however, that in terms of particular avoidance-pursuit pair ranking, a result set similar to this research presumably would be found only within very similar ethnographic settings (Gromm, Hammersley & Foster, 2000), although the importance of the study of relationships would have a much wider application.

While the generalisability of case study results may be difficult (Sturman, 1997), it is anticipated that the principles arising from the results of this research will have general application. This occurs through naturalistic generalisation (Gromm, Hammersley & Foster, 2000; Sturman, 1997; Stake, 1978), which Sturman described

100

as being arrived at "by recognising the similarities of objects and issues in different contexts" (p. 63). A confirmation of the finding of worldview and culture-linked avoidance-pursuit pair prioritisation signifies that similar prioritisations would be found in other contexts where similar worldviews are held. For example, similar results regarding the avoidance-pursuit pairs might be expected across the Andes region of South America and possibly more generally in South America, though the more general issue of relationships and culture would apply within any context. A further feature of naturalistic generalizability applies to the readers of the research. It is important that the lifeworld contexts in which the participants find themselves be considered fully in order to understand them (Geertz, 1973).

Ethical issues

The setting of this research had implications for ethical issues. Ethical complications arose from the research setting being on another continent and the research being conducted in Spanish rather than English. At the same time the research results have been published in English and on a different continent. The probability of anyone in Australia being able to recognise any of the participants or their institutions by references made to them in the thesis would appear to be so low as to be insignificant.

That having been said, the research was conducted with due regard for issues of ethics and privacy. Individual informed consent was obtained from each participant by way of a signed and dated form that accompanied a letter outlining the purpose of the research, the extent of the research, the publication of findings and a guarantee of anonymity in all reporting (Murphy & Dingwell, 2001). It was recognised that this guarantee of anonymity was perhaps of even greater importance to participants within a Latin American setting than it would be within Australia. Because of these sensitivities, the research participants were made aware that at any time they could request to have some or all of their data removed from the research project (Magolda & Weems, 2002).

Given the distance between the data gathering and the data analysis locations— Bolivia and Australia—generally, it was not possible to revise recorded interview data with the participants. It was also not possible for the participants to revise the analysed data as the analysis was in English and, apart from the foreigners to be interviewed, the participants did not have enough English to be able to fully understand the transcriptions. Effectively, the transfer of ownership of the data therefore occurred at the signing of the consent form.

During the interviews, care was taken lest participants feel uncomfortable, stressed or self-conscious. Interviews were conducted with "face-to-face contact, mutual respect, trust and mutual negotiation" (Magolda & Weems, 2002, p. 493). Within a Bolivian context, this appears to be particularly important. While Magdola and Weems referred to a warning by Soltis (1990) that "researchers have an ethical responsibility to be reflective about issues of harm and to engage participants in this process of reflection" (p. 504), the perception of "harm" within this research context was originally thought to have included almost any level of disclosure at a local level. The discomfort that could arise in this area would be due to a general lack of trust within the Bolivian society. It was felt that for leaders, a possible feeling of insecurity could have arisen from the fact that they would not want to be seen by the interviewer as not functioning effectively. So, either relating to the perceptions of their peers or concerns with the perceptions of the interviewer, particularly given the cultural context, the participants in the research were treated, as Hollway and Jefferson (2000) expressed it, as "defended subjects," who were "invested in particular positions in discourses to protect vulnerable aspects of self" (p. 26). As the interviews progressed, however, it became apparent that the participants were very content to talk about almost any issue without reserve, often relating quite personal issues or situations in which they had been perceived to have failed as leaders.

The perception of the researcher's rapport with the participants and of their ease in the interview situation was further complicated by perceived and actual power differentials (Magolda & Weems, 2002). Beyond the existence in interview situations of "asymmetries of power", to use Mishler's (1986) term, based on the interviewer's desire to construct a reality for research purposes, the asymmetries in the interview situations in this research added degrees of complexity. First, at a superficial and an expressed level, a certain degree of kudos is automatically afforded to foreigners. Though it may appear to be genuine, often it conceals a considerable reserve in the relationship or potential relationship. When interviewing participants with whom the researcher did not have a positive, even long-standing, relationship, the expressed kudos did appear to exist, and while it possibly could have covered a deep-seated distrust and antipathy of those considered to have come from colonising countries, this was never apparent. It was therefore not the case that a perceived power asymmetry on the part of participants ever led to a degree of resistance on their part—an equally important consideration in interview research (Weiler, 1988). Fortunately, Australians are generally well considered in Bolivia, but if there were a perception in the mind of the participant that an Australian is in some way linked with the United States, a restrained hostility could have existed in the interview. The only instances where a degree of antipathy was noted were with two leaders of *campesino* organisations who declined to be interviewed.

There was also an ethical consideration regarding the use of grammatical constructions in the personal approach of the researcher to the participants.

Conversation and interviewing must be done in a way that maintains cultural norms regarding social hierarchies and the implied power differentials. While acquaintance or friendship relationships existed with many of the participants, the Latin American culture complicates these relationships at several levels because the culture is much more communal or relationally based than Western cultures. For this reason, it was decided to use the formal second person pronouns and verb constructions as discussed above. A principal of a school, for example, may use the formal grammatical forms during an interview because she perceives the situation to be a formal one or because she feels she does not have a strong enough relationship with the researcher for that particular situation to warrant the use of the familiar grammar forms. On the other hand, business leaders and politicians may automatically use the familiar form either based on the depth of the relationship they may have with the researcher, because they wish the researcher to converse with them as equals, or they perceive the researcher to be below them on the social scale. In each of these cases, sensitivity and reflexivity (Griffin, 1991) on the part of the researcher were required so that not only was accurate data obtained, but also so that the participants felt comfortable in acting and being treated with the appropriate courtesies demanded by their Latin American culture.

A final ethical consideration pertains to ethnocentricity. Participants were to be respected as valued individuals who work within respected institutions within an appreciated culture. The participants were not seen as being inferior in any way because their actions, lifeworld conditions, or beliefs were different from those of the researcher. *Weltanschauung* training within modern, western societies renders such objectivity extremely difficult, but in this research, every effort was made towards maintaining a descriptive relativist position. Western cultures have generally felt superior to the cultures in "developing" or "third world" countries, as implied in the distinguishing terminology that is used. Much of this is a consequence of an inculcated perception of the superiority of affluence. This is an area to which the researcher has become very sensitive and of which he was therefore very aware while conducting the interviews.

CHAPTER 4

Phase 1 Data and Analysis

Part I: Data collection and participant perceptions

Prior to travelling to Bolivia, arrangements had been made through a friend of the researcher for a teacher to work as a research assistant. The assistant worked in the morning shift of a school and was available in the afternoons to meet with the researcher to arrange the interview timetable and to contact potential participants. At first, the assistant was very shy and hesitant about contacting people who were community leaders, but as time progressed, she became very skilled at making the contacts and arranging appointments regardless of the status of the person. The assistant was first given the list of the Key Informants and suggested leadership roles from which participants could be selected—for example, the heads of civic institutions, politicians, and school principals. She was asked to provide a list of interview subjects that included a mixture of different roles, including leaders of both sexes, as many leaders from the country (*campo*) as possible, as well as leaders from both the Catholic and Protestant religious affiliations. This she was able to do with the following numbers of participants in the different categories:

Gender: Male 32; Female 10
Lifeworld: City 26; City/Country 11; Country 5
Employment: Business 6; Community 6; Education 12; NGO 3; Political 2; Professional 5; Religious 8
Class: Foreign 3; Mestizo 26; Quechua 5; "White" 8
Religion: Catholic 20; Evangelical 22

Notes pertaining to the Phase I participants

City/Country: The City/Country category was added to cover those participants who now lived in the city but had spent most of their lives in the country and those who lived in the city but had spent most of their working life in the country (for example, as a peripatetic doctor). Unfortunately, it was not possible for the researcher to travel to villages in the country away from the city of Cochabamba. Two possibilities were offered, but each would have involved significant time and travel. Another factor was that with the political situation at the time, it was difficult for the research assistant to arrange interviews with country leaders who had recently moved to the city or who were visiting. Two such interviews were arranged, but one was refused the day before, and the other on the day. At least in the second instance, the refusal appeared to be a power play involving *campesino* leaders who now felt that with the current government, they were now in positions of power and seemed intent on others being aware of the fact.

Classes: Bolivia is still a classed society, and the classes represented included foreigners, mixed race (or Mestizos), indigenous Quechuas and a number from the class known in Latin America as White. This last category consists of those who may consider themselves to be of pure Spanish origin, or their skin colour and/or social status places them "above" the Mestizos.

Gender: There were fewer women in the sample due to several factors. While almost half of the school principals interviewed were women, it is probably true to say that in the business community in the city, there would be more men in leadership roles. It also appeared to be less common for women to hold community leadership positions in the rural areas. Apart from the school principals, the women who were represented in the sample included a former diplomat, a former teacher from an international school, a retired school principal, and a politician of significant standing.

Employment: As the researcher and the research assistant both came from educational contexts, and because access to schools was readily available, the largest group of participants were school principals, and at least five of the participants listed in other occupations had had experience in education. One participant in the education category lectures at a tertiary level and, in the past, had served at a high level in the federal ministry of education. Apart from the *campesino* participants who were all community leaders, the other participants came from a range of occupations, though with a significant number working for religious organisations—two in an educational capacity as leaders of a tertiary institute and a seminary.

Race: The largest group of participants was in the Mestizo or mixed-race class. This is the largest group found in the city. The proportion of White participants far exceeds that found in the general community, but for the last four centuries, this has been the class that has dominated the leadership of the country in both business and politics. All of the foreign participants were Key Informants. The feelings of one class towards another vary. The traditional class structure of the society has instilled certain manners and procedures regarding the treatment of others. In general, the Mestizos seemed keen to work on a more equal footing with the Quechuas; the Whites also expressed this desire, though with varying degrees of condescension. The Foreigners seemed to relate equally well with the other groups. A number of the Quechuas, given the impetus towards self-recognition by the current government, seemed intent on demonstrating that there was a new order now in place and the traditional social structures were in the process of being redrawn. While the Mestizos and Whites were wanting to engage with the Quechuas, they were somewhat disconcerted by this restructuring of society and unsure of its implications for them.

Religion: The equal proportions of Catholic and Evangelical participants do not represent the proportion in the general population—where Catholics would make up 70-80% of the population. The difference was due to the fact that both the researcher and the research assistant are Evangelicals and therefore had more contacts within that community. The local saying, "to be Bolivian is to be Catholic," means that those with minimal commitment to the Catholic church or with animistic or syncretistic beliefs are still classified in the community under the heading of "Catholic".

Language: While all of the participants spoke Spanish, many of them also spoke other languages, and for some, Spanish was their second language. Forty of the interviews were conducted in Spanish and two in English. One participant who had English as a first language was interviewed along with a participant who spoke English as his second language, but in order for the latter to be more comfortable with the interview, the conversation was conducted in Spanish. Of those classified as having Spanish as their first language and without an indigenous language, at least nine had some English—several being very proficient. It was better, however, to conduct the interviews and have responses in their heart language.

Languages Spoken	Number of Participants
Spanish	16
Spanish and Quechua	17
Quechua and Spanish	4
Spanish, Quechua and Aymara	1
English and Spanish	1
English, Spanish and Quechua	2
Other, Spanish, English and Quechua	1

Key informants: Three of the Key Informants were foreigners who had lived many years in the country and had a profound understanding of the Bolivian culture—two working as missionaries and one as a diplomat. The other Key informants included a sociologist who is also an academic, and a psychologist who has studied in Bolivia and the United Kingdom. The majority of the Key Informants, therefore, have experience in at least one of the cultures in Bolivia as well as cultures outside the country.

The Phase I interviews

The interviews were conducted in many different venues—mostly in the homes or places of work of the participants or in rooms that had been borrowed for the purpose. One interview was conducted in the middle of a field in a farming community. Some of the school principals seemed a little distracted at first by what they may have seen as an interruption to their schedule. Certainly, the interviews in schools were characterised by many interruptions and a great deal of background noise from classes and physical education groups. Once the interviews were underway, however, all of the principals participated very willingly, and some wanted to continue talking past the allotted time. The school principals seemed preoccupied with the functioning of their school, but due to the political tensions in the country, many of the other participants wanted to talk about the tense political situation. One participant involved with the political life of the country had had threats against her family (he fled with her family the following week), and her discussion of the political and family situations resulted in a long interview, but one that had somewhat limited content relating specifically to the research questions asked.

Apart from the difficulties in hearing and recording interviews in schools due to the background noise, there was also an issue of language in several instances. Some of the *campesino* participants had limited Spanish or spoke with very strong accents, and at times used Quechua expressions or Spanish words with meanings other than those commonly encountered in the city. These words and phrases had to be explained by the participant, or another person was asked to explain them. Whereas most of the city participants were only too eager to socialise and talk, the demeanour of several of the *campesino* participants showed a shyness that could have been related to a feeling of inadequacy with Spanish, a deferring to someone whom they thought would hold a higher social status than themselves, or perhaps a feeling of suspicion and lack of trust.

Brief Phase 1 data analysis

This research was qualitative in nature, and the identification of the pair components and their pairings could not simply be accomplished by counting responses from the limited number of participants. That being said, a simplified matrix of responses was constructed, and this indicated a general shape to the responses of the participants that could then be checked with the coded data. The analysis of the reasons behind the responses and the links to worldview and culture then arose from the commentaries given by the participants. The general indications given in the data with regard to the perceptions of the participants from the two subcultures, of their own group and of the other, were as follows.

Perceptions of city participants of the city culture

The participants from the city saw honour and shame to be of considerably more importance than the other components for the communities living in the city. Justice/innocence and fear were seen to be of minor importance, while guilt and power were relatively insignificant, or secondary, for them.

Perceptions of city participants of the rural culture

The participants from the city saw power as being of some importance for rural communities, with justice/innocence, honour, shame and fear all featuring to a minor extent in their responses. Little mention was made of guilt as being important in the *campo*.

Perceptions of country participants of the city culture

The participants from the rural areas saw honour and shame as being significant for those living in the city, with the other components being quite insignificant.

Perceptions of country participants of the rural culture

The participants from the rural areas saw power and fear as being important factors in their communities. Some indication was also given that, to a minor degree, justice/innocence, honour and shame were also factors.

Perceptions of all participants of the city culture

Overall, the data from both groups of participants indicated the importance of honour and shame for those living in the city. Justice/innocence and fear were of very minor importance, and generally guilt was seen to be of secondary importance.

Perceptions of all participants of the rural culture

Overall, the perception of all of the participants of the concerns in the rural areas was that fear and power were important, though justice/innocence, honour and shame were also important, though to a lesser degree.

Other considerations emerging from the data

The most significant responses of Honour and Shame in the city and Power and Fear in the country would have been expected according to the literature, apparently confirming the observations of Muller (2006a), Hegeman (2006) and Blaschke (2002). Conclusions drawn from the data, however, must be considered within the participants' definitions and qualifications of pair component terms. In addition, these results only consider the pair components. The results for the prioritising of the pairs of components were also indistinct. Only ten of the participants paired Shame and Honour together for the city subculture, and only four paired Fear and Power for the *campo* subculture. Some of the variation seen in the data may be seen in the variations between the responses of the different participant categories. For example, there was a slight tendency for female participants to identify the shame and honour categories and for the men to identify the fear and power categories, though the differences were minor and did not impact the final results of the research.

Avoidance-pursuit pair components and religion

As the literature behind the avoidance-pursuit pairs used in this research had postulated the religious foundations of worldview to be significant in the prioritisation of the pairs, this category was examined in terms of the data. Both those who could be identified as being Catholic and those who could be identified as being evangelicals saw honour and shame as being important in the city context. The only difference between the two groups was that evangelicals tended to place a higher importance on the idea of power and fear being of more significance in the *campo*. Less than half of the Catholic participants indicated a priority for fear and/or power in the *campo*, whereas the majority (two-thirds) of the evangelicals felt that they were important.

Individual components of the avoidance-pursuit pairs: definitions and qualifications in the Phase I data

a. Power

Power was seen by most of the participants, particularly those in the city, as having both personal and political dimensions—purportedly being desired to overcome injustice or sought in order to rise above adverse circumstances. It was also linked, as mentioned above, with glory and honour. Leaders, political and organisational, were said to use their power to engender fear in the populace and hence increase their power over others. "The people look for power to be able to solve their problems, but the power is taken up by those who would take advantage of others" (Participant 4).

This was also mentioned by other participants. The promise of the use of power to overcome injustice was used by politicians while at the same time offering justice, and was used by them to gain glory for themselves. In this way, honour and power were linked in that honour and glory were said to be a part of power, particularly political power, and honour is often achieved through the acquisition of power. The Catholic and evangelical churches were also claimed to desire power.

One Key Informant believed that power was an important concept in the *campo*. This power was seen in terms of political power but could also be attributed to spiritual sources: divinities, spirit beings and ancestral spirits. This power of divine beings, particularly *Pachamama* [the Earth Mother deity], and spiritual forces, was the power to bless or curse crops and animals and to bring drought or floods. Effectively, the power of life and death was attributed to these beings. At another level, these beings were believed to have the power to control disease and health. These factors ensure that they were feared and revered, as discussed below, and the assistance of their power is sought through sacrifice and adoration rituals.

The concept of power in a *campesino* context, however, also included references to the gaining of political power and the empowerment the *campesinos* had under the current, indigenous-based government to make their own decisions. The declaration from many *campesinos* now was "We are the people!" This particular phrase in Spanish carries with it the implied meaning: We, the representatives of our particular culture, now define what it is to be Bolivian. This denoted a desire to return the country to a pre-conquest state where the country was, once again, populated by and ruled by indigenous Bolivians. This sentiment had brought about a rising sense of pride in the *campo,* but while positions of personal power were important in rural areas, there was still the possibility that such positions could be "bought" rather than democratically elected or inherited.

b. Fear

While not identified as the most important consideration when participants were asked to choose between the avoidance-pursuit pair components, expressions of fear were very common in many of the interviews with participants from the city. Fear was therefore given a more extensive treatment here than the other pair components. The two primary reasons for the fearfulness in the participants in the city were the uncertainty of the political situation and fear due to the rising incidence of assault or other crimes. The specific fears relating to the political situation varied among the participants.

While some fear expressed by participants may be described as "low level," for example, fear of not pleasing one's supervisor or arising from a lack of trust, others described fear as being "like a backbone in Bolivia" or directly linked to the political history of the country. In a country that has known one hundred and ninety-three coups from its independence in 1825 till 1981, where governments lasted an average of ten months, those in the population who supported the opposition of the moment were always fearful. At the same time, there was hope in the community that a just application of the law and the equitable righting of wrongs committed against the indigenous people would lead to a more stable situation. As one interviewee said: "Fear comes from the unknown". A fuller context of fear in a pluri-national country comes from a section of the interview:

> Because we, Bolivians, are living in one hundred and eighty years of history as a republic. We are living, er, after the arrival of others. That is to say, to someone, "who are you?" What type of person? I am a Bolivian like you. But I am brown skinned, I speak better Quechua than Spanish, or Aymara. We are only just recognising what in sociological terms has been quite obvious. They are plain. In this we see, Geoff, that I accepted the candidature of [leadership in the organisation] for the party of the *campesinos* because I had my childhood in a barrio a long way from the city and my barrio was full of *campesino* children. [Personal information given.] Fear comes from the unknown. How does he get angry? How do they get angry? Right. How are we going to react when we aren't in agreement? Are they going to kill us? Are they going to hurt us? We are only just recognising one another in this heterogeneous country. We have only just accepted that there aren't consonants in the east [of the country]. That there are only long vowels— instead of *pelado* they say *pelao*. And we are noticing that on the other side, there are no vowel sounds like those consonant sounds. From there, we are just noticing very complex questions. What is ethical, what is aesthetic, what is erotic? This is devastating. How does an Aymara girl flirt? We are just understanding that there is a teenage-hood, with pimples, in the Quechua world. Our writers in psychology have never told us of the adolescence of the Guaraní world. I believe that soon we will start to work on that. So, Bolivia is submerged in fear to a growing degree. Since 1952 and the National Revolution, when they issued the citizenship card, an occasion for everyone . . . for the *campesinos*. And now their grandchildren are living as presidents. So, who is Choquehuanca [a *campesino* name]? He is our chancellor. And who is, . . . well . . . . He comes from the Aymara people. And what does he know? Nothing. But we also do not know much. So, how . . . . [sigh] What decisions do they make? Still, we have to realise that to overcome fear, middle-class Bolivians, like me, of European descent, the Spanish were encouraged to vote for Evo [the current president]. Why? Because not voting for Evo signified confrontation. It seemed that Bolivians wanted to open the

door so they could come in, then close the door on them again. It seems to me that fear is a pillar that still stands among Bolivians. (Participant 23)

In the political climate in April 2008, when the interviews were recorded, nobody seemed to be able to predict what the next month held for the country, let alone the next year. In addition to this uncertainty, the rising rate of street crime added to the insecurity, uncertainty and fear in the city and in particular in the peri-urban settlements surrounding Cochabamba. Adults, and particularly children, were becoming more and more afraid of walking the streets, particularly at night. It was as Goldstein (2007) pointed out that "the general economic insecurity is compounded by the pervasive sense of physical insecurity, as crime and 'talk of crime' and its accompanying fear intensify, particularly in the poor urban communities (barrios) that ring Bolivia's cities" (pp. 50–51).

For centuries, there has been a constant stream of *campesino* migrants to the city and daily visits by *campesinos* to the city to trade. Despite living in relative proximity, however, perhaps the greatest unknown for the city participants was the culture and mores of the *campesinos,* as mentioned by Participant 23 above. This fear may also be seen in the context of the interview with Participant 35, who was fearful for her safety and that of her family because she did not know what the *campesinos* might do.

The specific fears relating to politics varied among the participants. Many appeared to be fearful of the particular political situation (Participant 40), with a referendum due within weeks that some commentators had said could lead to civil war in the country (*Los Tiempos*, 2008b) or a *coup d'etat* by the *Prefectos* [Department Prefects] of the so-called "Half Moon" of departments in opposition to the government. One participant feared, apparently with some justification, for her family and their home and said,

> There is a tremendous uncertainty. Nobody knows what will happen. It is day to day. I have fear for my children because they have told us that they are going to go to their school. There have been people who have gone to my children's school to see at what time they leave. (Participant 35)

She fled the country with her family within two weeks of being interviewed. Participants were also concerned for the future of the country under a new constitution and under an indigenous government that was perceived by some (such as Participant 35) to be incompetent.

In the peasant villages, "many *campesinos* have fear, but some no" (Participant 41). The primary concern of the villagers was with agriculture. Much of their meeting time as a community was spent discussing agricultural issues, and always there was the fear that the crop may fail or that some disaster may cut down their herd. This fear was compounded in that not only were these disasters feared, but there was also a fear of the forces (supernatural) that cause such failures and a fear that not enough would have been done to appease the supernatural beings so that a disaster would be averted. While this was important for older members, Participant 41 also noted that in the villages, the young people worry less now about the future—thinking more of the moment. Presumably, this was because they, more than previous generations, would understand that they would probably not live in the village much past their teenage years when they expected to move to the city for education and employment.

Fear and shame were also linked in that being shamed in a tight-knit village community was feared. As Participant 16 observed: "It doesn't matter if he has suffered pain, if it means that he isn't found guilty and [therefore] feels shame." *Campesinos* fear making a mistake, being wrong, or not achieving their objectives, "because we know that families, all in the family, always must achieve something and fear they won't reach their objectives." [Interviewer: This is connected to shame?] "Um, hum" (Yes) (Participant 34).

Fear was also strongly linked with power in the minds of a number of participants. Politicians were claimed to use uncertainty and fear as a weapon in order to gain power and to keep control. The fear was of "people who have the power to do them harm" (Participant 15). This also included the dead: "When a person is dying, there is quite a bit of fear in the Andean world regarding the relationship one has had with the deceased [and the impact this] will have on one now" (Participant 33).

The fear of spiritual beings includes spirits of the deceased, spiritual beings that may inhabit physical objects, demons or mischievous spirit beings and god-like supreme beings. One participant told of remote villages he had visited where this fear was very evident:

> Because for a lot of the time they live isolated there. When strangers enter there is always a fear . . . of who are they? So when someone arrives from outside it is a worry for all of the community. Because they have had experiences where, where they say: 'Who are these people? They are coming to us to control us. Control and see what we have.' It is a natural fear for them. They don't live with these people. And much more for foreigners. (Participant 27)

As Participant 27, dressed in a bright red and yellow jacket, had approached one particular village, the community became very frightened. It was only with some difficulty that he was able to negotiate accommodation for a night. The next day, he learned that someone from the village had recently seen a strange phenomenon in the sky and believed it to be an omen. On seeing Participant 27, dressed in very bright and different clothes, the villagers thought that he was a visiting spiritual being of some type. This type of fear is from childhood: "they have a fear that may be in their nature" (Participant 27).

Participant 28 told of the beliefs of the people in the *campo* in *Pachamama* [Earth Mother], and the spiritual entities linked with hills, the sun, the moon, and objects on a smaller scale. They believe that there are spirits in specific places, such as where

114

spring water flows, a large rock or a large stone, and in mountains. The villagers say, for example, that one can't sit on a particular rock because it is linked with a spirit. In one village that Participant 28 visited as an evangelist, there was a large tree:

> I asked permission to climb a tree to hang my speaker to evangelise the community from there—to preach the Gospel. Three or four men said to me, 'Sir, excuse us,' in Quechua, you see? 'Don't put your speaker there. Here, when one approaches this tree they die.' And, no. I'm not going to die. Don't be worried. It's OK. I'm not going to die, and nothing will happen to me. (Participant 28)

The villagers insisted that the tree was bad and that it had "eaten" many people and animals that had approached it so they had built a fence around it to keep animals or people away. Despite their protestations, Participant 28 climbed the tree and the villagers waited for him to die.

"Also, hills with walls around them—they look after them and sacrifice a llama or a lamb to it. Only the *yatiri* [priest or spiritual healer] can go to the hill once a year with a sacrifice," Participant 28 continued. He told the people in one such place that he would pray for them, saying that he would go onto the hill and sit down, and if nothing happened to him, then they should become Christians. He claimed that many communities had become Christian using this method.

Participant 28 also referred to the fear of spirit beings in the evangelical church: "There is still a little bit of syncretism in the church. In Challapata, there are educated people in the church, but they still believe in *Chupa Grasa* [also known as *callasiri* or *kharasiri*: a spirit being believed to approach people while they sleep and extract fat from their bodies], etc. They believe they are being watched." He tested them by doing things against the "spirits" after signing a document with the people containing a commitment that if nothing happened to him, they would change their beliefs.

> There are many ancestral, animistic, Andean beliefs still among the city people. But it is interesting that they aren't going to recognise [acknowledge] it. I know a family of a very high socio-economic level in Cochabamba, where if their small child cries, they will call their soul. That is to say, for their soul to return to their stomach. Where does that come from? It's Andean. A belief that when a person is sick, their soul leaves them. The *kallawayas* [Bolivian peripatetic spiritual healers] call for the soul to return. If you walk in certain areas in the county they believe that there are places called, literally, 'it calls the soul'. Even though they may have university degrees or are rich. There are many cultures present in the city. Lately, you can see them burning the *q'oas* [incense and other items burned as a smoke offering] on Friday nights—businesses that are boutiques or from the United States, perhaps of upper level [class]—still using the Andean

ritual. It is increasing. It is strange. You would need an anthropological or sociological study to understand it. (Key Informant 29)

[Interviewer: Perhaps the increasing practice of *q'oas* is because of uncertainty.]

Possibly . . . Exactly. One returns to the old practices/traditions for security. The first Friday is a very special day in the beliefs. All relate to a belief in the *Pachamama* [Earth Mother]—to not offend, to offer her an offering. (Key Informant 29)

Fears are dealt with by being able to be in power or leadership positions at a political level and by appeasing the supernatural beings (for example, making sacrifices to *Pachamama*, "who punishes"). "What they have is their traditions. This is their strength. So if they do their *q'oas,* their sacrifices, this is their strength. This is their, let's say, like a protection, as you say, offering to a spirit so that it can protect all" (Participant 27). According to Key Informant 42, this level of appeasement was seen in his village as being not so much related to an imminent fear but a more general, fatalistic fear of spirit actions beyond the control of humans. He did, however, tell of a more direct attempt at interaction with the spirit world in the case of a member of the village who had been injured when dynamite, which was to be thrown in the air to frighten away a hail storm, went off in his hand.

In spite of these fears, justice is also feared: "We all fear justice. The fear of justice is very present" (Participant 24). In particular, community justice (*justicia comunitaria*) is feared and is discussed in more detail below: "We fear justice. All of us . . . . Community justice is going to impose itself in the indigenous zones of Bolivia because it is faster, it is more transparent, it is public . . . . The fear of justice is very present" (Participant 27). It is feared in the city because it is seen by those in the city as being cruel.[17]

c. Shame

Honour, or being seen well in the eyes of others, was seen by participants to refer to two factors, which were sometimes linked, of how individuals wish to be perceived by others. The first was found in honoured social positions and social standing in the community, and the second was the pride that individuals and families feel due to the accomplishments of a family or community member. A very common example of the second facet was the pride families feel when a member is able to enrol as a student

---

[17] It was reported in the Cochabamba newspaper, Los Tiempos (2010), that the Vice President of Bolivia admitted that the greatest difficulty facing the administration of justice in Bolivia was finding some articulation of the statutory laws of the country with the *campesinos'* understanding of their *originario* laws. This was because these laws operated on different principles, standards and with different sanctions. This presented the government with a considerable challenge as they endeavour to not jeopardise the human rights enshrined in the Bolivia's Constitution.

in a university. For many families the degree was not important—just being able to enrol brings honour to the family. In those families where university attendance was more common, emphasis was placed on the study of medicine, law and more recently biochemistry, because graduates with undergraduate degrees from of these faculties were able to use the title 'Doctor'.

Respect was important (Participant 10) and was linked with honour: "Respect is huge. Honour is huge . . . . There is respect for the older ones—but not too old." In rural areas, the elected officials, such as the *correjidor* or *jilacata* [community leaders discussed below], were greatly respected (Participant 24). Some, according to Participant 8, used a variety of means in order to gain respect before their peers. They might say, for example, that they owned a car when they did not, or that they walked for health reasons rather than admit to not owning a car. An individual like this may become well known for "exaggerating his modesty".

Honour and shame, according to Participant 23, "are things that exist under the skin." They were a part of what it means to be human in a Latin culture, yet many had limited access to the means to obtain it. Participant 13 commented that parents of her school students from poorer communities felt shame because of their social position. In general, people desired social standing and prestige, they wanted recognition, and they wanted to see their photo in the paper.

Shame was seen to be important in Bolivia and, like honour, was a part of, or "under the skin" (Participant 23), of every Bolivian, but more so in the city where there was "much shame" (Key Informant 11 & Participant 40). It was common, therefore, that when asked who had done something, people would deny that they were culpable to avoid being shamed. Unlike guilt, which arises from an individual's belief regarding their guilt or innocence, shame involves one's belief about what others think regarding one's guilt or innocence (Atherton, 2003). This is particularly important in a society where honour is sought, and shame is related to being found and publicly proclaimed to be guilty.

Shame was seen in the context of guilt in the way the church defines sin: "Here, if no one has seen it, then it isn't sin. This was a way it is seen" (Key Informant 11). There was also the connection in the data with pain and fear in that, as Participant 21 explained, one had pain because of a fear that one would be discovered lying and the discovery would lead to shame. Apart from transgressions, however, failure was also a shameful thing. Migrants would not return to their cities or villages if they thought they had not succeeded in their new situation. Others would borrow money, even when they could not afford to pay it back, in order not to feel shamed before their family and friends.

In the *campo,* Key Informant 18 commented on the link between shame and guilt:

Also including guilt in the sense that in the *campo,* the idea of prestige, of good behaviour, with respect to the norms, is very present. So one can still see the act of punishment of a woman for adultery or punish someone who has stolen something, et cetera . . . . It is more for the theme of shame and the idea, let's say, that with guilt they have betrayed the trust all the community had in them.

Key Informant 42, however, spoke of a lack of shame in his rural village community:

Sometimes people do things that I [a foreigner] would be ashamed of, you know, but it doesn't really seem they are, and particularly being the leader of a community, but being publicly drunk and seen to be foolish—that ought to make them ashamed, but they [aren't] necessarily. I can remember one *corregidor,* Hermán, who got booted out of his job in May because of acting so badly, but then he shows up later on, and it's like, you know, nothing has happened.

Nevertheless, in general, the connection of shame to the city community was an obvious one, as the shame is experienced as a result of the perception one has of what others are thinking of one. In close, collectivist, urban communities, this can be particularly strong as Participant 16 and Participant 20 noted:

It doesn't matter if he has suffered pain, if it means that he isn't found guilty and feels shame . . . . That is how shame is. So that no one will say anything to them. Perhaps this has a strong impact on the lives of people. The shedding of light on something. (Participant 16)

Shame affects more. Because we live more with more external influences even in the church, there is more concern for shame . . . . In the secular world, shame has more power because shame covers many things. They live by appearance, let's say. But shame is strong. In the *campo,* let's say, if a woman becomes pregnant, she is worse off than in the city. For shame . . . . The man is forced to marry her . . . . If he accepts, the shame will be lost. It isn't so much that the pregnancy will be seen, but if she wants to be pregnant, there is a need to know who the man is . . . [otherwise people in the community will become suspicious of others].

It is because people have relationships with other people. We live under the influence of other people . . . because we always want to be better than the other person. But when there is a pain, a sickness, and no one should be happy about a sickness, it is a disgrace, or an accident . . . they do all that they can so that no one will know about it . . . not even the family . . . because they think that, if they are Christians, the accident will mean that they are in sin. If an accident happens in the secular world . . . they are going to see my disgrace. So, nobody should know. [This is] because they are going to keep advancing and they are going to beat us . . . . We live a lot under the influence of others, and it is because of this that shame has so much force. (Participant 20)

Participant 22 did not think shame would be important in the *campo*, however, because she believed that knowledge or education were prerequisites of feeling shame. Others did not hold this view, saying that within traditional, *campo* communities, which uphold traditional values, it was seen as a "terrible shame" to be found to be a thief, a liar, or to be lazy. This was because breaking the community law, *Ama suwa, ama llulla, ama q'ella* [Do not steal, do not lie, do not be lazy], constitutes a serious transgression against the community. Also, adulterous women were punished in the *campo* because this was seen as disrupting relationship structures in the community. (No such sanction appears to apply to men.) Other things considered to be shameful in the *campo* were those frowned upon for other reasons, for example, an old man marrying a young woman.

In cultures where avoiding shame is important, the very negative concept of lacking shame is also an important feature and is referred to as a state of being. Participant 12 spoke of a man who had caused problems in her school by saying, "This man does not have shame. I don't know what his objective is, but he is like that." Politicians in particular are described as being shameless [*¡sinvergüenza!*], of not having "face" or of having "the skin of a tapir" (Participant 9). Perhaps in the country's past, there had been more shame in politics: "In the past, government ministers would hide from shame, but now there is nothing of that. Today, they say something and tomorrow something different and without shame" (Participant 36).

d. Guilt

Guilt was not seen initially as being a very important factor, with only one interviewee identifying it as being important in the city context, though others saw it as being of secondary importance. In the city, an interviewee noted that there was guilt in the city, but only mentioned the context of men trying to escape the guilt associated with marital unfaithfulness. Another noted that parents of her school pupils felt guilty for not caring adequately for their children due to work commitments, and to relieve their guilt, they gave their children money.

In a rural context, one interviewee said that guilt did not seem to exist. Another, from an evangelical, religious vocation, appeared to have strong views on guilt but the guilt was very strongly linked with shame. A Key Informant thought that guilt was only of secondary importance. He noted, however, that in his mother's family—Quechua— there had been a sense of guilt because the Catholic Church made them feel guilty about many things, such as, for example, not looking after the children well.

> [This continued] till they had a lot of fear of being found guilty of not going to mass, etc., no. But at the same time, they, when they were doing something that wasn't good, in order to protect themselves, they hid themselves. Shame . . . . They do not want to feel guilty." (Key Informant 18)

Key Informant 18 was able to put this into context by explaining that in the *campo*, the idea of prestige, of good behaviour, with respect to the community norms, was very important so that a person may not feel guilt, but if the community imputes guilt, they will feel shame. Another evangelical interviewee noted that while in the city, in business, honour was sought, within the church, people seek justice and the minimising of guilt. In general, justice was seen as a way to minimise guilt, but at a personal level, individuals tried to justify guilty actions in order to avoid shame.

In the literature, guilt has been linked with justice to form a pair. In early interviews, the Spanish term for justice [*justicia*] had been used, but this was changed to the use of the Spanish terms for "righteous" or "just" [*justo*] and *inocente* [innocent] were used, and the issue of justice [*justicia*] was discussed in detail. While the participants had little interest in innocence and guilt *per se*, there was considerable interest in the theme of justice. Essentially, justice was seen as being concerned with the redressing of wrongs and was desired or sought at personal and societal levels.

The application of justice in a community was a means by which relationships, or the environment in which the relationships exist, may be maintained or restored. Through the appropriate application of just decisions by leaders or authorities, the network of trust and social bonding can be reworked to enable a return to 'harmonious coexistence': *pachakuti*. For example, the apprehension of, and sometimes capital judgment against, a thief from outside the village ensures that doubts and suspicions of community members against each other are assuaged. If the offender was from within the community, then each community member must then adjust their perception of the network of trust relationships so as to include the breaking of trust of the offender and a calculation of the possibility of future trust-damaging actions. Some of the difficulties encountered in this area were highlighted by one interviewee who noted that once a person had been accused of being dishonest, even if there was no proof, it would be very difficult for them to be given recommendations for other employment.

Apart from the fear associated with community justice, discussed above, both city dwellers and *campesinos* considered justice to be important. In the city, justice was sought to counter corruption, and in the country, justice was sought for the *campesinos* following centuries of feeling unjustly treated. Justice was seen by one interviewee as being the only hope for the future of which he was very fearful for his children. The need for social justice, for what was right for the *campesinos*, and in the fight against poverty, was seen as important, but the power of some sort was required in order to guarantee that justice was obtained.

In summary

The identification of the avoidance-pursuit pair components in this research, while valid in its own right, was distinguished from the pair components identified in the literature. In particular, the Bolivian participants were particularly interested in power and justice, but in terms of the abuse of personal power and the corrupt or inappropriate use of justice. While supernatural entities were feared, it was a fear of personal attack by some (such as the fat-sucking *callasiri* or *kharasiri*[18]) or the effect these beings may have on the sources of water and food. Shame and honour appeared to carry the same definitions and importance as the literature anticipated in collectivist societies. While guilt and innocence did not appear to be very important to the participants, fear, power, shame and honour all had the potential to influence the decisions of leaders.

Part II: The decision-making of leaders—taken from the data

a. Decision-making of leaders in the city

> One of the things that I suppose is very particular to Bolivia, since years ago, there is a strong socio-political pressure in Bolivia regarding decision-making. For a sports entity or educational or whatever other, it must organise itself with a governing body with a president, secretary, to make these types of decisions. It is a model that is spreading and influencing, and in particular, it is also in the [evangelical] church. (Participant 16)

Participant 16 also noted that the university's staff are teaching professionals who use this model of decision-making, and professionals in the evangelical churches want to use the model, though this may create pressure on the pastors. "It has reached the stage where husbands and wives can't make wise decisions in the home without a governing body to make it for them! . . . There is a perspective that someone is going

---

[18] The Cochabamba newspaper, *Los Tiempos*, carried the story on February, 2010, of a group of Aymara people who were being charged with trying to kill a presumed *kharasiri* in 2009. The depth of feeling about *kharasiris* may be seen in the following description from Forsyth (2008):

> The *kharisiri* was originally a spirit who stole the fat from the kidneys of unsuspecting victims during the dead of night. During the colonial period, the *kharisiri* was the ghost of a Franciscan monk who gave the fat to the bishop for the production of holy oils (Crandon 1991). Concurrent with increasing modernization after the Revolution of 1952, the popular image of the *kharisiri* changed to a person, usually a doctor, lawyer or politician, who sold the kidney fat either in La Paz, for production of soap to sell to foreign tourists, or for export to the United States where it was converted into electricity (Crandon 1991). (para. 3)

to help with making the decision" (Participant 16). Participant 16 thought that this situation had been exacerbated by the Catholic Church, where decisions were seen to be handed down from above.

The formal decision-making model has been adopted in both the rural and city contexts. In the city, for example, community groups such as *mancomunidades* [community associations] and OTBs (*Organizaciones Territoriales de Base*— organisations based in a particular location and made up of the local people) worked as local organisations to benefit their communities. The OTBs promoted the installation of infrastructure such as that needed for water, sewerage, roads, and electricity, using funds from the government that were available under the *Participación Popular* [Participation of the People] program. These organisations were strictly structured with a president, vice presidents, secretary, treasurer and delegates responsible for each of the projects under their control (Participant 38).

The procedures for decision-making in the city vary greatly, but generally, organisational, day-to-day decisions were made by the organisation's executive officer, the company business manager or school principal. Difficult decisions, particularly those involving staff and moral dilemma situations, were often handled by a board or some responsible committee. Participant 1 spoke of the difficulty she found with the decision-making process as a school principal. In particular, she related the difficulty surrounding decisions as to whether a disruptive student should be expelled from the school.

> At times, if you are thinking of the person, at times of the institution, whatever decision you make will damage one or the other. Suddenly, we decide that this young person [a problem student] stay [in the school] but at a cost to the institution. They say, " How is it that this young person is still in school? It brings the school into disrepute. You feel limited because of this. But if you look at it from the point of view of the honour of the student, perhaps you are, in inverted commas, saving his life. So what is more important? If you put it into a balance, which choice has the most importance? The life, the future of the student or the prestige of the institution?
>
> Each time it is more difficult. It is more difficult because you know that the decision you make is important and could influence and damage someone's life. So, who are you to make the more correct decision? So, there . . . only the guidance of God can help you to make the decision, because, if not, as a human being, who are you? Are you God to decide if this student stays or goes, or if this teacher stays or goes? You aren't anything. So you always run the risk that you aren't making the right decisions. At times, I do not want to decide, and at times, I have to consult with people whom I think are mature and trustworthy. This is the problem. What can we do? So you can get

different opinions and then decide. Because we can, I don't know . . . make mistakes. And if we make mistakes, sometimes the mistake is more serious than the other [i.e., making no decision]. [Laughs] (Participant 1)

The most reflection on dilemma situations was given by the educational leaders. This may have been because all of them showed a very particular and personal interest in their teachers and students. Community leaders, on the other hand, valued the advancement of their community as a whole and business leaders tended to be interested in the growth of the business and profit margins:

"Good decisions are those that bring more profit or build up the company. Bad decisions are those that are bad economically for the company" (Participant 2)

Participant 6 believed that leaders should make heroic decisions, not cheating the workers, but serving the workers and also making a profit.

Participant 9 went further, saying that profit is the only interest: "That the worker produces and that money is made. In general, in private business, they do not have a morality apart from that."

Decisions made by individuals were made on the basis of that person's values and convictions, and according to what was deemed to be a priority for the organisation, and for the best of others. At times, there were difficult decisions that could result in negative effects on others. Sometimes the decision was based on *antivalores* [negative values that are not a part of the cultural norms], on individualism, or *antivalores* that come from university business courses that could drive a decision. Some cultural groups were more suspicious of decision makers or might want to know what was in it for them. The negative response of Key Informant 29 to the university-based leadership courses and the *antivalores* he believed they promote would appear to come from the foreign origin of the courses, with their emphasis on individualism and profits rather than relationships and community.

Perhaps the most telling comment relating to decision-making was by a participant who works in rural and city settings as well as having considerable contact with Western management models: "We are learning how to make decisions" (Participant 4). This was not surprising given the colonial and feudal history of the country. For a number of leaders, the day-to-day decision-making in their business or organisation was claimed to be based on established procedures. Often, these procedures have a legal basis, but there is also the constraint of needing to follow the mission and vision statements and values of the institution, as well as social or relational pressures. Participant 23 also commented that it was important for leaders to have a knowledge of the history of the organisation and previous decisions and to learn from them.

In the cities in Bolivia, there still exists a *verticalismo* or autocracy, and not all decisions are made democratically, but where possible, democratic procedures are now sought. Some leaders even felt that they had been forced into a position where they had to make decisions in an autocratic manner, but wished they had the shared responsibility of more traditional forms of decision-making.

In business, good decisions were said to be those that bring more profit or build up the company and the best use of resources. In broader contexts such as the *Comité Cívico* [Civic Committee—something akin to a politicised Chamber of Commerce], consultations were held with the different sectors that debate the issue and present their conclusions to the Civic Committee, where decisions were made based on the possible effect on "common interests of a region" (Participant 6). Participant 6 saw three parameters relating to decision-making in the *Comité Cívico*: 1. "I need to conserve the social and political stability in the region so that it develops normally based on economic activities. So my object was to minimise the risks of confrontation, the risks of conflict in general, et cetera, et cetera," 2. "Incorporate criteria related to the design of a strategic development plan," and 3. Preserve the democratic nature of the institution.

Under the *reforma educativa* [education reform law], schools were encouraged to promote democracy as one of their core values. While school principals were expected to make many of the day-to-day decisions in an autocratic manner, they do try to be democratic where possible. This had been facilitated by the *Participación Popular*, as well as the *reforma educativa*, which insisted on the participation of all stakeholders in the decision-making in the schools. Principals, therefore, needed to work with, or in some cases contend with, *consejos de maestros* [councils of teachers], *juntas escolares* [school community meetings], and *juntas distritales* [district meetings]. In each of these, the principal of the school may be excluded from the process, but it was important that each person attending express their opinion, informed or not, before a consensus was sought and a formal motion proposed. This was also a part of the school administration ethos now, where every employee was considered to be important in the school. All needed to know the vision, mission and annual plan of the school so that they knew the direction of the school when making decisions.

In most organisations, there were boards or similar groups that voted on decisions. These groups, following the pattern set by governments, may decide by simple majority or, for significant matters such as changing a constitution, a two-thirds majority is required. Participant 15 said, however, that majority rule situations were still very much dependent on the leader. The leader may exaggerate his or her explanations or mislead the group, which depends on the honesty and sincerity of the leader.

While democracy has become a much-touted topic in Bolivia, the desired decision was one based on consensus. When each person had been able to give their opinion and the issues had been fully discussed, but a consensus was not evident, then the fallback position of a majority, or democratic, vote was accepted. Consensus, however, was always the ideal.

Participant 15 noted that for him, as a national leader in his organisation, there often was not time to seek consensus and he had to make a decision *ya no más* [and that is it]. He acknowledged that this was not democratic; it was imposed, but he tried to imagine what the particular group was thinking and what decision they thought he should make. "But in our country, there are two classes of leader . . . up to four or five classes. One is those who look for consensus." In his organisation, the governance was from the constituency up, so that what was decided in the assembly or in a group, the executives did.

> But in many cases, the leaders decide. In some pueblos, for example, there is autocracy where one person says and the rest obey. But in that case, they are submissive, or that is to say, they fear the leader. They do not want to contradict him even though they aren't in agreement, but he can punish, he can sanction, so for fear of him, they say, yes, whatever the leader says. (Participant 15)

There were many constraints on the decision-making processes, however. These may have come from political, denominational or personal interests, and at a family level, may include the interests of family members who had emigrated and who had sent remittances home. In extreme, though common, cases, political pressures in the decision-making process might have been so great that any opposing argument was not tolerated.

> There are places where another philosophy or another political party does not enter. For example, a pueblo like San Julian . . . . They don't permit it. There have been clashes, they have chased them, they have killed them, and they have beaten them. And they know now. (Participant 15)

A good deal depended also on the capacity for influence that people had or how much they controlled the purse strings. At times, influence might be benign, but it could also be dictatorial and, at times, a brutal abuse of power.

The patience of the Bolivian people in situations where they have decisions imposed on them seemed to be due, at least partly, to their long-term view of the situation:

> There are people who are commanding [imperious], who love to dominate, to give orders, and they lead according to that. But they don't last long. Finally, a moment will come when they [the people] are going to change them [the leaders]. You will see an election, or they will get tired. In the end, the people rebel, in the end they complain and protest or simply abandon [the organisation]. People don't attend meetings, they don't anymore, because they don't like the leader. There are places like this where the leader is left all alone. (Participant 15)

While businesses were run as in other contexts, churches and denominations used local and national level assemblies in which they tried to make decisions based on biblical values—with love, of care in the application of the decision-making process, and making sure that people understand the issues.

Relationships and decision-making

The participants, particularly school principals, emphasised following structures and guidelines in the decision-making process, but at the same time, there was the sense that in the legalistic following of these procedures, an effort was made to try to learn how to make decisions the way they are made elsewhere: that the guidelines they have been given were foreign and imposed structures. The maintenance of personal and intra-institutional relationships, however, was still of great importance.

> When we speak of leadership, well, it is people and here enters the issue of culture in the way things are done. In our Latin American culture, interpersonal relationships are the priority. Not so much rules. This [the rules] arrived with the missionaries . . . . This is important . . . . But for us, no. Yes, in its place, but the priority is relationships. And because of this, our emotions have a stronger voice in our decisions. (Participant 36)

So even though there had been considerable dynamic and rapid change in the way decisions were made since Bolivia became a democracy almost thirty years ago (Participant 26), there was still a perceived need for decision-making structure but structures that allow for the arrival at a consensus, structures where all were free to voice their own opinions—even though in the final analysis, "people will listen to the person who speaks the most" (Participant 15).

This process of working towards mutual understanding, where all members of the community have not only expressed opinions but have talked through and around the issues, perhaps for hours, meant that all participants were led to understand the context, import, consequences, benefits, disadvantages and constraints of the decision being made. The importance of the maintenance of relationships in this context was seen in the way the participants thought through solutions to real and hypothetical problems, particularly moral dilemmas.

In dilemma situations, often involving the possible dismissal of staff, maintaining relationships in the decision-making process was so important that confrontation was to be avoided "at all costs" (Participant 36). As already quoted: "The main point isn't the issue—it's the relationships" (Participant 37). Participant 37 added that there was a recognition of the imperfection of all human beings, so when peace could not be guaranteed, accommodations were made. In these situations, biblical principles such as grace and mercy were cited to justify the decision. If a committee was involved in the decision and agreement could not be reached, Participant 1 suggested that "we need to work more on their [the committee members'] character."

In order to ensure the maintenance of relationships and to indicate fairness on the part of the leader, it was felt to be very important that the evidence of both sides was listened to fully and the leader was not seen to be partial. Once all sides had been heard and considered and if there was proof of culpability, efforts were usually made to restore the culprit. If these failed, as in cases mentioned by Participants 7, 8 and 20 where teachers had problems such as drunkenness, the hard decision had been made to remove the individuals from the organisations. The decisions spoken of by these participants seemed to be particularly difficult because there was a genuine care for people. In the case of both Participants 7 and 8, this meant empathy for teachers with a drinking problem because of the shame they were under and also thinking of the honour of the schools that were being damaged.

It was interesting to note that Participant 8, working in rural areas, said, "We are going to change the teacher," saying that there was a need to help people with difficulties. It was a matter of conjecture that the rural connection and traditional "laws" (do not steal) might have influenced his much harder attitude to another teacher who had over-claimed expenses. In this case, he said that his decision had been made on the basis of the "values" of his "faith". Key Informant 11 noted that evangelical churches could operate in this way, saying they could be very *tajantes* [sharp or legalistic] and pharisaic.

The time taken to process difficult or moral dilemma decisions may be extensive. Key Informant 11 believed that in European countries or Australia, there were clear norms that guide the process. In Bolivia, however, there was more "flexibility"— particularly in order not to shame or "crush" the individual. Another reason for delays in the process came from the election of people who were not *idonea* [fit or capable] to positions of responsibility. A further reason was given by Key Informant 11 who said that *directorios* needed to be patient and that where trust had been *consumida* [consumed, eaten away], one needed time to recover. Where there was no incontrovertible proof of the guilt of a presumed offender, the whole process was confused further by the existence of rumours.

To further complicate the situation, there was the retardation or disruption of the decision-making process by the perception of the status of the accused or those involved. Sometimes, for example, the perpetrator or wrongdoer might have been protected at the victim's expense, particularly as the accused would often make themselves out to be the victims. Participant 16 believed that the outcome depended on the power and influence of the person, so that even though someone might know the truth, they did not speak because of this. People of *impacto* [those who make an impression] or *trayetoria* [rising socially] were respected and would be feared by those given the task of determining guilt, and who would therefore find it difficult to confront the situation. In these cases, those responsible for the decision would wait and either hope that everything would settle and be forgotten or, if they had the courage, would step in and make the decision based on the belief that if they did not, then the situation would deteriorate for the organisation. Adding to the difficulty was the awareness of the likelihood of the truth not being told: "In our culture, it is very easy to lie. Someone could make an accusation, let's say, because that person does not have access to the money the treasurer manages and so makes an accusation" (Participant 16).

The importance of relationships and the use of conciliation to heal relationships were also highlighted when dealing with moral dilemma situations involving school leadership:

> Firstly, the restoration [of relationships]. In every case, brother, restoration. Because we do not want confrontation. Rather, see where the roots of the problem are. Listen to one, listen to the other and from there to confront them and make it so that instead of moving away, they come together more. They come together more, and from there the knowledge of one or the other starts to mature and increase in reality [move towards the truth]. Because it is what the school does, and it is what we want to do. Listen to each one, to their versions of what happened, and from there reflect, orientate [guide], help and conciliate. (Participant 13)

Participant 37 commented on the difficulty the board leadership in an organisation often had when confronted by a situation where a member of staff should be fired or sanctioned. Often in this situation, the board would vote for dismissal, but months later, nothing may have happened. As mentioned above, Participant 37 said, "The priority is relationships."

> And because of this, our emotions have a stronger voice in our decisions. So you say this person is doing this and this and this, what happens is that the emotions of these people in the board rise . . . and arrive at the point where there is anger . . . . Finally, the anger rises above everything, and they say, all right, we will remove him. ¡Listo! [Finished!] Decision made. But the emotions rise and fall. After two weeks, this emotion no longer has the same force. It has decreased. So there isn't anything pushing the execution of the decision. That has been lost. And you won't see it done until, once again, the emotions rise. And once again, yes, he needs to be removed. What needs to be done in this situation is to proceed [with the dismissal] at that moment when the emotions are high, proceed. The negative side of this is that the person will be put down and [claps his hands]—he will be destroyed. So, for this reason, it isn't uncommon that they have made the decision and, in that moment, all are in

agreement. It has to be done. Certainly. But one day, two days later when things have died down . . . well . . . . (Participant 37)

Latin American cultures have been described as "high-context" cultures (Hall, 1981), where factors surrounding a communication carry as much or more communication content as the words used and these comments by Participant 37 show the importance within the culture of the relational context. As Plueddemann (2009) wrote:

> In a high-context culture, it is preferable to delay a decision rather than to agree on what is seen as unwelcome news. It may be quite obvious that a policy needs to change, but if this policy has the potential to cause disruption, no firm decision will be communicated. "We are still studying the matter" is one response that frustrates leaders who are accustomed to efficient decision-making in low-context cultures. They would prefer to tell the bad news and get it over with, while high-context leaders prefer not to disappoint people, telling them to wait instead. (p. 82)

b. Decision-making in the *campo*

Traditionally, in the pueblos, which may have from fifty to one hundred and fifty inhabitants, *reuniones comunitarias* [community meetings] were held once a month, although in emergencies they may meet at other times. "Generally, there is a meeting that they have in the community, and they call together all of the population. To call together all the population, they use *pututos* [horns of animal bone or horn] or, more recently, dynamite" (Participant 27).

> Let us say from a meeting of fifty, one person from each family must attend. So, they elect the board. The syndicate president, is like . . . . then the secretary, then, also, one in charge of irrigation, another, agriculture, another, roads. Like that. And they are elected. So, they give authority (to them), they put them into their positions and they have the right to them for one year. (Participant 14)

Participant 41 described the leader in his rural community as a *dirigente* [leader or manager], and these were elected normally for two years. Following the *dirigente* was a *menor dirigente* [second in command], then a secretary, then a *secretaria de actas* [minute secretary], then a *vocal* [committee member]. In his community, the *vocal* advised everyone of the meeting using dynamite or animal horns. "When the people have arrived, they call a roll, and if someone doesn't come, they have to pay a fine next time . . . Bs20 to Bs50. In the city council, they charge Bs50—in the villages, perhaps Bs10 or Bs20."

Participant 27 said that in the rural communities, they tried to get the widest participation possible—both in attendance and in the discussion—to give everyone an opportunity to express their feelings and also to see the possibility of identifying new leaders. He added that this was primarily male-oriented. There were women present, for example, widows, or representing a husband who was ill, but they did not participate because, according to Participant 27, the perception seems to be that women had neither the education nor the reasoning capacity to participate fully. Despite this perception, Participant 14 noted that in community meetings which he had attended where husbands and wives were both present, often the women had influence over the men in the meetings, and when they needed to vote, many men looked to their wives for a signal—particularly in economic matters.

Participant 27 also noted that in the meetings, "there are arguments and disagreements. But generally, what benefits the community prevails. What will benefit the majority, or what is the most correct?" Repetition was seen as being very important in the meetings. If a number agrees with one point of view, then they would participate and share their thoughts—even if they were just repeating what had been said already. "It is very necessary to hear them. If one stops someone from speaking, this won't work for them" (Participant 27). The last words spoken in the meeting were from the older people because they are perceived to have the most important things to say.

There has been a growing trend, particularly in the past twenty years, for these meetings and the decision-making processes in the *campo* to conform to structures dictated by a form of rural trade unionism with pueblos being organised as *sindicatos* [literally syndicate or trade union but here referring to the formal meeting of a rural community]. (Prior to the 1980s, if one started to organise communities like this, they would be seen as being a form of government in opposition to the central government.) In the city, the function of these groups was maintained by the OTBs (*Organizaciones Territoriales de Base*) and in villages such as that of Participant 40, an hour's drive from the city, the terms *sindicato* and OTB appeared to be used synonymously.

The members of the *directorios* were given their responsibilities for one or two years and often, particularly at the village level, took turns in the various positions. The responsibilities of those holding these positions may have *comisiones* [commissions] with which to work, and often they must go to the city to speak with local or state-level government officials concerning funding projects and resources such as school teachers for their communities. Participant 10 noted that all projects were approved by the *sindicato,* and if approved, they were acted on. There had been, however, a change in the process that has been seen to have taken place in some villages: "There isn't consensus—consensus disappeared about 10 years ago. By majority now. Always majority. They have common needs. They ask who is in favour. Each person has to give their opinion first" (Participant 14).

130

At a national level, community leaders from the different *Departamentos* elect a *directorio* that meets weekly to discuss internal and external issues. For major decisions at a *Departamento* level, they always endeavour to listen to the *bases* [the grass roots representatives from the syndicates]. Then, for all decisions, they "enter into detail, listen and make an analysis until a decision is made" (Participant 31). Participant 31 stressed the importance of the workers being united in what they saw that the government should do for them: "The workers are not isolated."

While decisions in the *campo* often were motivated now by politics, in many of the pueblos it appeared that they took decisions based still on their culture and their understanding. Participant 24 said that decision-making was still more community-based in the rural areas, though he noted that, though that was starting to change, people in the country have more respect for authority and do not question decisions as much as in the city.

Decision-making in the evangelical churches appeared to follow a similar pattern. According to one interviewee, the churches in the *campo* used a congregational governance model with the church assembly being the highest authority. Pastors and deacons had a level of decision-making responsibility, but if they could not make a decision, it was taken to the assembly. There were also regional and national assemblies, although it was noted that fewer representatives from the *campo* were attending national assemblies because of the cost, and they also might have felt intimidated. While it was claimed that this model came from the culture, copying what they do in the communities and giving the ultimate decision-making responsibility to the *bases* [the people], the model could have been introduced a century ago by Western missionaries as one interviewee claimed, and many Western evangelical churches used this model.

Constraints on decision-making in the *campo*

The growing politicisation of rural communities under an "indigenous" government was a concern for some, and this may have changed the topics discussed in community meetings. While these meetings have traditionally been concerned primarily with agricultural themes, broader development issues involving, for example, the development of significant, modern infrastructure to serve villages and *ayllus* [groups of villages] were now discussed. Presumably, given the decision-making structures of the *sindicatos* and other indigenous groups at a national level, more time would be spent now on discussion of national constitutional issues and other political concerns.

Another factor influencing the making of decisions was the recognised existence of 'natural leaders.' Natural leaders were said to be very strong and did not necessarily have the title of *correjidor* [here the title was used in its older Spanish meaning of civic leader], or *jilacata* [traditional leader], but were always behind the nominated leaders and "commanding" them. It was believed that even the current president, Evo Morales, was controlled to some extent by a natural leader—someone who may not even be in the government. It was claimed that these natural leaders at times stood in the way of justice, as the authorities would not stand up to them. "In Quechua, Aymara and Guarani cultures, it is *who* says, not *what* they say, that is important. Everyone could be speaking but everyone will be waiting to hear what the natural leader—who has the influence—says before they make a decision" (Participant 20). Participant 20 thought that the natural leaders gained the respect of the community because they were known as those "*cumpliendo sus palabras*" [honouring their words or doing what they say they will do]. From what Participant 20 had seen in his work, natural leadership seemed to be linked with prosperity in that often these leaders would have more llamas or more sheep, but he also noted that natural leaders could use intimidation and even violence to impose their will on decision-making.

The communal or relational nature of decision-making in the rural villages was highlighted in the *campo* communities, where decisions to convert to Christianity were more likely to be taken as a whole family rather than individually. Certainly, it would be difficult for an individual to convert to Christianity if the rest of the family did not agree with the decision, and particularly if it were felt that such a conversion might imperil their standing with *Pachamama* on whom they felt they depended for their crops and livestock.

The relational nature of the decision-making processes, both for the *campo* and in the city, was further explicated in the range of values, or virtues, that were identified by the participants.

Decision-making and participant-identified virtues

Apart from the value placed by participants on religion and relationships mentioned above, valued virtues held by the participants fell into several broad categories: caring and cooperating, obedience to rules, spirituality, work, community development and values *per se*. Most of these values are connected to working and living in a harmonious relationship.

i. Caring and cooperating

Twenty-six of the interviewees referred to the need for democracy, to work together in solidarity, to have compassion and think of others, and to respect others and have tolerant attitudes. These participants were evenly distributed across the participant categories. The most common comments were those related to working together and doing things for the best of others.

ii. Obedience

Perhaps it is not surprising that six of the thirteen interviewees who spoke of the importance of obeying rules and laws were educators. The particular areas of concern were responsibility and punctuality, then morality, sobriety, honesty and the "*Ama llulla, ama qilla, ama suwa*" [Do not steal, do not lie, do not be lazy] traditional law of the rural areas.

iii. Work

Having work was a value expressed by seven interviewees. This interest or concern could be connected to the economic climate, where the economic growth and resultant upward mobility socially meant that a stronger "keeping up with the Joneses" mentality was developing. With the improvement of travel to and from the cities and the reach of communications media—at times one could see satellite television dishes on tiny adobe houses in villages where there is electricity—Participant 4 believed that *campesinos* were becoming jealous of the possessions of those living in the city, and this required paid work.

iv. Development

Four of the five interviewees who lived in country villages placed a high value on the development of their communities. This development involved the building of infrastructure and the supply of utilities to the village as well as access to education and health services.

v. Values (virtues)

A number of interviewees who were school principals spoke of the importance of "values" in the training of students and spoke of the rise in the youth culture of *antivalores* or values that were not compatible with the traditional values of the society. The emphasis on values for educators also comes from the Ministry of Education's insistence that the schools teach a set of state-determined values across the curriculum.

The virtues that were identified by the participants could be applied in general terms to all members of the Bolivian communities. It was acknowledged, however, that not all lived by them, and it was a perceived lack of respect for these values that seemed to have drawn the attention of the participants to them. While some of the school principals appeared to be a little more legalistic in this regard, and concerned for the image of their schools, the desire of the participants in general was that these espoused values should be controlling values in the decision-making processes of leaders within the country.

It may be noted that the virtues identified by Starratt (2005)—authenticity, responsibility and presence—were viewed somewhat differently within the Bolivian cultural context. Authenticity equated with the virtue of integrity, or wholeness, and this was felt to be of particular importance as discussed below. Responsibility was something that was felt by the participants to be an important consideration in the work, though the responsibility had a particular significance in terms of the bureaucracy under which they worked and the responsibility to maintain the relationship structures. The concept of presence was not discussed with the participants, but the outworking of Starratt's idea of presence as a virtue that affirmed, critiqued and enabled may be complicated by the class structures of the Bolivian society and also the relationship structures to which all leaders in the culture must attend.

Decision-making and leadership

Leaders are expected to be able to make decisions. Apart from the issues discussed above with regard to the function of leadership in Bolivia, a number of factors influenced different types of leaders in Bolivia as they made decisions. One of these was leadership style and the participants in this research recognised that there were different styles of leadership such as autocratic or democratic. The classes of leaders that were identified, quite naturally, were distinguished by the relationship between the leader and his or her followers. Respect for leaders may be important, particularly as they are the ones who, after all of the discussion, make the final decisions. Key Informant 11 pointed out, however, that leaders must also respect their followers, but Participant 36 noted that: "There are two types of leaders. One who works *por* the people, *para* the people[19] and the other group that uses the people to climb higher. The people below him do not interest him. He is not there to help the people. Rather, that people help him to rise [socially]." Participant 2 and Participant 28 also expressed this view, saying that for some leaders, political ambition and personal interests will drive decision-making. Others, according to Participant 5, will also be looking after the interests of family and friends. A common term in Bolivia, particularly around the time of election, was *pegas* [from *pegar,* meaning to glue to]. This term refers to those followers who have supported a candidate for leadership and, in return, expect favours. Obviously, nepotism and *pegas* can have a very significant effect on any decisions that are made. Compounding the process was the almost ubiquitous corruption that leads to injustice.

Character was seen, therefore, as an important part of good leadership, particularly in churches where honesty and sincerity, biblical values, and spiritual development

---

[19] Participant 36 used here two words for the English word "for". The first (*por*) is a word that indicates a reason—he or she is a leader because of the people—and *para* implies a direction for the action, and could be translated as: for the benefit of the people.

were seen as priorities. The wisdom to be able to discern the truth in school leadership situations was emphasised by Participant 21, who recognised that this was very complicated. A lack of education on the part of leaders also made this more difficult.

In general, as they made good, ethical decisions, leaders in Bolivia, particularly educational leaders, would endeavour to use the guidance provided by the organisational documents or established mores. These may have been based on requirements from the government, internal organisational regulations, actions or practices mandated by a church, or following an adherence to long-established cultural practices. In many instances, however, while claiming to be following these guidelines, leaders made decisions based on what they think they can get away with, and the local papers frequently included stories relating to some official or leader who was being sought or charged with corruption, nepotism or embezzlement. These actions, often engaged in shamelessly and without expressions of guilt, provide insight into connections between the avoidance-pursuit pair components and the worldviews and subcultures.

In summary, an aim of this research was to examine the decision-making of leaders in the two subcultures in Bolivia to determine whether the priorities given to the avoidance-pursuit pairs affected the decisions leaders made. In most cases, the participants did not make a direct connection between the pair components and the decisions that were made, though influence could be inferred. In some cases, however, a direct link was made. Two educational leaders spoke of the shame of teachers in their schools who had drinking problems and indicated that they felt sympathy for the shame they experienced and the importance of maintaining the honour of their schools in the decision to fire the teachers. Participant 1 spoke of schools where honour was considered a priority and the importance of maintaining honour would have influenced decisions.

The other factors that influenced decisions were:

a. Best use of resources and the making of profit in the business community.

b. Power politics in the rural communities (Participant 4), in the Catholic Church and evangelical churches.

c. Maintenance of community norms in rural communities and legalism.

d. Personal power in the city—particularly on the part of politicians.

e. Respect for others who may be affected by the decision.

f. Respect for the one affected by a decision if that person was a "natural leader".

g. The maintenance of interpersonal relationships.

Part III: Relationships: Connecting the avoidance-pursuit components to worldview and culture

Shame and honour were identified as being important in the lives of Bolivians, particularly the city dwellers in Cochabamba. Shame and honour, however are only found within a relational context with others and therefore the Bolivian understanding of relationship needs to be understood. Before considering the significance of relationships in the city and the *campo*, however, a caveat is in order regarding the changing nature of Bolivian culture. Some urban interviewees expressed concern with the rise in recent times of individualism and from rural experience, one linked individualism with the growing desire for goods and indirectly linked individualism with *antivalores*. As people became more individualistic, and more self-centred, according to Participant 4 they were saying, "I don't care what happens to my country. I care what doesn't happen to me." Participant 26 saw individualism as applying to all levels of society in the city arising out of a desire to see change to improve the prosperity and access to goods and services that an individual has—comparing the desire for change to the Obama pre-election slogans in the United States.

While the concerns of these two participants were very real, there was not a general feeling expressed by participants that individualism, at least among adults, was heavily affecting the relational nature of the culture. This may change with the coming generations and grave fears were expressed, particularly by school principals, for the values of these young people. However, where delinquency and the fear of delinquents was mentioned, the context was almost always as group activities involving *bandillas* [gangs] which were, by their nature, strongly bonded.

Relationships in the city

Relationships were central to both the city and pueblo cultures and while there were differences between the two cultures, and the types of relationships that exist, through historical context and immigration, the relationships in tho *campo* had affected the city to an extent. Even though the city environment did not have the intense, daily, interpersonal contact that was inevitable in rural villages, in the city, it was noted that people establish bonds and they like them to be long term. School principals spoke of the relationships within their schools between teachers and students and one also said that principals needed to show love for their teachers and not try to relate to their students by the use of rules.

The reasons given in the interviews for the maintenance of relationships varied. Often there was a wariness of the power another person might have in the community with the implication that if that person were to be offended they might cause trouble for

136

those who had decided against them. Conversely, there was the consideration of what one may gain from maintaining the relationship. For example Participant 2 said that in his father's hacienda they had worked to maintain a good relationship with the *campesinos* and their farm was not as affected as much as others with the 1952 agrarian reform laws that saw many haciendas turned over to *campesinos*.

Other participants saw the importance of relationships in a variety of contexts. Some of these included:

- within the family and extended family.

- within a school staff, where the principal needs to love the teachers and where the reconciliation of relationships was seen to be a high priority.

- in politics, where friends and relatives are given positions.

- in the organisation of communities where the governing body has a "secretary of relationships" (i.e., with other organisations, the government, etc.).

- in the rural areas they know each other because they see each other every day and they are all related in some way.

- in rural areas where the familiar forms of personal pronouns are always used.

- in the specific vocabulary used to describe the intensity of a relationship.

- in the manner in which people establish bonds and desire that those relationship bonds continue.

- in the fear some rural people have of the spirits of the dead returning to seek vengeance on those with whom they did not have a good relationship.

- in the pleasure found in the *campo* "when in a community there is a living together [*convivencia*] in a way that is healthy, a harmonious living together, a living together where a unity of opinions exists, of mutual help, of *solidaridad* [solidarity, community]".

- in the gangs of young people that form.

- in the importance attributed to what was said by others.

- in the constant attention given to creating new friendships or fictive relationships.

- in the concern regarding issues of trust between people.

Relationships were also seen to be important within religious contexts, where church groups could be considered to be similar to common interest groups. At the same time, it was noted that people who shared a supposed friendship bond in the workplace may not share the same bond when in church together. (This would relate to the in-group/out-group functioning in a collectivist society.) There was an acknowledgement that God has spoken in the Bible but also the realisation that we are all imperfect, so, in order to keep the peace, biblical principles such as grace and mercy are used to justify the making of decisions that maintain relationship even though the decisions may not be perceived to be just.

Relationships in the *campo*

Apart from the collectivist, in-group bonding, the city relationships often revolved around common interests (for example in the work place, in churches or in clubs), but the perception within the city was that relationships in the *pueblos* in the *campo* may be strong within the extended family—and in the pueblos where "everyone is your uncle" (Participant 14). The socialisation process within this context was said to begin when a child was very young. "When a child's hair begins to grow they invite the community and invited persons to cut a little bit of the child's hair and give a gift to the child. It was a part of the socialisation process for the child—acceptance into the community" (Participant 14). As well as familial and community ties, *compadrazgo*, relationships that have no blood or legal basis, were common in rural areas as well as in the city. These included the fictive relationships of *parientes simbólicos* [literally "symbolic relatives"] such as *padrinos* [godparents]. These relationships were strong and carry significant responsibilities.

The comment was made that in rural villages some may at times place a higher priority on community development than on maintaining interpersonal relationships. Even in development, however, relationships must be maintained as groups worked together to accomplish tasks. For agricultural pursuits, families used the system of *ayne* where families helped each other and shared tools and equipment, particularly at times of sowing and harvest and *pasanacu* [passing (lending) money between themselves]. Key Informant 29 noted in this regard that "In the country they were *más comunitario* [more communal]." For development projects communities worked cooperatively under committees and where large projects were concerned, *mancomunidades* [associations which may involve a number of communities] were formed to coordinate the project.

Relationships in these settings where people moot every day had many implications that influence levels of friendship and trust:

 i. "When you visit a friend you don't arrange it—you just turn up . . . not like in the city" (Participant 14).

 ii. A system of money lending called *pasanacu* was used. This involves a simple transaction without documentation, based on trust in another's word.

 iii. The familiar form of the second person singular personal pronoun (tu) was used exclusively within the rural communities. When both parties in a conversation use this form: "*Tu a tu* means at the same level" meaning that

138

there was no confrontation—because they are at the same level (Participant 29).

iv. When an unmarried girl becomes pregnant there was a great need to find out who the father is—because everyone was "related" in one way or another and doubt about paternity can cause mistrust or suspicion to grow thus harming relationships.

v. Many say that the word "please" does not exist in Quechua (as claimed by Key Informant 18) because their relationships are so close that it was not needed but there is a term, *allichu*, though it appears to be little used. Likewise, Key Informant 18 claims that "thank you" does not exist but the formal term, *anchata agradisiyki* exists though it has Spanish roots.

vi. Contentmentseen in a social context: "They consider it good when in a community there was a *convivencia* [living together] that was healthy, a harmonious living together, a living together where a unity of opinions exists, of mutual help, of *solidaridad* [solidarity, community]" (Participant 34).

vii. "There are systems predicated on sharing—the *ayne*—the way that they share labour, share tools, borrow things back and forth, have dedicated hours to community projects" (Participant 33).

Greetings and terms used in relationships in Quechua use added suffixes to reflect the depth of relationship, friendship or endearment. For example the greetings *Imaynallan kashanki, Imaynallan kakuishanki,* and *Imaynallan kapuwashanki* increase in familiarity or intimacy, as do the words used for father, *papa, papito, papitay.*

Where a pre-existing relationship did not exist there would be, at least initially, expressions of distrust. Once relationship and trust had been developed they were maintained by mutual obligations, by the *correjidor* whose judgements were designed to maintain harmony, and by the common saying (referred to as the Three Inca Laws) "*Ama llulla, ama qilla, ama suwa!*" [Don't be a liar, don't be lazy, don't be a thief (and some versions add, don't be dirty)]. According to the Glossary of Terminology of the Shamanic & Ceremonial Traditions of the Inca Medicine Lineage (O'Neill, 2007), traditionally these laws were in a positive form *tukuy munayniyoc,* [focussing on the positive, and loving rather than holding on to anger and resentment], *tukuy yachayniyoc* [refine your intuition and inner knowing to experience wisdom], and *tukuy llank'ayniyoc* [recognition of work as service to the divine] or Desire well, Learn well and Work well. In their current form they are constantly referred to and are intended to promote personal responsibility and maintain harmonious relationships within an efficient community.

The disruption or termination of relationships, for example when people fight or someone dies, was painful for the community. Death, however, may have another powerful influence on relationships:

Care is taken with relationships because someone, through relationships, through witchcraft or in the afterlife could come back to cause difficulties. When a person is dying there is quite a bit of fear in the Andean world regarding the effect the relationship one has had with the deceased will have on one now. (Participant 33)

Religion: relationships between people and supernatural beings

Religion is a significant part of a person's worldview, and therefore, some attention was given to the religious background from which the participants came.

In the city, the Catholic participants in this research did not express strong religious views but, rather, indicated that they came from Catholic families that they were educated as Catholics or that they were "Christians at heart . . . Catholic" (Participant 35—though she did note that they had sent their children to an evangelical school, as did Participant 9). Participant 9 remembered that in his strict Catholic school education, "everything was prohibited" and that near his school there was a "house of the devil" [a Presbyterian church] in which, he wryly noted, his daughter recently had been married. While it was recognised that most Protestants attended church regularly, of the eighty per cent of the city who claimed to be Catholic, only around twenty per cent of them attended mass on a regular basis.

The evangelicals interviewed appeared to be more strongly connected to their faith and their denomination or local church, though many of them would have had a Catholic upbringing, and the ancestor of one of them had been a very famous Catholic priest in Cochabamba. This upbringing is significant in that the formative lifeworld of many evangelicals was either Catholic or animist. This has led to a degree of syncretism in the evangelical worldview, just as many Catholics also still held syncretistically to animist beliefs.

While one interviewee thought that evangelicals were often found in the poorer barrios surrounding the city, this would not appear to be borne out by the number of large evangelical churches in the centre of the city. Until perhaps thirty years ago, the persecution of evangelicals had been common, and a number had been killed. At the time of the research, with much higher numbers and a broader acceptance of the beliefs of others, strong persecution was not common, though one interviewee complained of non-evangelical members of her school staff planning various forms of "attacks" against her.

A perception of biblical values was seen to be quite strong for evangelicals involved in education, including the need for moral teaching, prohibition of folkloric dancing—presumably because of the strong links between this form of dancing and animistic rituals—and the importance of commandments such as do not steal. There was a feeling that "Christian values come from faith in God and consequences. Convictions are important" (Participant 11). Perhaps these were enforced in the church for those who had respect for God or *temor* [fear—as a basis for prudent action] of God. The social work of the evangelical church was seen as being important by a number of interviewees, but the use of the Gospel to bring worldview change in rural communities was mentioned by only two of them. Participant 41 said that when this happened, people changed and gave the example of a *correjidor* who judged justly and was not corrupt.

Of the panoply of gods associated with traditional Incan, Aymara and Quechua worship, the most common one was *Pachamama* or Mother Earth. The relationship the people had with *Pachamama*, according to, was one of respect and love, and she was not feared. She was prayed to at all important agricultural events, such as when sowing and harvesting, and offerings were made to her of *challas* [oblations], *q'oas* (smoke offerings) or sacrifices (often of llamas, though there are rumours of human sacrifices). "They have quite a lot of faith in *Pachamama*" (Participant 27).

> Most of the offerings to appease *Pachamama* occur with events that have to do with the use of the *Pachamama* and to some degree also with sickness caused by *Pachamama* when she is upset because of a lack of respecting [her]. (Participant 33)

According to one interviewee, *Pachamama* is strongly linked with what he termed 'supernatural' events: wind, heat, cold, rain and rainbows. He referred to these events as the *brazos operativos* [operating arms] of nature, which will determine how people will behave and gave the example of a farmer who believed that lack of rain was punishment for something he had done, but when it rained, it meant that he had done things well.

> Pachamama is the supreme being that gives life and must be respected. Our perspective [in the city] is that God is a super being charged with looking after values—ethical and moral. In their [rural] perspective, it is the earth, nature. Their beliefs lead them to defend their territory. (Participant 2)

As with many religions, and perhaps taken largely from colonial Catholic beliefs, there were also "negative" supernatural beings. Apart from the diabolical and demonic characters played out in Carnival procession before Easter, perhaps the best known in Bolivia is probably the *Dios mono* [the Monkey god] or *Tio diablo* [Uncle devil] of the mines in Potosi. The miners give offerings of cigarettes and coca leaves to its image in the mines and seek the blessing of this being, asking it to help them and to protect them as they draw wealth from its territory beneath the earth. Participant 27 added that

> They believe in bad spirits in the *campo*—not in many spirits—more of the dead that visit at times. There are demons as well. When something strange happens—like a lightning strike or a natural disaster—they will believe that

there is something spiritual behind it, of an evil spirit, or a punishment. They still believe these things.

The earth is considered to be sacred, and dividuation exists, and that also includes a holistic view being taken of everything in the environment—humans, animals, plants and inanimate objects—each belonging to the other in some way. The beliefs in spirits that inhabit inanimate objects or ancestral spirits, though apparently widespread, were not universal: "Here [in Valle Alto] no. In some places, there are trees where they believe that there are demons in the trees, and if you touch them, you die. *Gato Blanco* [the white cat)] yes. And a dog. No ancestral spirits here" (Participant 39). Participant 14 also said that he had not seen evidence of it, though he had more of a belief in *Pachamama*, "because the earth produces, gives fruit. One has to revere the earth, things like that. Water too, there is a preference given to water because it is involved with production."

From the Spanish conquest to the rise of evangelicalism to the pervasive presentation of Western, secular humanism in the communications media, attempts have been made to change the religious worldview beliefs of the Bolivian people. Changing worldview beliefs is, however, not an easy task. Participant 28 claimed that it was almost impossible, and others also commented on belief change.

The pueblos that haven't been evangelised still believe in the spirits. Still there are *creencias ancestrales* [ancestral beliefs] and these are hard to get rid of— even though the Catholic church has influenced the communities—particularly with their ceremonies. Many times, the *autoridades originarias* [indigenous authorities] have a lot of influence. What they do, the whole pueblo does— whether Catholic or evangelical. In some radical communities, this has led to repression of those with different beliefs and for not participating in the community activities. They lock them up, punish them—though you do not see this much. "If we receive some benefit, you will not participate in it." There is still this. (Participant 27)

As the Catholic and then the evangelical churches have done in the past, the indigenous political party currently in government is attempting to promote belief changes, particularly through education under the new constitution passed on 25th January, 2009.

In the new constitution, there is no official religion for the country—as there is Catholicism now—but they are putting in and emphasising *"religión communitaria ancestral"* [ancestral community religion]. They are going to propagate this in the schools. But this is a dead religion. Very few people believe in it . . . perhaps in Orinoca [the President's birthplace]. A few people still sacrifice llamas to *Pachamama*—but this government wants it propagated through the whole country because it is the religion of the *campo*.

> Evangelicalism is imported from Israel, from the USA, from other countries. The religion here is the adoration of *Pachamama*. Some worship the frog, others lizards, as in Oruro, others condors. These are things they have invented, but they say they are from our country. These beliefs are worse than the Catholic Church—which at least believes in God and in the Bible, in the Holy Spirit, in Jesus Christ. They are closer to us. (Participant 15)

Some areas in the *campo*, however, appeared to have "forgotten *Pachamama*" (Participant 41), mainly due to an evangelical short-wave radio station, and the impact in the communities of the Catholic and evangelical churches but in many ways ancestral beliefs still formed a part of the worldview of Bolivians in the city and in the country; including in the Catholic and the evangelical churches. This syncretism involved beliefs such as the conceptualisations of the afterlife, rituals, and figures of adoration and worship.

> *Pachamama* was the protector, the provider, the producer . . . so relied on to sustain your life. The Catholics come with a different worldview and say *Pachamama* is the Virgin Mary. In the iconography, now we see a large statue of Mary with the baby Jesus. Who is the most important? Mary. Looking at Bolivia, what festivals attract the most people? In La Paz, the *Virgen de Copacabana*; in Oruro, the *Virgen Maria del Socavón*; in Cochabamba, the *Virgen de Urkupiña*; in Sucre, the *Virgen de Guadalupe*; in Santa Cruz the *Virgen de Cotoca*. Masses of people celebrate. It is interesting that the Catholic church presents Jesus as a baby or crucified. Who is going to worship someone crucified, dead? The most powerful image in the Andean worldview is the Virgin Mary, so it is hard for them to see Jesus Christ as the Saviour. (Participant 3)

> Pope Benedicto XVI was wrong when he said that the conquest of the New World was without pain—it is a lie. Indians who did not accept the cross were killed. The Catholic Church brought all these saints that the people did not know. Syncretism grew. You can see a cross with the sun [instead of Jesus]—a mixture. *Pachamama* is the principal [goddess] because the people depend on the earth. Interesting that she is a woman. After that, the *tatas* [masters or lesser deities]—*tata inti* [the weeping god], *tata sol* [the sun god] . . . because they know that without the sun they could not live. (Participant 8)

While the participants in this research seemed to agree that traditional animistic beliefs were held less in the country than in the past, one noted that many people in the city were now talking about them and celebrating *challas, q'oas* and other rituals, even though it was suggested that these were cultural and not necessarily indicative of strong religious beliefs due to the influence of the beliefs of the Catholic church. While the specific worship of *Pachamama* may have diminished in the city, this mixture of animism and Catholicism has led, according to Participant 14, to the demise of "pure culture." The "pure culture" to which he referred had its sources in the ancient civilisations of the region, but the Spanish conquest, the Roman Catholic and Evangelical churches, and the media have added new layers to the culture and new conceptualisations of religion. While for practical and geographic reasons, education, at least at the secondary level, is not available universally in Bolivia, education has played a significant role in the development and maintenance of cultural constructs, including religion.

Education and culture

The use of education to ensure that culture is preserved was ubiquitous and may have been given constitutional status. Older Bolivian constitutions made little or no mention of education, but with the adoption of the Education Reform program in the late 1980s, education became enshrined in the constitution as a significant role for governments and was included in a number of rights that were to be preserved. Article 77.1 stated that *La educación es la más alta función del Estado, y, en ejercicio de esta función, deberá fomentar la cultura del pueblo* [Education is the highest function of the state, and, in the execution of this function, should promote the culture of the people] (Congreso Nacional de Bolivia, 2004). This is an area much discussed in education circles where schools, apart from religious schools, were conceded to have become places where "anti-values" [*antivalores*] have developed, and the culture is perceived to be changing in undesirable ways.

As mentioned in Chapter 2, the various editions of the constitution of Bolivia have also seen changes in the attitude towards religion. The earliest examples precluded traditional religions and protestant faiths, while the current version purports to be all-inclusive as applied within an educational context:

> [*Artículo 86. En los centros educativos se reconocerá y garantizará la libertad de conciencia y de fe y de la enseñanza de religión, así como la espiritualidad de las naciones y pueblos indígena originario campesinos, y se fomentará el respeto y la convivencia mutua entre las personas con diversas opciones religiosas, sin imposición dogmática. En estos centros no se discriminará en la aceptación y permanencia de las alumnas y los alumnos por su opción religiosa.*]

> Article 86: In schools, freedom of conscience and faith and the teaching of the religion and spirituality of the original rural people will be recognised and guaranteed, and mutual respect and coexistence with people of diverse opinions and religions will be fostered, without being imposed dogmatically. Schools will not discriminate in the acceptance or retention of students on the basis of their choice of religion. (*Congreso Nacional de Bolivia*, 2008)

The impact the new constitution will have on schools, particularly private, confessional schools, is not yet known. New laws relating to education had been drawn up and were due to be promulgated following the adoption of the new constitution. Participant 32 strongly expressed his views by saying that the government wants to "ideologise" learning in these schools by including teaching that would clash philosophically with that of the school. An example he gave was that "instead of teaching from Genesis 1, the children would be told, this stone and this stone had sex and . . . ." In this process, he said the animistic government is trying to inculcate a "different worldview." For him, the government's policy of decolonisation meant "ridding the country of all the Western ideas that have arrived through the evangelisation process" as well as replacing scientific beliefs with indigenous beliefs.

The culture and worldview of the present and future Bolivian citizenry is therefore being pressured by these changes to the governance and constitution towards a more animistic orientation, while, at the same time, the globalised media are exerting pressure towards a consumeristic secular humanism. The impact these two forces are likely to have on the future priorities given to the avoidance-pursuit pairs considered in this research is unknown, but presumably would be different from the present situation.

CHAPTER 5

Phase II Data and Analysis

The analysis of the data from Phase I of the research indicated the importance of an understanding of relationships as a means to understanding the role of the avoidance-pursuit pairs in decision-making, and particularly shame and honour and fear and power. This understanding included the types, strengths and formation of relationships within the two different subcultures. The Phase II data indicated that the relationship networks found in the two groups were very distinct, with each having a culturally driven perspective in their formation and maintenance. The implications of the qualities and strengths of relationships for the avoidance-pursuit pairs and the decision-making of leaders were affected by issues of trust, integrity and obligation. These are set within the context of a form of collectivism, though of a type different from that found in Asia (Uskul, Oyserman, & Schwarz, 2009).

The data in Phase II were collected in April 2009 in the form of recorded follow-up interviews with four of the participants and two of the key informants from those in Phase I. Unfortunately, it was not possible for contact to be made with the other two key informants, as neither was in the city at that time. After reviewing the findings from Phase I, both of the key informants were able to add considerably to the understanding of the data and particularly their insights added significantly to the understanding of relationship structures in the city and rural communities.

The Phase II interviews were loosely structured to enable the interviewees to expand on their responses, but to cover the necessary details. The focus of the interviews was to provide some clarification or deeper understanding of culturally contextualised concepts such as shame, justice, friendship and extended familial and fictive relationships, as well as the cultural context of the concept of relationships in general. The conversations were therefore guided with questions to elicit clarifying responses.

Two areas of concern were specifically targeted in the interviews in Phase II. First, the participants were given the opportunity of responding to the general findings from the data from Phase I. This involved the presentation of the sample graphical representations of the data relating to the pair components and a general discussion of the context of each. The participants were then asked to explain the existence, strength and function of the various interpersonal relationships that existed within their subcultures. This included those within the nuclear and extended families, relationships between individuals in different classes, how relationships were initiated and maintained, and factors that could lead to the breaking of relationships. Within the city context in particular, these relationship structures established the framework within which shame and honour are experienced.

Shame and honour in the Phase II data

The evidence from the Phase I data was that within the city culture, shame and honour played a very significant role, and this was confirmed in the Phase II interviews. "Shame and honour are the things that move relationships . . . in a positive or negative way . . . the mechanism for motivating us to do something or stopping us" (Héctor). Shame and honour in this context, he added, had the most power in relationships. Héctor went on to explain that a group of people with whom an individual related formed, through shame, an external control over behaviour. When the relational group was no longer present, there were no controls over behaviour.

A further clarification of this was given by Alberto, who said that people worried about what others think and even feel that others were always watching them. The *mestizos* and Catholics, he felt, were particularly susceptible to this and feared being seen badly by others, especially by those in the family with whom the closest relationships existed. When students performed poorly in school, when a girl became pregnant or arrived home late at night, these things brought shame to the family. The shame was less with those on the periphery of the family, but it still existed. An example Alberto used was of university students from Cochabamba who, some years ago, went to Oruro to study engineering. Away from their family and others, they behaved particularly badly—at times being found lying drunk in the streets. This is something that almost never would happen where they might be seen by relatives.

As a school principal, Reina was concerned about the negative impact on students when they have been shamed in front of the school community or, more importantly, in front of their families. She believed that giving honour to a child was, in effect, saving its life. For her, the honour of the student was more important than the honour of the school, though she admitted that there were schools where the honour ('the good name') of the school was to be protected regardless of any damage that may be caused to students.

Héctor spoke of the power of shame to exert control over behaviour and said that the use of guilt within the urban culture had no effect in this regard and only caused resistance. Shame, on the other hand, was used as a unifying force to keep cultural groups together. This shame, however, had two other features. First, it was not an absolute and was dependent on the norms of the particular group. Something that may not be seen as being shameful within one's own group may be seen to be shameful in another group. This dualism is discussed further below. The second feature was that the strength and incidence of feelings of shame were diminishing in the culture due to the influence of such things as television and foreign visitors, such as missionaries, introducing individualism to the culture.

Relationships in the Phase II data

"Interpersonal relations are the base [of Bolivian society]." (Héctor)

Having been seen to be a significant factor in the Phase I data, the theme of relationships was explored with the Phase II participants. Each of the participants and Key Informants was asked to consider the role of relationships in the different communities and how these may have influenced the results relating to the prioritisation of shame and honour in the city and fear and power in the *campo*.

In Hernando's pueblo in Valle Alto, the relationships within the family were said to be strong, but other relationships existed within the community with those who lived nearby and those with whom one worked. Apart from the nuclear family, Hernando felt that perhaps the relationships with one's work companions were the strongest: based on shared customs and tasks. Two other factors affected the quality of relationships in his village, however, and both were resource-driven. The first was that the more wealth a person had, the more friends they would have, and the second was that many people would leave the community to find employment or better wages in other places, particularly in Argentina. This migration dramatically affected the network of relationships, both through an individual bringing more wealth into the community and therefore meriting more friends, and also because when the migrants returned to the pueblo, they would bring different customs and a different vocabulary, as well as being now somewhat out of touch with their original culture.

Another scenario was presented for the peripheral barrios such as Quillacollo—which had once been a town ten kilometres from Cochabamba but which had grown into a city in its own right, being at the time of the research, ten to twenty times larger than it had been twenty years before. According to Reina, a *Quillacolleña*, the

Quillacollo area has been settled by many migrants from mining areas in rural Bolivia. These people have brought their relationship networks from the *campo* but have formed new structures on the edge of the city, and there was a feeling, at least among the older inhabitants, that whereas once everyone knew everyone else, now "nobody knows anyone", and the strong relationships from before were gone. Many of the existing relationships were dysfunctional due to the dislocation from cultural roots, the ready availability and consumption of drugs and alcohol and what Reina saw as the inherently rebellious nature of the miners being passed on to their teenage offspring. In a school in which she had taught night classes for many years, Reina had also seen an added complication of the impact of migration. Many *Quillacolleños* have left to work in Spain, and high school students may be left on their own. One teenage girl in one of Reina's night classes had two children of her own that she was trying to bring up while both her parents were working in Spain. Most of the children in her classes were from families divided by divorce or migration, leaving many of the children "like orphans." Students in the night school, from situations where nuclear families were being destroyed, could not study well in school. The families of students in classes held during the day might have found themselves in more favourable conditions, but the general impression given by Reina was that of a very significant deterioration of relationships at all levels in the community.

In the very different setting of a very isolated village in the *campo*, Key Informant, Estuardo, found some similar patterns emerging regarding migration and was able to throw considerable light on some deeper relationship dysfunction. He gave as a context for this the fact that twenty to thirty years ago, transportation had been by foot or by mule, and the village did not have roads leading to it. With the advent of a good quality road connecting the village to other villages, and to the provincial capital some hours away, migration to find work had become a significant factor in the life of the community. Often, husbands would leave their families in the pueblo and go to Argentina to work, sending money back to their families, even though at times they had begun a new family in Argentina.

While this appears to present a very significant rupturing of relationships, it is, according to Estuardo, an extension of relational dysfunction that seems to have existed for a considerable time in the culture of his particular village. This situation was seen at the most fundamental of societal structures:

> Family life seems like it was a nightmare back in the *campo* when, you know, there was no *defensoría de niñez* [equivalent to a child welfare department], there was no police. Every husband was totally king of his own house, and the domestic violence, especially under the influence of alcohol, which everybody drank, just reached nightmarish levels, it seems. And even today, one of the things that we have always tried to promote in families and in churches is Bible

reading together. But they always say, well, there is never time. The families just don't eat together. They don't have the . . . Eating is what we do to get energy, it is not a social time like it is for us, you know . . . I have not been impressed with close-knit family relationships in the part of the *campo* where we were. (Estuardo)

The dysfunctional relationships in the family, the lack of bonding and the frequent beating of children—"The stories are horrendous" (Estuardo)—lead to many children as young as eight or nine years old leaving their homes and going to a city or even another country to work and live. One example Estuardo gave was of an eleven-year-old child who was beaten so much at home that he hired himself out to someone who was passing by on the way to Argentina. He worked there for a year without his family knowing where he was. The lack of relationship in these cases appears to have been primarily with the father. Another account was of a young teenager who left to escape and to find work, and nothing was heard of him for four years. When he did arrive back in the pueblo, it was to learn that his mother had died while he was away and that she had cried for him every night. It may be that the mother-child relationship in the pueblo families still existed in a fairly strong form. Despite this, Estuardo could not think of any good family models in his village and said that seventy per cent of the young people in the village were growing up without a father figure in their lives.

From Estuardo's perspective, as someone who has lived in the small pueblo for many years, within the village, friendship, *per se*, did not seem to exist. All of the inhabitants knew each other, and they knew each other's history. The villagers would stop and chat, but they did not seem to spend time together relaxing in a social setting. For the men, the only situation where they were in close social contact was when they were working together. Work, in their fields or orchards, or on communal projects, took most of their time and energy, so there was no time left to relax with "friends." The women in the villages, on the other hand, did have time to share together in their *clubes de madres* [mother clubs] that meet each week. This activity, however, was compulsory rather than being voluntary and based on relationship or friendship and women were fined if they did not attend.

Estuardo commented that, unlike Western cultures, friendship relationship situations were always spontaneous rather than planned. Where a friendship bond did exist between people, they would arrive uninvited to chat and without a set time or place. Instances where a time and place were given for people to meet would automatically be assumed to be for the purpose of discussing business or a problem. Estuardo gave examples of an awkward evening spent with a couple whom they considered friends but who came, invited, to dinner expecting that there was some problem that had to be discussed. On the other hand, one member of the couple would call in to the medical centre where Estuardo worked and "hang around" and talk, seeming oblivious to the fact that Estuardo, as a Westerner, was busy and did not want to be interrupted. Relationships in the *campo* thus seemed to operate in a relatively informal and unplanned manner.

Relationship formation in the city

Apart from the collectivist relationships within the family, in the city, relationship formation at the edge of the collective was seen to be important in childhood and adolescence as well as the workplace. As an important Key Informant with expertise in Bolivian sociology, Alberto was able to reflect at length on the relationship structures in the society. As adults, there were opportunities for the upper classes to form relationships through such things as card groups, tea groups, golf clubs, and the country club. These activities were more expensive and more sophisticated but, unlike the other classes or those in the *campo*, these classes of people had the free time to be able to pursue these activities and therefore the concomitant relationships.

At a more general level in the society in the city, many people would meet with work companions or a select group of friends to play sports or drink. On a less regular basis, Alberto and Hernando both noted the importance of celebrations: in particular, fiestas, religious festivals, marriages, baptisms, anniversaries, and funerals. These were times when relationships were strengthened both in social contact and, as seen below, in the obligations that were inherent in the invitations.

Situated relationships

In the city, relationships within the Bolivian cultures may be seen as being strongly situated. Relationships were strong within the strict confines of the nuclear family: "If you have to choose, you always stick with family. You won't back a friend over family" (Eliana). Outside the family, as Alberto explained, while people may be very good friends within a shared working environment, may play sports together and share family news with each other, they probably would never go on picnics together, and if they saw each other in the street, they might only greet each other with a polite hello. Estuardo gave the example of a work colleague with whom he developed what he considered to be a very good friendship in his medical centre. When they were both elected to a committee in their church, however, the friendship did not appear to exist in that context and, indeed, appeared to be replaced by antagonism. When asked to reflect on this, Alberto explained that this would have happened probably because the relationship in the clinic was one of dependence, whereas in the church committee, they would have been considered as equals, and so the co-worker would not have bothered to foster the relationship within that situation.

As indicated earlier, a very significant component in interpersonal relationships in Bolivia, in both the country and the city cultures, was reciprocity. In the workplace people were befriended, particularly if they had some social standing or wealth, and invited to family functions. This might involve attendance at a birthday party, or it could mean being named Godparent of a child. In these cases, the expectation was that the favour would be returned. These actions had very significant social implications. For example, there was kudos to be gained if someone with a higher social status were to become the Godparent of your child and further kudos from being invited to be the Godparent of the other's child.

This reciprocity extended to the lending of money or other resources and, in Alberto's situation as a university lecturer, relationships were often fostered with him in order that at some stage in the future he might be able to assist a son or daughter to get into the university. Reciprocity was seen as being a powerful means by which relationships were established and maintained, and is further discussed under obligations below.

Factors that strengthen or weaken relationships

The strengthening of relationships within the city culture is something that was undertaken consciously and intentionally. Actions were undertaken that were specifically designed to bring prestige to the family, and these included throwing, organising and paying for at least part of a good party, buying costumes for dancers in parades, or facilitating the building of a school or other public infrastructure. Honour would also be brought to the family by association with someone with social prestige, for example, having the mayor or a politician, or someone considered by the community to be important, present at a family event. These, according to Alberto, would bring more acceptance (tighter bonding) within the family and also enhanced leadership power.

The things that tended rather dramatically to weaken or break relationships included competition for limited resources or other economic stresses that lead to migration. Blanca felt that the most important factor was the betrayal of friends or relatives and the consequential breaking of any trust that might have existed. This betrayal may relate to a breaking away from the assumed beliefs of the family or group. For example, voting for a different political party from the rest of the family could cause a serious disruption of relationships and might lead to individuals being isolated from the group. This might be the case, particularly if the dissenter's party were to lose an election. Reflecting on this level of relationship breaking, Alberto used the illustration of a past Vice President of the country, Victor Hugo Cardenas. Cardenas had changed his name from an Aymara name to a Hispanic one so as not to be excluded from enrolment in university and had risen to be the first indigenous (Aymara) Bolivian to reach such a high level in politics. Since his time as Vice President, Cardenas has lived in an Aymara community near Lake Titicaca and decided to stand for the presidency in the elections that were held in December 2009. This meant that he would have been standing against the incumbent, indigenous president, and the inhabitants of his pueblo showed their displeasure by demonstrating outside his house, eventually driving him and his family from it and from their community. Cardenas was perceived to have betrayed the trust of his village by siding with the opposition. Other relationship-strengthening or weakening factors identified by the participants in Phase II were trust, integrity and obligation.

i. Trust

A key component in relationships is trust, and trust was a very significant issue in Bolivian cultures. A lack of trust makes stable relationships difficult to maintain. Héctor suggested that, in terms of complete (100%) trust, you could not even trust the person inside your own shirt! Christians may trust God 100%, and mothers, he said, could probably be trusted to about 90%. There is the feeling that "God . . . I may not understand but I will trust" (Héctor) and "Mum may lie to me, but it is basically because she loves me and wants the best for me" (Eliana). In general, Héctor felt that there were levels of trust that one had to have in relationships, and these stayed in place until the trust was broken in some way.

In the barrios around the city, there was generally less trust because trust takes time, and it takes a long time to be accepted in the barrios. Reina noted that trust was being lost in Quillacollo and in the city. She saw the outworking of this in Quillacollo in the commercial activities in which she saw ninety per cent of that community involved. These people did not seem to care whom they hurt, caring only for their personal interests. And once someone had broken your confidence, the lesson learned was that you would not trust them again.

In his small village about forty kilometres from Cochabamba, Hernando believed there was a high level of trust between family members and even extended family members. Between friends, he said, there was not much trust, and this was a delicate area. The friend may or may not keep his or her word. In more general terms, within the community, Hernando cited *ayne* as an example of an expression of trust, and this relates to obligations and the fulfilment of one's word by complying with the obligation to act.

Key Informant Estuardo was asked to reflect on the issue of trust within the context of his particular *campo* village. His response was simply: "*No hay!* [There isn't any!] That was an easy one." Estuardo used the illustration of elderly people who came to his clinic to pay their accounts with counterfeit currency that they had been given for their produce. He went on to explain that "There is really a sense that if you don't watch

154

out for yourself, nobody else will. They'll take advantage if they possibly can. And I think that goes to the *no hay confianza* [a commonly heard expression—there isn't any trust] stuff."

ii. Integrity

Eliana asked if there might be a connection between the lack of trust in general in the community and the issue of integrity. The noun, *integridad*, which may be translated as integrity in English, has the sense in Spanish of moral integrity, but also maintains its original intention of being well integrated. The word therefore may be translated in English as wholeness and may even be used in the context of virginity. When speaking with the participants in Phase II of the research, it was obvious that most of them saw *integridad* at least partially in the sense of wholeness rather than exclusively in terms of moral integrity.

A person had integrity, according to Alberto, if they were not corrupt, respected the principles of their position, completed their plans, did not buy positions or use business resources for personal purposes and had respect for others. He added, however, that people recognise that "*Es un tonto que no aprovecha las oportunidades*" [It is a fool who does not take advantage of opportunities] and that a person may be considered to have integrity even though they were not *integro* [complete, honest or upright] because that person has a bright personality or is an intelligent leader. This would work as long as the person involved did not do something too far beyond the mores of the group, as this would bring shame on the group, and that person would not be trusted in the future. Leaders in politics, according to Héctor, had particular problems in this regard and he claimed that it was very, very difficult for someone in politics to be *integro* and there was an attitude in the community that for many it is a matter of "*Hecha la ley: hecha la trampa*" [This saying may be translated as: Where there is a law, there is a loophole].

There were those, however, particularly elderly people of sixty or seventy years of age, who would be said to have integrity according to Héctor. People were also seen as having integrity in the Bolivian culture if they accepted themselves and then those around them for who they were. This was not an easy process, according to Blanca, and the acceptance of others was based on the integrity or wholeness of the other.

Within the rural communities, Hernando linked integrity to completing one's duties to the community. In particular, he used the illustration of a well and associated irrigation channels that had been dug for the community water supply and all those who fulfilled their obligations to the community were said to have integrity. For him, *integridad* is *cumpliendo* [completing what one has said one would do or completing one's obligations]. Estuardo saw integrity in his village community as being associated with loyalty and loyalty to the beliefs of the community or group in particular. He illustrated this by referring to the *Masistas* [those who are loyal to the governing MAS political party] being loyal to the party and the *cambas* [people of the lowlands] almost universally despising the *collas* [people of the mountains and valleys]. A different perspective on integrity in his community was seen as the ability of a leader to be able to accomplish something for the community. This may include such projects as the construction of a basketball court or other infrastructure, which lead the community to believe that they have managed the local economy well. This is strongly related to the concept mentioned above of *cumpliendo*: keeping one's word or fulfilling one's obligations.

iii. Obligation

Collectivist societies in Latin America, structured as they are around tightly defined groups between which there is little trust, operate under a strong sense of obligation and *quid pro quo*. Obligations may take various forms from those dictated by authoritarian leadership to social, interpersonal obligations based on community mores and at all levels, they affect the decision-making of individuals.

Obligations imposed from outside the immediate community often involve politically motivated actions. These may be in response to government or union groups and could involve considerable danger where riotous behaviour was involved. Alberto gave the example of the *cocaleros* [coca growers] in the Chapare region, where there was a very vertical and authoritarian political leadership. All those in the region were obliged to participate in demonstrations, and those who refused could find themselves punished or fined. These obligations also applied to syndicate meetings and other community leadership meetings, as mentioned by some interviewees in Phase I. Estuardo pointed out that a common saying: "*Sin sanción nosotros no hacemos nada*" [Without sanctions we will not do anything], applied to such meetings and this meant that when meetings were called, those who were obliged to attend must calculate whether the money they would lose from leaving their work for a day would be more than the fine that would be imposed. Often this meant that, as Estuardo remarked regarding marches and demonstrations, "what at first glance seems to be patriotic spirit, you know, people who are really into participating in democracy, it is all coerced. All of it." At a national level, one interviewee had the perception that everything from the government was done by force, and according to Héctor, the *campesinos* have been used by the government, through obligation or forced through fear, to ensure its election.

Another effect of obligation on the community and individual decision-making of *campesinos* is inherent in the concept already mentioned of *ayne*.

> Ayne is one of the things that people always admire about the Inca culture. One of the things that gets held up as community solidarity and so forth, but, again, it's . . . I mean, I used to compare it to an Amish barn raising . . . everyone pulling together. But again there is this obligation, you know. It is not a freely

given thing. It is not grace at all. It's—I'm going now either because you helped me before and I'm obligated or because I want to obligate you to me . . . . It's like, in the *campo* the economy always, traditionally, worked by *treuque* [barter]. You know, I bring my salt blocks from Uyuni down to the valleys, and I trade my salt for corn. And that's always been the preferred way to do business in the *campo*, though it has been replaced by money now. But it's the same idea. You have something I need. I have something you need. It's not a gift really, it's not, you know, out of the goodness of my heart that I am helping, which is kind of at first brush, you might see, but it is always, we understand that there is recompense. And I'm doing it more out of an obligation than because I want to help you. (Estuardo)

Rather than existing across the entire community now, in his village, Estuardo suggested that due to the constant division of the land over generations, *ayne* was now limited to within families and close relatives. Also, in these remote communities, no taxes were paid, and therefore, few services were available. If roads need to be maintained or water channels cleaned, this work must be undertaken by community members. One day each week is therefore set aside for all to work on community projects. According to Estuardo, the reduction in land size and the role they had been told they were obliged to play in the community had led to many young people being dissatisfied with life in the *campo,* and so they had moved to the cities.

For those in the middle class in Cochabamba, Alberto spoke at some length and with a number of personal illustrations regarding obligations that revolved around such things as friendship or sympathy for a cause. While the sympathy for a cause may apply to political and other demonstrations, obligations had a much more immediate expression at an individual and family level, where the feeling of obligation might be manipulated. People, including his university colleagues, would use a variety of actions or activities to provoke a *quid pro quo* response. To do this, they might have given gifts or given invitations to parties, barbeques, weddings and special family events. The obligation from these may be effectively buying votes for an election, securing obligated support for a promotion, or, especially when directed towards those higher on the social scale, used to acquire social esteem or the possibility of being able to use influence in the future. Through these mechanisms, networks of relationships were developed, thus forming broader collectives than the narrowly defined collective of immediate and extended family.

Collectivism

A form of forced collectivism in and around Cochabamba was evident in a number of different forms—both in construction and in action. Non-family, forced groupings such as those used for demonstrations or in unions, had led to a situation where, quoting a term used by sociologists, Alberto said "*el sujeto está borrado*" [the individual has been erased or ignored]—becoming subjugated and becoming merely an indistinguishable part of a group. These groups were then manipulated in a dictatorial fashion to fulfil the wishes of their leadership. Often this involved opposition to another group (out-group) in the society: having a different social status, ethnic background, political affiliation or different religious beliefs.

A traditional form of collectivism, particularly within the city, was based on the family as the fundamental unit. These units were maintained as within each unit, there would be at least a degree of love and friendship, as well as trust. Beyond the family unit, links of different types, including "old school tie" networks (Estuardo), were used. These were essential in order for commerce to function in the city.

The formation of strong bonds within family and other groups in collectivism in Latin America may have a number of sources. Alberto mentioned the role of the dominance of the Moors in Spain and the turbulent period of Spanish conquest in Latin America, when, presumably, people were forced to form tightly knit groups against common enemies. Given recent violent unrest in the city, Blanca, who had been fearful in Phase I of the research, was convinced that the *campesinos* were intent on destroying the city people whom she referred to by the term *civilizadas* [civilised], by way of contrast with the people from the *campo* who had closed sections of the city with violent protests for five days in January, 2009, resulting in two deaths. The conflict, Blanca claimed, had strengthened the bonds in the relationships in nuclear and extended families.

An important consideration with regard to collectivism, at least as it was expressed in Bolivia, was the existence of a moral dualism. This was highlighted by Estuardo, who said that what may be permissible to do to the out-group may not be permissible within the in-group. While it would not be in the in-group's best interests for a member to destroy property belonging to the group, the group may consider it to be quite permissible, and even the honourable thing to do, to destroy the property of another group or of members of that other group. This would be the case particularly where there had been a dispute between the groups. Alberto noted that within groups, the rules may be very strict and strictly adhered to, whereas a different morality applies regarding actions of group members outside that group context. In terms of moral direction, as Héctor said, what was said by your clan or group is important to you, whereas what was said by another clan, another family group, did not carry much weight. This moral stance, as well as the leader's position in a collective, would be important influencing factors on their decision-making.

158

The decision-making of leaders

The interpersonal relationships that existed in the family and that were formed with others, appeared to have a significant effect on the decision-making of all individuals, including leaders. The strength of these relationships was also important. Alberto noted that where there were factions and not much unity, the leader would feel weaker and must act more prudently and not make decisions that were too radical. When the group was united, the leader would have more confidence and his decisions would be more progressive and be broader-based. Within the group, subgroups would press for the implementation of their particular projects and try to ensure that the project met their specific needs, even though the project might benefit the whole group.

The importance of decision-making by leaders in order to meet needs was a very important aspect of the culture as indicated in the saying: *wawa que no llora, no mama* [the baby who does not cry, receives no milk].

> If you think about it there is a lot behind [the saying] if you unpack it. First of all it's that we are *wawas* [babies] . . . . We're not responsible for our welfare. We're dependent on somebody else's largesse. And we assume that that person isn't interested in helping us, you know. We don't think it's a mother who wants to nourish us. We think it is somebody who is indifferent to our well-being. And so the only way to get what we want is to be as obnoxious as possible, you know. We'll start with little things, and if we don't get what we want quickly on our list then we will go *tomar la alcaldía* [take over the council buildings], which means, you know, go nail up the doors or actually take over the offices and sit in there till we've got what we want, you know. That's, well, it's another way, it's a masculine way of conflict resolution, you know, as opposed to negotiation or something like that. So, given those presuppositions, that we are helpless to improve our condition, that we depend on handouts from somebody else, that's where *muñeca* [influence] comes in. If you have some way to gain some degree of influence, you know, on somebody, then you are a person of power too in the eyes of the people around you. (Estuardo)

Despite these complexities in decision-making in general, Reina noted that decision-making was difficult for her in her particular setting as school principal. She expressed concern about the decisions she had to make on a regular basis regarding her teachers and pupils. Decisions affect people, and she said that she needed God's wisdom because, after all, "Who are you to make the right decision? . . . You are talking about lives." She felt that in some ways she was placed in a position where she had to make decisions as if she were God and where the consequences of making the wrong decision might be worse than those of making no decision. This very heavy responsibility, she felt, should be shared to ease the burden. Reina had endeavoured to spread the decision-making across a leadership team in the school, granting responsibility to those who had proved that they could be trusted.

The role of educational institutions, such as Reina's, was important in a collectivist society, as already noted, in the development of "old school tie" networks for use in the future. Reina also noted that schools are important in the inculcation of ideas and ideologies. These would provide a source of cohesion for the culture group through commonly shared beliefs. At the same time, these distinctions provided the defining otherness for the group, contrasting it with other groups (out-groups) and other beliefs. The distinctions were seen between Catholic and Evangelical schools, but also between the perceived social status of the schools. Within schools, however, there could also be class differentiation and discrimination. Blanca illustrated this with references to children from families of *comerciantes* [shopkeepers] who, due to changing economic circumstances, were now able to enter schools that previously had been the preserve of middle and upper-class families. In these schools, the children of *comerciantes* were, reportedly, suffering from being isolated and discriminated against by other students. The non-family collective to which they would normally have been aligned would be found in a government school.

CHAPTER 6

Research Findings and Discussion

The findings of this research emerge from the analysis of the data that explored the question: What worldview and cultural factors influence the prioritisation of affective domain avoidance-pursuit pairs and do they affect the ethical decision-making of leaders in different subcultures—in this case, in Bolivia? Specifically, the findings with regard to the research question originated in the analysis of data collected from interviews with the purposively chosen interviewees and Key Informants in the two phases of the research.

In order to be able to answer the research question, the following subsidiary questions were posed:

1. What defines and differentiates the two Bolivian subcultures in this research?

2. How does leadership function within these cultures?

3. How do leaders make decisions?

4. What determines the "right thing to do" in the decision-making process?

5. What priorities do the members of the subcultures place on the avoidance-pursuit pair components (guilt, shame and fear as opposed to justice/innocence, honour and power)?

6. Do the prioritisations of the pair components indicate culturally-based pair prioritisations?

7. What are the worldview and cultural sources of the prioritisations?

In addition, the following assumptions had been generated from the literature with regard to the avoidance-pursuit pairs and their prioritisations and these were tested in this research:

Assumption 1. That the pair components (guilt, innocence, shame, honour, fear and power) are identifiable as being important to the people in the two subculture groups studied and that there is an observable sub-cultural variation in the levels of importance attributed to them and to their pairs: guilt–innocence, shame–honour and fear–power.

Assumption 2. That these priorities flow from culturally embedded worldview sources, including religious beliefs.

A further assumption was added that was not generated from the literature:

Assumption 3. That the prioritisation of the avoidance-pursuit pairs affects the decision-making of leaders.

Within the data, the responses to the first four subsidiary questions provided the context for the analysis. Subsidiary questions five, six and seven provided the specific data relating to the research question. The following classification of the significant findings emerged in response to the research question, the subsidiary questions and the testing of the three assumptions:

Finding #1: The avoidance-pursuit pair components

Finding #2: The avoidance-pursuit pairs

Finding #3: The avoidance-pursuit pairs and decision-making

Finding #4: Contributing factors

Finding #5: The cultural and worldview sources of the avoidance-pursuit pair prioritisations

Finding #5: The cultural and worldview sources of the avoidance-pursuit pair prioritisations: Collectivism, animistic dividuation and colonial law.

Finding #6: The key to understanding the affective domain avoidance-pursuit components and pairs: relationships

The first two findings were from direct responses in the Phase I data (Chapter 4) and the other findings arose from the analysis of the Phase I and Phase II data (Chapters 4 and 5).

Finding #1: The avoidance-pursuit pair components

Priority was found to be given for the shame and honour components in the city subculture and fear and power in the country subculture. Very little concern was expressed by the research participants for guilt and innocence.

The results from interviews have shown in both Phase I and Phase II of the research that honour and shame were significant for leaders in the city, and fear and power were significant for the *campesino* leaders living in country villages, though these often were not linked as specific pairs for the individual. For example, a participant from the city may prioritise shame and power rather than shame and honour. In general, this confirmed Assumption #1 that had been derived from the literature. Issues of being deemed to be guilty or just/righteous or innocent, however, appeared to be of less significance. While this last result was not expected from the work of Muller (2001), given the influence of the Catholic and Evangelical churches over many years, it is an important finding in that it appears to indicate that religion, per se, at least imported religion, may not have a strong, direct impact on the avoidance-pursuit pair prioritisations within the Bolivian context. On the other hand, if the term *religion* is taken to connote something of its original meaning of binding together—either people, as in a monastic setting, or people to a deity—then this would give a relational framework similar to that found in this research.

In general terms, however, the identification of the individual pair components of shame, honour, fear and power confirms the similar findings in the literature of Muller (2006a), Hegeman (2006) and Blaschke (2002). It should be noted, however, that unlike the African and Middle Eastern contexts of the work of Muller, Hegeman and Blaschke, in the Bolivian context, fear and power, while related at times to spiritual dimensions, were more strongly expressed in relation to other factors. Certainly, in the *campo* [rural areas], there was fear of the supernatural, of the unknown and of the natural forces over which the *campesinos* [those living in the rural areas] have no control, though they believe supernatural powers control them. Fear, however, was seen also to exist as fear of others or of other groups and of a lack of the necessities of life, as well as the spirit world. Power, also, did not pertain exclusively to the domain of the supernatural, and leaders were seen to seek and exercise degrees of personal power and the political power that may be generated by mass groupings is very well understood and practised. This appears to have become more evident in recent times with the national-level rule of a *campesino*-led government.

In the city, in general, shame was seen to be something of considerable importance both personally and within the collective in-group and at times was linked to fear because of the fear of being shamed and of bringing disgrace to the family or in-group name. It was also found that where relationships were not strong or non-existent, the effect of shame may be limited or even seem to be non-existent. Given the concerns of the participants regarding growing individualism in both the country and city societies, it would appear that the shame-based characteristics of the Bolivian culture may diminish in the future, along with collectivism as it has been defined traditionally for Bolivia or Latin America. Participants in this research did remark, however, on the current importance in their culture of reducing shame or saving face. In order for Westerners to understand more fully the values, attitudes and actions of individuals from collectivist cultures, it is important, obviously, that there be some understanding of the importance and depth of this value.

Commenting on the results of the Phase I data, Key Informant 18 made the following observations:

> I think that in the city, in the urban world of Latin America, and specifically the Bolivian world here in Cochabamba, there is a great worry, a big "concern"—about who is watching, what others are saying, what they think of us? So shame and this honour come to be very important because perhaps in all of these interactions, inter-relationships, that you mentioned, there is a good deal of: "everybody is watching everyone, to see how we are." And rumours and comments become very important because they affect us around the idea of how we are seen by others. So, perhaps in a more modern society or more agrarian, but I think that in general, in a more Western society, life for each person is a little more advanced. That is to say, here is my life and it has pressures, but here we worry also about the lives of others, but also in the sense of . . . one can't judge, but, to appreciate, to value and to comment on what is good and what is bad, what is shameful and what brings us honour. I think that perhaps it is the Catholic training that creates this. But I think it is a particular trait of the *mestizos*—that it is shameful to be seen to be bad. To be . . . not devalued, or necessarily have a stigma attached but to be seen to be bad by others. (Key Informant 18)

When asked about shame and the importance of the family, Key Informant 18 added:

> Fundamentally, it is the family. That is to say, the son who misbehaves in school and calls attention to himself, and when the father knows that he has lost a year because they have expelled him or they have punished him in school, it is shameful. But also, in terms of gender, much . . . let us say, for example, the theme of a girl who has a child while still very young, or stays out late at night because she doesn't have good friendships. This is changing here. They are starting to drink from when they are very young. And this [is shameful], at a family level, and perhaps also with the extended family, with an uncle, a relative, a cousin. They could end up in gaol, they could have problems with debts . . . . It affects, let's say, the family a little more. Until, perhaps, one is part of a group of friends, shame can be caused by a friend, also, in a way, but I say that it is more at the level of the nuclear family.

Shame and honour, therefore, relate directly to the setting of the individual's lifeworld and the source of their worldview formation: the nuclear family and the extended family.

Finding #2: The avoidance-pursuit pairs

This case study confirmed the existence at a cultural level of the prioritisation of the avoidance-pursuit pairs in two Bolivian subcultures. This added to earlier studies of the phenomenon in West Africa, Asia and the Middle East.

The literature had pointed to the existence of these affective domain avoidance-pursuit pairs and their prioritisation in other cultures in West Africa, Asia and the Middle East but this research has been the first to identify them in a Latin American context and to describe the cultural differences between two subcultures in Bolivia. This confirmed Assumption #2 that had been derived from the literature. The low number of participants also meant that the analysis and the conclusions reached in this research focused on the individual pair components rather than the defined pairs per se. A larger study may be able to clarify further subcultures and subculture distinctions. For consideration in future studies in this area, it should be noted that the pair linkage of the particular set of avoidance-pursuit pairs used in this research may be a peculiarly Western worldview construction, coming as it does from the literature which was almost entirely produced by Westerners such as Muller (2000), Hegeman (2006a) and Blaschke (2001).

The results from this research, however, demonstrated a sub-cultural prioritisation by city dwellers, of both shame and honour, and by those from the *campo* for both fear and power. Little evidence was found in either the city subculture or the rural subculture that perceptions of personal guilt and innocence played a very significant role. While the literature had indicated the identification of the pairs at a culture level, this research, with a limited number of participants, found the pairs to exist at a general, subculture level but there was limited evidence at an individual level for the existence of the specific, linked pairs and their ranking, though the discrete components were ranked by individuals and an overall image was generated for the represented subcultures. This lack of clear identification of the specific pairing predicted in the literature, however, may be due to the nature of the limited, convenience-based sampling of participants used in this study. A further factor that may have resulted in the distinctions being less clear than expected would be the fact that a number of the participants live within a city-*campo* continuum rather than having their worldviews formed entirely within one of the subcultures. In terms of the reflections of the participants on the subculture other than their own, even where strong distinctions between the subcultures were made by the participants, there was an indication that attempts were made by those in the city to understand those in the *campo*.

> Years ago, most of the people in the city were middle-class. When we were young, we went out with friends who were of the same social and racial group. We would have friends from other groups in the school, but not outside the school. Influences have come from Europe and North America. In school, there was not a strong influence from Spain, nor Chile—because they stole the sea. Now there is much from Spain because of the emigrants. It is the mother country. But most of us feel the influence of all Latin Americans. There has always been a relationship with the *campo*. My uncles speak Quechua perfectly . . . . When my mother died, my relatives had land, so there was always contact with servants [farm workers], and they had to speak the language [Quechua], and my brothers, when they arrived at the properties, they said that no one could speak Spanish because my parents said that my brothers had to learn Quechua. Now, as "white" people, we are all educated, and people wonder how we can speak Quechua so well. The *gente morena* [brown-skinned people] were humble, good people and were taken into the family as family.

> We don't differentiate between the city and the campo. In both groups, people can think about justice, have correct ideas, but also in the country, there are people who are negative and only think about money . . . . Now in the campo, they are waking up. Some of them have the right now to be someone but don't know how to talk [i.e., speak correct Spanish], don't know how to live, don't know how to behave themselves, cannot reach, sadly, what we can reach. The changes need to recognise this. They are people, not animals. But they want to get into power, but they don't want to study or improve themselves. (Participant 9)

Finding #3: The avoidance-pursuit pairs and decision-making

The decision-making of leaders was affected by the relational context within which they found themselves in terms of the priority given to the avoidance pursuit pairs.

It was evident in the data in this research that responses to the affective pair components inform the decision-making of leaders in Bolivia to a significant extent, and this confirmed Assumption #3. The responses of the participants were related to the relational structures, particularly interpersonal, in which they lived and worked. It was seen that decisions were made with conscious or unconscious consideration being given to the reduction of shame or the acquisition of honour, or to the reduction of fear and the gaining of power. While not every decision that was to be made was governed by the ranked pairs or pair components, their effect was woven through the communities and the thinking and acting of the community members, being an integral part of their worldviews.

Apart from within an education context, where strong, situated, workplace relationships existed, these would overrule procedural concerns. These relationships may have been natural in terms of physical proximity in the workplace or may have been what could be seen as imposed or artificial. These imposed relationships were not the forced relationships of, particularly, the *campo,* where involvement in group activities was enforced, at times using threats of physical force or fines, but those that had been developed artificially by others, possibly outside the direct workplace, in order to exert influence at some future point in time. To initiate and maintain this type of relationship, the person in a position of power or influence would be invited into a fictive or similar relationship with the family. While there is a degree of cultural obligation to comply with these requests, there is also an implicit obligation to reciprocate and thus strengthen what may be seen as an artificial bond.

In general, those in leadership considered relationship networks to be very significant. For leaders, the strength of the interpersonal relationships that exist between the leader and his or her followers, as Maxwell (2007, 2010) has pointed out, will determine the level of influence the leader has, and this, in turn, will be a measure of the level of leadership the leader has. The making of decisions by democratic processes was also important in terms of maintaining community as well as respecting others within the family, the in-group and the broader community within which the participants lived and worked. Participant 26 commented that, "to know how to make decisions and understand how to make decisions, one needs to look at what the [decision-making] path is," and it would appear that the decision-making processes also influenced the decisions that were made. With each person being obliged to give their opinion on decisions made in the rural *ayllus*, all community members have an opportunity to hear how others feel and what they are thinking, and thus developing a strong *sensus communis* approach to decision-making. It may also be true, however, that the use of democratic processes released leaders from having to make difficult decisions that had relational implications, as implied by one interviewee. The resorting to legalistic methods by leaders, and by those participants in education settings in particular, may also be seen in this context.

A note regarding educational leaders

Within the specific context of schools, the formation of fictive relationships such as those in offices and businesses was not evident in the data. The work-place relationships of the educational leaders were strongly determined by the priority given to the necessary compliance with regulations while attempting to maintain functional, educational institution context relationships with teachers and parents. From the data that was gathered, the decision-making of school principals was seen to be strongly influenced by the rather strict bureaucracy of the education system and of the governance structures set in place by the *Reforma Educativa* education reform laws that involve *juntas escolares* [school committees]. Principals implied that one of the bottom lines in their decision-making was that they must comply with the substantial number of laws and regulations that govern education, as well as school committees that could be difficult entities with which to negotiate. Those in private schools were also answerable to their school boards. There was evidence in a number of places in the data that at times these pressures carried with them a degree of threat of the potential termination of employment.

The school principals generally did not express concern for their own honour or shame but were concerned for the name of their school, and some were also concerned for the personal relationships they had with their staff, with the parents, and with the students. Principals appeared to have particular difficulty with the moral dilemma decisions where choices had to be made between the "right thing to do" as determined by the government or school policy, and the "right thing to do" in terms of maintaining stable relationships. While a school principal may not have strongly bonded relationships with all within the school community, where the principal may be seen to be out of step with the desires of school community there was considerable concern regarding having to face the angry, and socially powerful, massed will of the school family. Perhaps, also, principals in the quotidian functioning of their school sub-societies have to deal with more interpersonal conflicts and decisions relating to interpersonal relationships than those in other leadership positions.

Finding #4: Contributing factors to the decision-making of leaders

A number of contributing factors to the decision-making of leaders were identified in this research: trust, values, profit, political power, legalism, personal power, respect, and respect and fear.

Eight other factors that also influenced the decision-making of the leaders were identified in this research. While there are many cultural and situational factors that influence decision-making in any culture, the following were seen in the data to be of importance for the participants in this research.

a. Trust

The relationship structures within the city subculture appeared to have existed within the collectivist in-groups in Cochabamba at least throughout the living memory

168

history of the country, and probably much longer, dating back to before the Spanish conquest. As noted by Key Informant 18, from a Bolivian perspective, one of the features of the relationship structures in collectivist societies is the level of trust between individuals. The situations described by Huff and Kelley (1999) and O'Toole (2008), regarding trust in collectivist cultures, were very similar to those found in Bolivia, where trust was something reserved for the very closest of relationships. In general, however, the society in the city was marked by a lack of trust—that may even extend to relationships within a nuclear family.

b. Values

The value sets and the relationships within which they functioned, and which drove decision-making, provided the basis for the significant findings in this research. Schwartz (2006) commented that values could be central features that add cohesion to a culture because they shape and justify the beliefs, actions and goals of individuals and groups. At a general level, values espoused by the participants in this research were frequently connected to the specific cultural values of working hard, being obedient, caring, cooperating and living in a harmonious relationship. They also included the value of having values (or virtues) by which to live, as opposed to anti-values [*antivalores*] that were seen as being, by definition, anti-social. Each of the highlighted values has a strong connection to interpersonal relationships and the bonding of the community for both the existence of the community and the quality of living that it provides. While caring and cooperating may flow from human affective or pragmatic sources, not working hard, being disobedient and promoting disharmony were seen as shameful, an important component of the avoidance-pursuit pairs and therefore had an effect on the results of this research. Perhaps contrasting with the individualistic orientation of many Western societies, the emphasis on "getting on" with each other within a collectivist environment was very highly valued by the participants.

c. Profit

Less significant, though related to values, was the importance of making the best use of resources and making a profit in the business community.

d. Political power

Power, as it relates to politics, was seen to be an important determinant in the decisions made in a number of different contexts. In the rural communities, it was significant and gaining in significance under the current government, but its importance was also identified as existing in the Catholic Church and also Evangelical churches.

e. Legalism

A legalistic framework for decision-making was noted in some situations such as schools, due to the necessary adherence to Department of Education rules and school board decisions. In rural communities, a rigid adherence to the traditional community norms (*Ama suwa, ama llulla, ama q'ella* [Do not steal, do not lie, don't be lazy]) was also a consideration that had quite legalistic overtones. Legalistic attitudes to decision-making were also noticed in the setting of a Non-Government Organisation by one interviewee. Despite this, the following reflection was added by Key Informant 18 in Phase II of the research with regard to making decisions for a local community in-group and also adherence to externally imposed legal requirements:

> Where there are factions and not much unity, the leader will feel weaker and must act more prudently and not make decisions that are too out there. When the group is united, the leader will have more confidence and his decisions will be more progressive and broader. Within the group, subgroups will push for their projects, even though it will benefit everyone, but it will be particularly beneficial for the subgroup.

f. Personal power

The seeking of personal power was seen to be of particular importance for politicians in the city and might be presumed to influence the decisions they may make.

g. Respect

Respect for others who may be affected by a decision was seen as a significant factor, particularly by educational leaders and was closely linked with honour. It would appear that in the contexts in which most of the participants in this research worked and lived, respect for others was a high moral value.

h. Respect and fear

A different form of respect that influenced decisions was seen in situations, particularly involving difficult, moral dilemma decisions that required the firing or sanctioning of someone on the basis of accusations of misconduct. This form of respect was one where the accused was seen to be a "natural leader" or even if it was thought that perhaps they might be. Leaders, as individuals or as committees or boards, struggled with making difficult decisions in this context for fear of the consequences that may arise should the accused gain the support of others or threaten legal action.

Finding #5: The cultural and worldview sources of the avoidance-pursuit pair prioritisations: Collectivism, holistic animism and colonial law.

Finding #5 was a partial confirmation of Assumption #3 as religion did not feature as a *source* for the prioritisations. The two significant avoidance-pursuit pairs identified in this research were shame-honour and fear-power. There were significant differences in the worldview and cultural, including religious, backgrounds to each of these, as there are between the two subcultures. Conspicuous by its absence as a significant part of this finding is the lack of importance accorded to guilt and innocence issues.

The three avoidance-pursuit pairs were seen in this research to be linked with collectivism, holistic animism and colonial law.

Collectivism: Shame and Honour

As with the "face" collectivist cultures of Asia, shame and honour in the Bolivian city subculture arose from the human relationships within which the participants found themselves. Close relationship ties existed in the nuclear family with progressively weaker ties in the extended family (including fictive relations), the in-group, those in the workplace, and those in the subculture. Each of these groups held to its own set of norms for behaviour, and breaking these norms brought shame on the individual and the group. Shame was used in the subculture as a sanction and a "brake" on permissive behaviour.

Dividuation and Animism: Fear and Power

Fear in the city subculture had its roots in the unknown. In particular, there was a fear of what the rural subculture members may do in the future because many of those living in the city do not understand the *campesinos* fully or know how they may react in particular circumstances. In this regard, there was a great deal of concern expressed about the misapplication of *la justicia comunitaria* [community justice], which, in some instances, equates with lynching mobs.

In the rural communities, fear was expressed in terms of the unknown and particularly where the unknown may have some supernatural origin. There was also a deep concern expressed regarding the adequate production of food, and as this was linked with the supernatural, sacrifices and offerings are made to *Pachamama* and other deities or spirits.

Apart from the "power" attributed to appeasement sacrifices in the *campo*, power was also seen in both of the subcultures to have political and personal power dimensions. The origins of these were linked to seeing honour and the new political context of the country as governance is restructured across most levels under an indigenous, or *originario,* national government.

Colonial Law: Guilt and Innocence

Another, and unexpected, factor in Finding #5 was the lack of a specific relationship to religion in the modern, English sense of the word. As mentioned in Chapter 2, research by Hofstede (1984) had concluded that religion was primarily consequential rather than influential in decision-making processes. This has also been illustrated in the data of this research. If religion had been the primary influence on the social norms, one would have expected that the four centuries of a ubiquitous Roman Catholic Church and the rising influence of the evangelical church would have produced quite different results, highlighting the importance of guilt and innocence in at least the city community. While of much less importance to the participants, and some said that guilt did not seem to exist, a number of them felt that it was of at best to be of secondary importance. One participant linked feelings of guilt with the Catholic Church in that people were afraid of being found guilty of not attending Mass.

As mentioned in Chapter 2 and below, the most important perspective given in this finding is, in fact, the *lack* of responses to the guilt-innocence pair that was seen in the initial examination of the data. While there had been some confusion in early interviews because the term *justicia* [justice] had been introduced rather than *inocencia* (innocence), because the literature on which the research was based had used specifically the guilt-*justice* pair, but even when this had been clarified, most of the participants expressed a preoccupation with justice but little attention was given to the importance of being seen to be innocent.

A re-examination of the data showed that the most noteworthy references to justice or fairness came not from religious sources but from references to the law. As one participant said, the concept of guilt "came with the Spaniards," who were the ones to introduce and impose a foreign legal system. Perhaps the attitude to foreign laws imposed by conquerors may be evident also in a lack of respect historically for colonial authority figures, and this may have had some influence on the uprisings that have led to the many coups and attempted coups in the country. Some participant reflections that relate to this finding are seen in the following comments:

> [The parents of school students] try to follow the law, but they look for honour. (Participant 1)

> The authorities, in the country communities and in the city, usually don't punish the leaders of lynchings for fear of the community [because they are natural leaders]. In each community, there is protection from the community so that community members will not cooperate with authorities if they try to find or prosecute natural leaders. (Participant 13)

> The *curraca* looks after culture and traditions [which would include community lore]. He is a leader born from inside the community. (Participant 27)

Participant 35 indicated her view of a disregard for the colonial laws when she spoke of the *campesino* president of the country having deceived the country because "he has not complied for a moment with the national statutes, with the political constitution that governs the country."

172

Finding #6: The key to understanding the affective domain avoidance-pursuit components and pairs: relationships

> The relationship networks—interpersonal, between individuals and the metaphysical, and between individuals and their physical environment—provide a significant framework that may be used to understand the pair component prioritisation and influence in different cultural contexts.

The data from Phase I of the research indicated a network of factors that were interconnected. These interconnections were mapped and a number of combinations were explored until it became obvious that the one element that provided a context for the various factors that emerged in the research was relationships. In a similar manner to the relational epistemology model discussed in Chapter 1, the relationships included interpersonal relationships as well as relationships with the supernatural and with the physical environment.

This network of relationships that was embedded in the worldview of the participants was seen to form the deontological framework for the decision-making of leaders and others within the subcultures. These relationship structures also provided the framework that supported the existence and valuation of the avoidance-pursuit pairs and components within, and differences between, the subcultures. The ranking of the avoidance-pursuit pairs and their components within the subcultures correlated directly with the perceived importance of the vertical or horizontal relationship structures of the subcultures.

The maintenance of these extant relationship networks in the cultures was important, and where damage to them occurred, restoration was seen as being of particular necessity: "It is what the school does, and it is what we want to do" (Participant 13). This is an important concept in Bolivia, where the specific Quechua term *pachakuti* is used in this sense to represent the restoration of things to the way they were. But in order to be able to restore relationships or to understand the processes involved, relationships themselves, natural, contrived, interpersonal, and holistic, must be understood in their cultural and social artefact contexts. The naturally formed structures included those of birth, natural sociation within neighbourhoods, and workplace relationships of convenience. Contrived relationships were those formalised in the culture through fictive relational structures or through religious practices, to bond individuals who would not otherwise have had a strong relationship within the collectivist culture.

Elements in the holistic epistemology model, as well as in the concept map of the results of the research—environment, individuals and the perceived ontological source—are connected and may be considered to be interdependent. These relationships form essential components of the holistic framework of the individual's *Dasein*, or concept of being-in-the-world. This model is explicative in terms of the personal knowing and interconnectedness of individuals in the city and their relationship with the God of the Catholic and evangelical churches, as well as of the people in the *campo* who had a strong connection with the natural environment—though they also recognised a role that their perceived ontological source played in the physical realm.

In both the city and the country, other structuring of relationships came within formal patterns as prescribed in the laws, regulations and policies of government, business, institutions and *mancomunidades* [associations or groups working together for common benefit] that function at a local, civic level, and were reinforced by a thriving bureaucracy. The *verticalismo* [vertically structuring of hierarchies] that existed particularly in the city society was an important way by which relationships were clearly defined between individuals who did not have a familial or in-group relationship. These structures became blurred, however, through nepotism and *pegas* [a *quid pro quo* agreement whereby those who have supported someone, such as a political candidate, may expect to be given a position in the institution or government]. Direct access to leaders had a very significant effect on decisions being made through influence [*muñeca*] and in terms of the Quechua principle of *wawa que no llora, no mama* [the baby who does not cry, receives no milk]. The inequity that these may have produced, resulting from the decisions that were made, was a common source of complaint in the Bolivian media.

On the other hand, leaders could play an important role in defining and securing relationships within the community. Goldstein, Mignolo and Silverblatt (2004) noted this in the barrios surrounding Cochabamba that are comprised of immigrants who had arrived from the mining communities around Oruro. These, they claimed, played a significant role in the brokering of important relationships between residents and the various powers existing outside the barrio. Participant 38 was one such leader in an immigrant barrio, and he was proud of the work that he had done in this regard for members of his community. The decisions made by him flowed from this context as well as his values and worldview that had been developed in a mining community and from his lifeworld in his barrio in Cochabamba.

This mediatory role of leaders such as Participant 38 on the periphery of the city (in the *barrios periféricos*) is also seen in the *campo*. This has also been noted by Strobele-Gregor (1996), who referred to the important role of the *jilakatas* [community leaders] as intermediaries between *ayllus* [groups of local communities]—often accomplished through the organising of festivals and participation in rituals. One might speculate as to whether the structured decision-making processes of the *campo* communities, with their inherent, sometimes enforced, democracy, might be at odds with the national concept of a parliamentary democracy where only those who are elected are in a position to express an opinion. This might explain the number of protest marches in Bolivia[20] as the people assert what they see as their traditional right to express their views on decisions of leaders in government at local, department and national levels, in the same way that in the villages all families would be involved in the discussion and decision, or law-making.

Relationships: Towards a theory

In this research, it was seen that within the family, and within a family business, decisions were made with familial relationships in mind, and family members would be trusted much more than non-family members. In other work contexts, such as in a university faculty or in a business office, decisions were made both on the basis of relationships and on the basis of institutional procedures. The maintenance of all of these interpersonal relationships was seen to be of very considerable importance to the participants. The making and maintaining of interpersonal relationships was to be actively pursued, and the breaking or damaging of relationships was to be avoided, almost at all costs. This was a very significant factor in the data in relation to the making of difficult decisions involving moral dilemmas and staff members within the leaders' organisations.

A very significant finding of this research was that the data strongly indicated that these relationships were a key to understanding not only the role of the affective domain pairs, but many of the thought processes and actions that are involved in decision-making by leaders: "In our Latin American culture, interpersonal relationships are the priority" [Key Informant 36]. The differentiation seen in this research between the city and the *campesino* participants related directly to the importance of personal-to-person relationships in the collectivist culture in the city, and the person-to-deity-to-environment, holistic relationships in the *campo*.

A third construction that was also important in this research was the relationship the participants had with the laws and norms under which they lived. Ruth Benedict had observed that guilt was important for individuals and that each individual sought expiation privately. In the collectivist subculture, however, where there was little significance ascribed to imposed, foreign laws, and where those related closely to the

---

[20] Research by Barometer of the Americas in early 2008 (Los Tiempos, 2008a) showed that more people engaged in protests in Bolivia (29.3% in the previous year) than in any of the other twenty-two countries in the Latin Americn survey.

individual did not see the breaking of one of these laws to be problematic, then there may be no shame attached to it, nor guilt.

In the research data, a number of participants made direct or indirect references to guilt, and a Key Informant explained guilt in terms of breaking the community laws. Educators, perhaps naturally, seemed to be interested in obedience to set rules and norms for behaviour and would have been very aware of the strict codes enforced by the government through the Department of Education. At the same time, in Phase II of the research, Alberto noted that the legality of what was being decided by a leader was secondary. The most important things were group needs and what would benefit the group. The importance of the legality of the decision object was only in relation to possible repercussions, such as fines or other sanctions, and the effect these would have on the group.

A significant finding regarding colonised peoples

An interesting finding from the research that has implications for all those living in, or in contact with, cultures that have been colonised, including Australia, is the relationship to law. The laws imposed on the *originario* peoples of the country by the *conquistadores* did not seem to be "owned" by them, not having come from their history and their culture. The people did not relate to these culturally foreign, imposed laws in the same way that they related to and highly esteem the *ama suwa* moral lore that was so important to the *campesino* people in particular. The lack of esteem given to the foreign laws of the land in the two subcultures could be seen perhaps in the corruption that existed, along with the many ways that were sought to circumvent them. This has meant that the government has had considerable trouble with some *alcaldes* (mayors or leaders) in the *campo* because they have ignored the laws to suit their community. Alberto used the expression of people going "the wrong way up a street" in order to get to where they wanted to. The foreign law, therefore, was seen not as something requiring obligatory obedience but often something that should be worked around where possible. This was certainly seen in the use of the *muñeca* and *coima* forms of bribery and corruption that were endemic in the country. The quality of the relationship with the law was therefore a determinant in terms of the importance of feelings of guilt or innocence.

The importance of community members having ownership of, or a relationship with, a law, was seen particularly in the decision-making processes that function in the *campo*. As discussed earlier, decisions were made by representatives of each family in the community meeting and discussing the issue until there was consensus or at least a very clear majority in favour. This method ensured a strong understanding and personal commitment on the part of each community member to the decision being made.

The key feature is relationship frameworks

Based on the areas discussed above, a table may therefore be drawn indicating the types of relationship identified in this research and the avoidance-pursuit pair to which each corresponds.

RELATIONSHIP TYPES	AVOIDANCE-PURSUIT PAIR
Interpersonal	Shame-Honour
Human to Physical/Metaphysical	Fear-Power
Human to Law (Indigenous Lore or Foreign Law)	Guilt-Innocence

These relationship frameworks form the most significant worldview and cultural links with the affective domain components defined by affective responses to the culturally imbued worldview of the participants. Shame and honour have their roots in the networks of interpersonal relationships that exist between community members, while fear and power in this research tended to be linked, though not exclusively, to the relationships that Bolivian *campesinos* had between the community members and the spirit realm and that which they believe the spirit realm controls—namely, the earth and the weather. Guilt and innocence appear from this research to have their source in the law, and the participants related that concept to the imposed legal system of the Spanish conquerors, which flows from a Western conceptualisation of a Justinian Body of Civil Law [*Corpus Juris Civilis*], as well as in church law.

The strength and direction of these horizontal and vertical relationships defined the two subcultures and explained much of how they functioned and the decisions that were made. Within the setting of the Bolivian subcultures studied, relationships also at times exhibited a high degree of asymmetry rather than equality, for example, as seen in human and nonhuman relationships in the *campo* and the existence of the cross-class, *compadrazgo*, fictive relationships in the city. They were also strongly situated, with at least the interpersonal relationships varying markedly from one context to another.

The use of power differentials to maintain order or to oppress provides yet more contextualised relationship structures with vertical and horizontal dimensions within the communities. In both the rural and the city communities, horizontal relationships may be forced into existence in order to develop an opposition to a common enemy, survive during resource scarcity, or undertake agricultural pursuits requiring cooperation (Triandis et al., 1993). They may also be based on other factors, such as a survivalist recognition of the importance of appeasing those in a vertical relationship who are higher on the social scale and therefore more powerful, as well as spirits and deities, including both those of animistic origin[21] and the God recognised by the Catholic Church. These cultural artefacts are embedded in the worldview of the participants. As well as institutions such as churches, nuclear and extended families and schools have been used in Bolivia, as elsewhere, to inculcate these worldview components into each successive generation. From these lifeworld origins, they then form integral parts of each individual's worldview and, as a subculture may be represented as the collective worldview of its members, these factors are embedded in the culture.

This research has gone some way towards meeting the need that Fitch (1998) had written, saying that "the road between cultural beliefs and interpersonal relationships has not been a well-travelled one to date, at least in the sense of detailed consideration of culture as a symbolic resource with which people construct their relationships throughout their lives" (p. 3). Because of the emergence of this relational perspective in this research, the research participants cannot be considered to be isolated individuals. Each is embedded within a meaningful matrix of referential and functional relations and the relational constituents of his or her culture. It is these factors that define so much of who the individual is, what is their *Dasein*, their sense of *Befindlichkeit*: of existing within the context into which they find themselves to have been put. To understand this, as the British anthropologist Macfarlane (1970) pointed out, one cannot use an ego-centred approach, but, rather, the researcher needs to learn the map of social relationships just as the participants have had to learn it. These relationships, however, vary within the general classifications of cultures. For example, it should be noted that the relational frameworks identified in the collectivist culture of suburban Cochabamba were qualitatively different from the *guanxi* of Chinese collectivism, though these differences are yet to be explored.

Other relationship considerations in this research

i. Governance structured relationships

As mentioned in previous chapters, the democratic system employed in the country villages was in a very different leadership context from that in the city. Here, a rotating

---

[21] While *q'oas* (smoke sacrifices) are normally made once a month, they are of particular importance naturally in Spring:

> The Pachamama (Mother Earth) wakes in August and is ready to fertilize everything that comes from within her. She rested since the last harvest in February and now must return to the beginning of the agricultural cycle. After months of rest "she has her mouth open," she is hungry. . . . The q'oa is one of the formulas most used to calm the hunger of the soil and to scare off or maintain harmony with the supernatural beings. (Vásquez, 2009, para.para. 1, 3)

leadership model was used with each person expressing their opinion on each decision, which had been fundamental to the governance of villages for centuries. This governance model was extended by representation to groups of villages [*ayllus*] and regions. Since the agrarian revolution of 1952, this model has been coloured by the introduction of the *sindicatos* [syndicates or unions] and the strict formalising of all relationships and positions available for governance. Silvia Rivera Cusicanqui (1990) was quoted by Albaro (2006) as saying that the newer version of democracy was, in fact, another form of domination of the villages by a governance structure that was imposed and of foreign origin. Whether this is true or not, it was evident in this research that both the *campo* villages and the city of Cochabamba have very clearly structured sets of relationships that support governance and decision-making, and these are supported largely by democratic processes in the villages and bureaucracies in the cities. These relationship structures, imposed or indigenous, were a significant part of the Bolivian subcultures studied in this research and for the relational framework that illustrated implications for the decisions made by leaders, but these relationships have a culturally embedded meaning that is distinct from many Western conceptualisations.

ii. Constraints on the relationship structures

Alford's (1999) arguments regarding the distinctions between shame and guilt cultures were of interest in the Bolivian collectivist setting. In one sense, the guilt of which he wrote as being against cultural norms in an individualistic culture seems to have a similar definition to shame in the collectivist, city culture in Cochabamba, but different in that the cultural norm against which the transgression is enacted is that of promoting and maintaining individual, family and in-group honour at all costs. The Freudian sanction of loss of love may be a significant factor in a collectivist culture but the sense gained from the data in this research was that it was not love *per se* that was the issue, as perhaps might have been be the case in an individualist culture, but the need for group bonding, whether for mutual support, for protection, or for some other reason. Within the collectivist culture, the breaking of this bond was seen to be serious, even though behaviours that were allocentric in nature may not be evidenced. Further research could be conducted on the differences between love relationships in the contrasted cultures, but the researcher's experience in Bolivia, and particularly as noted in the comments of a Key Informant with regard to family relationships ("Family life seems like it was a nightmare back in the *campo*"), would indicate that the commitments of love were different—at least between adults. Certainly, the stereotypical, Latin, *macho* male, who had an in-group to which he was bonded and that protected him, appeared to have the conquest of the women as an ideal, perhaps rather than the more protective, mutual bonding that may be found in individualistic cultures. That being said, there appeared to be strong survivalist concerns within the subcultures and a fear of being excluded or cut off in some way should relationships be broken: relationships with others broken or a relationship with supernatural powers broken. These distinctions in the perception of collectivist cultures when viewed by Westerners are important in understanding this research and in furthering our understanding of other cultures.

Implications for further research

In order to further explore the phenomena described in this research, anthropological studies may be conducted within the two settings in Bolivia, mapping the relationships more extensively. Such a study would draw the boundaries and map the complexities of the Bolivian *Gesellschaft*, and with further analysis, the depth of the *Gemeinschaft*, in the subcultures examined in this research. In addition, further studies are required that would concentrate on the sense of *communitas* experienced by the migrant dwellers of the *barrio periférico* suburbs lying around the city of Cochabamba. These Bolivians, caught in many ways between two cultures, experience a degree of cultural *liminosidad* [living at the margins]. The relational structures that may be examined, therefore, include not only interpersonal and inter-in-group relationships but the broader relationships between the city dwellers and the *campesinos*, as well as with the bi-cultural migrant groups. Rather than these being considered as discrete groups, however, they should be seen as integrated systems: "as the local termini of a web of group relations which extend through intermediate levels from the level of the community to that of the nation" (Wolf, 1956, p. 1065). This also raises the question of the degree to which one can generalise at a national or pan-cultural level.

While highlighting both the form and the function of relationships within the subcultures involved, this research has seen evidence of the effect of three waves of cultural forces on each of the groups: Hispanic conquestation, indigenisation and globalisation. One factor in each of these has been the religious context that each has brought: Catholicism, animism and Western, individualistic secular humanism, along with evangelicalism. Further research may be indicated in this area, as well as on the additional effects on decision-making of these three cultural forces on the imported and imposed representational democracy model of governance and legislation.

The literature also indicated that further research is necessary in several related areas. Heine and Norenzayan (2006) claimed that most of the research carried out so far in areas related to comparative psychology has been from a North American viewpoint, and most has involved the contrasts between the United States and Asian cultures. They suggest further research involving other cultures and also an examination of the use of language, citing the Whorfian hypothesis that language influences thought. Whorf's proposal was that there existed a principle of linguistic relativity between dissimilar languages (such as Spanish and Quechua) "which holds

180

that all observers are not led by the same physical evidence to the same picture of the universe" (Carroll, 1956, p. 214). While in this research the Spanish and Quechua vocabularies surrounding leadership, guilt, shame and fear were of particular importance, further linguistically based anthropological studies may generate a greater depth of knowledge of the relational bases of the cultures.

The linguistic and worldview variation between the cultures begs the question of the universality of values. While work has been undertaken by philosophers, anthropologists and ethicists on the identification of universal ethical principles, there appears to be a need for research to be conducted into the strength of the so-called universal principles in different cultural contexts. This may include further research on the avoidance-pursuit pairs, their nature and definition, as well as the definition of a more exact set that forms the matrix. Given the globalisation process and the facility of travel, synchronous communications and the activities of the international business community, this research indicates that more information is required on the cross-cultural differences based on the avoidance-pursuit pair hierarchies and over a range of cultures. This would include an exploration of the principles, universal, penuniversal or otherwise, behind the formation of the avoidance-pursuit pairs and their ranking.

Where such suggested studies include an examination of cultures beyond Australia, as well as subcultures within Australia, a much deeper understanding could emerge that would enhance the appreciation of the cross-cultural contexts of other pluricultural and multicultural societies, such as Australia, substantively. The results of such studies could provide an explicative framework for understanding the in-group and cross-cultural relationships, communication processes within and between groups and the reactions or responses of individuals from different subculture groups to different situations. This should lead to an enrichment of the cultural groups represented, as each would be able to understand more adequately the lifeworlds, worldviews, values and relationship structures of the other groups. Such a study would prove valuable in politics, in commerce and industry, and in educational contexts where migrant students may need to be considered more socio-holistically rather than as individuals.

The literature surrounding leadership at an international level would also indicate that further studies should be undertaken within Latin America on the influence of globalisation on the changing role and function of leadership within Latin societies. In particular, there is a need to understand the cultural changes to collectivist cultures that may be initiated by imported individualism.

Conclusion

This research set out to investigate the proposed existence of the affective domain pairs shame-honour, guilt-innocence and fear-power, their prioritisation in different subcultures, the influence this prioritisation may have on the decision-making of leaders and the worldview and cultural roots of the prioritisations. The research found evidence of the existence of the pairs and their prioritisation in the different contexts: shame and honour in the city subculture, and fear and power in the rural villages. It also revealed that there were many factors that played a role in defining the concepts for the participants who were interviewed and the implications this had within different cultural contexts. The research did not find strong evidence or a strong prioritisation of the guilt-innocence pair, as had been predicted in the literature, but it found that the different prioritisations of all three of the pairs were derived from culturally imbued networks of relationships. These included interpersonal relationships, person to elements in the physical and metaphysical worlds and relationships with imposed colonial law and traditional lore.

These relationship structures were entrenched in the cultures, being a part of the lifeworld of Bolivians and as such, they were embedded in their worldviews as part of their value systems. The decisions made by leaders within the cultural contexts would therefore be guided or informed by a logic pertaining to a leader's negotiation of the different types of relationship networks in which they find themselves. Cultural members were therefore seen to rank the avoidance-pursuit pairs or components on the basis of an affective response to the relationship framework of their cultural setting. The differences in the pair prioritisations and their distinctive cultural roots form a context that at times is difficult to understand or negotiate for either sub-cultural group in a country that is so often torn by political discord, mistrust, fear and, frequently, physical conflict. In order for the two subcultures to better understand each other, to communicate better and to work harmoniously, each must make an effort to understand the rich worldview and lifeworld contexts of the other.

The implications of the research, however, extend beyond the Bolivian context and apply perhaps to those in our immediate neighbourhoods, as well as to culture-to-culture or state-to-state understanding. In a globalised world, where communications, travel and commerce frequently reach beyond the confines of individual cultures, the need is increasing for a better understanding of, more efficient communication with, those from other cultures and more effective leader-follower relationships across cultures.

GLOSSARY

The following is a glossary of Spanish, Quechua, German and some uncommon English terms as they are used in this research:

Ahijado - Godson

Alcalde – Mayor

Alcaldía – Local government council

Allichu – Please (Quechua)

Ama Suwa, Ama Llulla, Ama Q'ella – An ancient moral code in Bolivia: Do not steal, do not lie, do not be lazy.

Anchata agradisiyki – Thank you (Quechua)

Antivalores – Anti-values, values that would be seen as having a negative influence in a society

Autoridad – Authority

Ayllu – A village in the country

Ayne – The practice of helping each other out—particularly in rural settings

Bandilla – Gang (usually of youths)

Barrios periféricos – The suburbs lying on the edge of the city

Befindlichkeit – Living within the context into which one finds oneself "thrown"

Brazos operativos - the operational arms or organisations

Cabildo – Meeting of the community where decisions regarding governance issues are discussed

Cacique – Local political leader, chief, perhaps a tyrant

Callasiri (or ***Kharasiri***) – A spirit being that is believed by some Andean groups to suck fat from people

Cambas – People from the lowlands of Bolivia

Campesino – Someone living in a rural area, not in the city and of the Quechua, Aymara or Guaraní races

Campo – The country—as opposed to the city

Caudillerismo – Government by a *caudillo*—a person in authority, one who monopolises control

Caudillo – Leader or commander

Challas – Drink offerings made to deities

Cholo – Someone with at least one Spanish grandparent

Ciudadano – A city dweller or citizen

Cocaleros – Those who grow coca plants (Coca leaves are mildly narcotic and are chewed but they are also the source to cocaine and thus a significant part of the drug trade in Bolivia.)

Cochabambino – Resident of the city of Cochabamba

Coima – A bribe

Collas – People from the highland areas of Bolivia

Comerciante – Shopkeeper

Comisiones – Commissions

Comite Civico – A civic committee, largely comprised of business people and responsible for decisions at a state (*Departamento*) level

Compadrazgo – The network of "godparent" relationships

Compadre - Godparent

Confianza – Trust

Conquistadores – Conquerors (the Spanish)

Consejo de maestros – Council of teachers

Convenio – Agreement or contract

Convivencia – Living together

Corregidor – A village leader who is responsible for village discipline but in some cases has a broader leadership role

Culpable – Culpable, guilty

Cumpliendo – Completing what one has said one would do or completing one's obligations

Curacas – Overlords in the Spanish feudal system in Bolivia

Dasein – Heidegger's concept of our sense of being-in-the-world

Decolonizar – Remove the influence of colonisers (may refer in Bolivia to Spanish or North American influences)

Departamento – State (of a country)

Dios mono – Monkey god

Directorio – The board of an organisation or institution

Dirigente – Leader

Dividual – An expression for the wholeness or connectedness of others (as in a collectivist society) or to all things including supernatural beings and the physical environment—as opposed to in-dividual which connotes the separation of entities

Dividuated animism – This term is used in this research to denote the defining of individuals by the relationship they have for each other and for spiritual and physical beings.

Eidos – Essences (German)

Erklären – Explanation (German)

Fictive relationships – Relationships such as godparents-godchildren or patronage.

Ganqing – Feelings (Chinese)

Gato blanco – White cat, a spirit being in the Quechua worldview

Gemeinschaften – Communities (as distinct from *Gesellschaften*)

Gesellschaften – Societies (as distinct from *Gemeinschaften*)

Guanxi – A Chinese expression for a network of human relationships within society

Guanxiology – A term coined by Man and Cheng (1996) for the study of *guanxi*

Harmatia – Sin, missing the mark (Greek)

Idonea – Capable

Inocencia – Innocence

Integridad – Integrity, wholeness

Inti – A deity of the Incas

Ius romana – Roman law

Jilacata – A village leader in the Aymara culture

Junta distrital – District meeting

Junta escolar – Meetings of the community members associated with a school

Justicia – Justice, fairness

Justicia Comunitaria – Literally Community Justice. In practice this has come to mean a group of people taking into their own hands the ascertaining of guilt and meting out of punishments—often severe.

Justo – Righteous, fair

Kallawayas – Medicine men, healers, who often travel from village to village

Kharasiri – See *callasiri*

Lebenswelt - Lifeworld

Líder – The Spanish word, taken from English, for leader

Liminosidad – living at the margin (of the city or of the community for example)

Los Tiempos (The Times) – A newspaper in Cochabamba

Machismo – The Latin concept of the supremacy of males

Malkus – Leaders

Mama t'halla – A female leader of a village community

Mancomunidades – Groups of communities working together

Masistas – Those who are adherents of the MAS (*Movimiento Al Socialismo*) political party—the left wing, *campesino* party currently in government in Bolivia

Mestizaje – The mixture of races (particularly Spanish and indigenous people)

Mestizos – Mixed race people—of the Spanish and indigenous races

Muñeca – Manipulation, the use of relationships to influence people to do something

Nomos (Nomos) – Law (Greek)

Normal or ***Normal superior*** – A teacher training college

Organizaciones Territoriales De Base (OTBs) – Organisations of local communities that work to provide local infrastructure

Originario – Of the original (indigenous) people of Bolivia or Latin America

Pachakuti – A term signifying the restoring things to the way they were

Pachamama – "Big Mother" or "Earth Mother"—the female goddess of the Earth who is believed to be responsible for productivity

Parientes Simbólicos – Fictive relatives such as Godparents

Participación Popular – A government program whereby local communities can select and organise local works for which government money is supplied.

Pasanacu – The informal lending of money between group members

Patrón – A patron, landlord or master

Pegas – The relationship (from the word for glue) people believe they have to someone they have helped. (For example, those who help a political candidate to become elected expect to be rewarded with a position in the public service after the election.)

Prefecto – Political head of a *Departamento* or State

Q'oa – An oblation offered to deities

Quillacolleño (or ***Quillacolleña***) – someone from the city of Quillacollo on the outskirts of Cochabamba

Reforma Educativa – The education reform program—similar to that implemented in other countries around the world in the past forty years

Religión communitaria ancestral – The religious practices of the original, pre-Spanish communities

Reunion comunitaria – A community meeting

Secretaria de actas – Minute secretary

Sensus communis – Common sense, or a general agreement by community members on a particular understanding

Sindicato – Union

Sinvergüenza – Without shame

Tajante – Sharp, caustic or legalistic

Temor – Fear (as the basis for prudent action)

Tinku – An encounter each year between two *ayllus* in Bolivia. The encounter involves fighting and often results in deaths.

Tio diablo – Uncle devil

Tu – Personal pronoun You singular (informal) (The use of *tu* varies in different cultural settings but in the city of Cochabamba it is used between family members, between close friends or when speaking with someone on a lower social level.)

Tutear – To speak to someone with the informal, more intimate personal pronoun *tu*

Usted – Personal pronoun You singular (formal) (The use of *usted* varies in different cultural settings but in the city of Cochabamba it is used in formal social contexts such as meetings, between acquaintances, or when speaking with someone on a higher social level.)

Vergüenza – Shame

Verstehen – Understanding (German)

Verticalismo – Autocracy—as opposed to democracy

Viernes del soltero – The tradition for some married men to declare themselves to be single on a Friday night

Weltanschauung – Worldview

Weltgeist – The universal spirit

Wirracocha – Supreme deity of the Andes region

Yatiris – Spiritual leader in the animistic communities

REFERENCES

Abramson, N. R., Keating, R. J., & Lane, H. W. (1996). Cross-national cognitive process differences: A comparison of Canadian, American, and Japanese managers. *Management International Review 36*(2) 123-147.

Adelman, C., Kemmis, S., & Jenkins, D. (1980). Rethinking case study notes from the Second Cambridge Conference. In H. Simons (Ed.), *Towards a science of the singular* (pp. 45–61). Norwich, UK: Centre for Applied Research in Education, University of East Anglia.

Aguirre, N., & de la Paz, A. M. (1998). *Juan de la Rosa: Memoirs of the last soldier.* (S. G. Waisman, Trans.). New York: Oxford.

Albaro, R. (2001). Fictive feasting: Mixing and parsing Bolivian popular sentiment. *Anthropology and Humanism, 25*(2), 142–157.

Albaro, R. (2006). The Culture of Democracy and Bolivia's Indigenous Movements. *Critique of Anthropology, 26*(4), 387–410.

Aldrich, V. C. (1939). An ethics of shame. *Ethics, 50*(1), 57–77.

Alford, C. F. (1999). *Think no evil: Korean values in the age of globalization.* Ithaca, NY: Cornell University Press.

Anderson, L. W., Krathwohl, D. R., Airasian, P. W. et al. (2001). *A taxonomy for learning, teaching, and assessing: A revision of Bloom's taxonomy of educational objectives.* New York: Longman.

Archondo, R. (2006). ¿Qué le espera a Bolivia con Evo Morales? *Nueva Sociedad, 202*(3-4), 4–12, Retrieved from http://www.nuso.org/upload/articulos/3332_1.pdf .

Argyris, C. (1982). *Reasoning, learning and action.* San Francisco: Jossey-Bass.

Argyris, C., & Schon, D. A. (1984). Organizational learning. In D. S. Pugh (Ed.), *Organization theory* (pp. 352–372). Harmondsworth: Penguin.

Aristotle, (W. D. Ross, Trans.). (2009). *Nicomachean Ethics By Aristotle, Written 350 B.C.E.* Retrieved from http://classics.mit.edu/Aristotle/nicomachaen.3.iii.html

Atherton, J. S. (2003). *Doceo: Shame-Culture and Guilt-Culture* [On-line] UK.

Retrieved from http://www.doceo.co.uk/background/shame_guilt.htm

Au, K. Y. (1999). Intra-cultural variation: Evidence and implications for international business. *Journal of International Business Studies, 30*(4), 799-812.

Audi, R. (Ed.). (1999). The *Cambridge dictionary of philosophy.* (2nd ed.). Cambridge: Cambridge University Press.

Australian Bureau of Statistics. (2007). *2006 census table: Australia.* Canberra, ACT: Author. Retrieved from http://www.censusdata.abs.gov.au/ABSNavigation/prenav/ViewData?breadcrumb=LPTD&method=Place%20of%20Usual%20Residence&subaction=-1&issue=2006&producttype=Census%20Tables&documentproductno=0&textversion=false&documenttype=Details&collection=Census&javascript=true&topic=Ancestry&action=404&productlabel=Ancestry%20by%20Country%20of%20Birth%20of%20Parents%20-%20%20Time%20Series%20Statistics%20(2001,%202006%20Census%20Years)&order=1&period=2006&tabname=Details&areacode=0&navmapdisplayed=true&

Baier, A. (1997). Doing things with others: The mental commons. In L. Alanen, S. Heinämaa & T. Wallgren, (Eds.), *Commonality and particularity in ethics.* Bassingstoke: Macmillan Press Ltd.

Barkow, J. H. (1975). Prestige and culture: A biosocial interpretation. *Current Anthropology, 16*(4), 553–572.

Barth L. C. (1998). *Honour, shame, and the rhetoric of 1 Peter.* Atlanta, GA: Scholars Press, Society of Biblical Literature.

Basabe, N., & Ros, M. (2005). Cultural dimensions and social behaviour correlates: Individualism-Collectivism and Power Distance. *Revue Internationale De Psychologie Sociale, 18*(1), 189–225.

Bass, B. M. (1985). *Leadership and performance beyond expectations.* New York: The Free Press.

Bass, B. M. (1990) *Handbook of leadership: Theory, research and managerial applications.* New York: The Free Press.

Batista Gumucio, M. (1978). *Cultural policy in Bolivia.* Paris: United Nations Educational, Scientific and Cultural Organization.

Battiste, M., & Henderson Y. J. (2000). *Protecting Indigenous knowledge and heritage: A global challenge.* Saskatoon, SK: Purich Publishing.

Beck, C. (1999). Values, leadership and school renewal. In P. T. Begbey & P. E. Leonard (Eds.). *The values of educational administration.* London: Falmer.

Bedny, M., Caramazza, A., Grossman, E., Pascual-Leone, A., & Saxe, R. (2008). Concepts are more than percepts: The case of action verbs. *The Journal of Neuroscience, 28*(44),11347–11353.

Begley, P. (2005). *Ethics matters: New expectations for democratic educational leadership in a global community.* Rock Ethics Institute, The Pennsylvania State University. Retrieved 18th September, 2006 from http://rockethics.psu.edu/resources/education.pdf#search=%22%22Ethics%20Ma tters%3A%20New%20Expectations%22%22

Begley, P. T., & Hodgkinson, C. (1999). *Values and educational leadership.* New York: State University of New York Press.

Begley, P. & Johansson, O. (Eds.). (2003). *The ethical dimensions of school leadership.* London: Kluwer Academic Publishers.

Bell, B., Gaventa, J., & Peters,J. M. (Eds.). (2002). *We make the road by walking: Conversations on Education and Social Change: Myles Horton & Paulo Freire.* Philadelphia: Temple University Press.

Benedict, R. (1934). Anthropology and the abnormal. *Journal of General Psychology, 10,* 59–82.

Benedict, R. (1946). *The chrysanthemum and the sword.* Boston: Houghton Mifflin.

Biggart, N. W., & Hamilton, G. G. (1987). An institutional theory of leadership. *Journal of applied behavioural science, 23,* 429–441.

Bilsky, W., & Koch. M. (2002). On the content and structure of values: Universals or methodological artifacts? In J. Blasius, J. Hox, E. de Leeuw & P. Schmidt (Eds.), *Social science methodology in the new millennium: Updated and extended proceedings of the fifth International Conference on Logic and Methodology, October 3-6, 2000.* Cologne, Germany:

Bird-David, N. (1999). "Animism" revisited: Personhood, environment, and relational epistemology. *Current Anthropology, 40,* 67–91.

Bird, G., & Jindibah, G. (1996). *Mijah: Indigenous people and the law.* Leichhardt, NSW: The Federation Press.

Blaschke, R. C. (2001). *Quest for power: Guidelines for communicating the gospel to animists.* Ottawa, ON: Guardian Books.

Bloom, B. S. (1984). *Taxonomy of educational objectives.* New York: Longman.

Blum, L. A. (1988). Gilligan and Kohlberg: Implications for Moral Theory. *Ethics, 98*(3), 472–491.

Blumer, H. (1969). *Symbolic interactionism; perspective and method.* Englewood Cliffs, NJ: Prentice-Hall.

Bogden, R. C., & Bilken, S. K. (1992). *Qualitative research in education* (2nd ed.). New York: Allyn & Bacon.

Bolívar, A. (2001) *Liderazgo educativo y reestructuración escolar.* Conferencia en el I Congreso Nacional sobre Liderazgo en el Sistema Educativo Español. (Córdoba, 28-31 de marzo de 2001) (pp. 95-130). Departamento de educación de la universidad de Córdoba. Publicado en Actas del congreso.

Bolívar, S., Fornoff, F. H. (Trans.)., & Bushnell, D. (Ed.). (2003). *El Libertador: Writings of Simón Bolívar*. Oxford University Press.

Boroditsky, L. (2009). How does language shape the way we think. In M. Brookman (Ed.). *What's next: Dispatches on the future of science* (pp. 116–129). New York. Vintage Books.

Bourdieu, P. (1980). *The logic of practice*. Stanford, CA: Stanford University Press.

Brislin, R. W. (1980). Translation and content analysis of oral and written materials. In H. C. Triandis & J. W. Berry (eds.), *Handbook of Cross-cultural Psychology* (Vol. 2). Boston, MA: Allyn and Bacon.

Brown, D. E. (1991). *Human Universals*. New York: McGraw-Hill.

Burnett, D. (2002). *Clash of worlds*. London: Monarch Books.

Burnett, D. (1988). *Unearthly powers*. Nashville, TN: Oliver-Nelson Books.

Burns, J. M. (1985). *Leadership.* New York: Harper & Row

Burton, D. (2000). *Research training for social scientists: A handbook for postgraduate researchers*. Thousand Oaks, CS: Sage Publications.

Buttery, E. A., & Wong, Y. H. (1999), The development of a guanxi framework. *Marketing Intelligence & Planning. 17*(3) 147-54.

Cable News Network. (2006). *Pope's Islam comments condemned.* Retrieved 10 Oct 06 from http://edition.cnn.com/2006/WORLD/europe/09/15/pope.islam/index.html

Cano Tiznado, J. G. (2001). Globalización, calidad y liderazgo dducativo. Notas introductorias. *Acción Educativa: Revista Electrónica del Centro de Investigaciones y Servicios Educativos, 1*(1) Retrieved from http://uas.uasnet.mx/cise/rev/Num1/

Carr, D. (2000). Education, profession and culture: Some conceptual questions. *British journal of educational studies, 48*(3), 248–268.

Carroll, J. B. (Ed.). (1956). *Language, thought and reality. Selected writings of Benjamin Lee Whorf.* Cambridge, MA: MIT Press.

Carter, W. E., & Mamani, M. (1982). *Irpa chico: Individuo y comunidad en la cultura aymara.* La Paz, Bolivia : Librería-Editorial Juventud.

Catholic Encyclopedia, The (1907). *Bolivia.* New York: Robert Appleton Company. Retrieved 12 December, 2006 from http://www.newadvent.org/cathen/02627a.htm

Chambers, S. C. (1999). *From subjects to citizens: Honour, gender & politics in Arequipa, Peru 1780-1854.* University Park, PA: Pennsylvania State University Press.

Charon, J. (1979). *Symbolic Interactionism.* London: Prentice Hall.

Chase, S. E. (2005). Narrative inquiry: Multiple lenses, approaches, voices. In *Research design: Qualitative, quantitative, and mixed methods* (3rd ed.) (pp. 651–679). Thousand Oaks, CA: Sage Publications.

Chhokar, J. S., Brodbeck, F. C., & House, R. J. (2007). *Culture and Leadership Across the World: The GLOBE Book of In-depth Studies of 25 Societies (4th ed.)*. Mahwah, NJ: Lawrence Erlbaum.

Chilcott, J. H. (1987). Where are you coming from and where are you going? The reporting of ethnographic research. *American Educational Research Journal, 24*(2), 199–218.

Chomsky, N. (2007). *Responsibility and war guilt: Conference Interview with Noam Chomsky, The* Massachusetts *Institute of Technology, Mon. June 25, 2007.* Retrieved from http://www.zcommunications.org/responsibility-and-war-guilt-by-noam-chomsky

Cobern, W. W. (1995). *Worldview theory and conceptual change in science education.* A paper presented at the 1994 annual meeting of the National Association for Research in Science Teaching, Anaheim, CA, March 26-29. Revised August, 1995.

Cohen, L., Manion, L., & Morrison, K. (2000). *Research methods in education* (5th ed.). London: RoutledgeFalmer.

Commonwealth of Australia. (1998). *Northern Territory: Prime Minister's visit. The Senate Adjournment Speech.* Canberra: Author. Retrieved from http://parlinfo.aph.gov.au:80/parlInfo/genpdf/chamber/hansards/1998-03-25/0163/hansard_frag.pdf;fileType%3Dapplication%2Fpdf

Congreso Nacional de Bolivia. (2004). *Ley No. 2650. Constitución Política del Estado.* Retrieved from http://www.presidencia.gob.bo/leyes_decretos/constitucion_estado.asp

Congreso Nacional de Bolivia. (2008). *Nueva Constitución Política del Estado. Texto final compatabilizado. Versión official, Octubre, 2008.* Retrieved from http://www.embajadadebolivia.com.ar/nueva_cpe_textofinal_compatibilizado_version_oct_2008.pdf

Congreso Nacional de la República de Bolivia. (1826). *Texto completo de primera constitucion politica: 19 noviembre 1826. Versión modificada en algunos aspectos de la ortografía para conformarla con el uso actual.* Retrieved from http://www.geocities.com/derechoconstitucional2001/cpe1826.htm

Contreras, M. E., & Talavera Simoni, M. L. (2003). The Bolivian Education Reform 1992-2002: Case Studies in Large-Scale Education Reform. *Education Reform and Management Publication Series, 2*(2).

Copleston, F. S. J. (1994). *A history of philosophy, Vol. 7: Modern philosophy from the post-Kantian idealists to Marx, Kierkegaard and Nietzsche.* New York: Doubleday, Image Books.

Crain, W. C. (1985). *Theories of development.* Englewood Cliffs, NJ: Prentice-Hall.

Cranston, N., Ehrich, L., & Kimber, M. (2004). *'Right versus wrong' and right versus right': Understanding ethical dilemmas faced by educational leaders.* Paper prepared for the 2004 Australian Association for Research in Education Conference. Retrieved from 11 December, 2007 from http://eprints.qut.edu.au/archive/00000967/01/cra04031.pdf

Creswell, J. W. (2005). *Educational research: Planning, conducting, and evaluating quantitative and qualitative research.* Upper Saddle River, NJ: Merill/Prentice Hall.

Crotty, M. (1998). *The foundations of social research: Meaning and perspective in the research process.* London: Sage Publications.

Cunningham, L. S. (1987). *The Catholic faith: An introduction.* New York: Paulist.

Dahl, S. (2004). *Intercultural research: The current state of knowledge.* Middlesex University discussion paper No. 26. Retrieved from http://ssrn.com/abstract=658202

D'Altroy, T. N. (2003). *The Incas.* Oxford: Blackwell Publishing.

Den Hartog, D. N., House, R. J., Hanges, P. J. Dorfman, P. W., & Ruiz-Quintanilla, S.A. (1999). *Emics and etics of culturally-endorsed Implicit Leadership Theories: Are attributes of charismatic/transformational leadership universally endorsed?* A working paper of the Reginald H. Jones Center, The Wharton School University of Pennsylvania.

Denzin, N. K., & Lincoln, Y. S. (2005). *The SAGE handbook of qualitative research.* Thousand Oaks, CA: Sage.

Derks, S. (2010). *Power and Pilgrimage: Dealing with Class, Gender and Ethnic Inequality at a Bolivian Marian Shrine.* Vertag Münster: LIT.

DeSilva, D. A. (1999). *The hope of glory: Honour discourse and New Testament interpretation.* Collegeville, MI: The Liturgical Press.

Dey, I. (1993). *Qualitative Data Analysis: A user-friendly guide for social scientists.* New York: Routledge.

Dodson, M. (1995). Opinion: From 'Lore' to 'Law': Indigenous Rights and Australian Legal Systems. *Aboriginal Law Bulletin.* Retrieved from http://www.austlii.edu.au/au/journals/AboriginalLB/1995/1.html

Dostal, R. J. (2002). *The Cambridge companion to Gadamer.* Cambridge: Cambridge University Press.

Douglas, J. D. (1985). *Creative interviewing.* Berverly Hills, CA: Sage.

Dower, N. (1998). *World ethics: The new agenda.* Edinburgh: Edinburgh University Press.

Dooyeweerd, H. (1960). *In the twilight of Western thought.* Philadelphia, PA: The Presbyterian Reformed Publishing Company.

Duignan et al. (2003). *Contemporary challenges and implications for leaders in*

194

frontline human service organisations. Strathfield, NSW: Australian Catholic University.

Duignan, P., Burford, C., Cresp, M., et al. (2003). *Contemporary challenges and implications for leaders in frontline human service organisations.* Strathfield, NSW: Australian Catholic University.

Edwards, C. P. (1985). *Rationality, culture, and the construction of "ethical discourse": A comparative perspective.* Lincoln, NE: University of Nebraska. Retrieved from http://digitalcommons.unl.edu/psychfacpub/1

Elmer, D. (2002). *Cross cultural connections: Stepping out and fitting in around the world.* Downers Grove, IL: Intervarsity Press.

Escalera, S. J. (2006). Industrialización de hidrocarburos en Bolivia. Autonomía Ya! *Autonomía no es separatismo, autonomía en el marco de la unión de Bolivia.* Online journal. Retrieved from *http://autonomiaya.org/?p=449*

Evans, N., & Levinson, S. C. (2009). The myth of language universals: Language diversity and its importance for cognitive science. *Behavioral and Brain Sciences, 32,* 429–492.

Evers, C. W. (1991). Schooling, organizational learning and efficiency in the growth of knowledge. In J. Chapman, (Ed.). *School-based decision making and management.* London: The Falmer Press.

Evers, C. W., & Lakomski, G. (1995). *Science in educational administration: A postpositivist conception.* Invited Address, Division A (Administration), to the annual meeting of the American Educational Research Association (San Francisco, CA).

Federal Research Division of the Library of Congress. (2007). *Mestizos and cholos.* Retrieved 11 June, 2007 from http://countrystudies.us/bolivia/32.htm

Ferguson, J. (2003). *Latin American places and themes: Rich legacies, uneven development.* Latin America in the International System. The Department of International Relations, SHSS, Bond University, Queensland, Australia. Retrieved from http://www.international-relations.com/WbLatinAmerica/WBLA-Lec1-2003.htm

Fessler, D. M. T. (2004). Shame in two cultures: Implications for evolutionary approaches. *Journal of Cognition and Culture, 4(2),* 207–262.

Fincher, C. L., Thornhill, R., Murray, D. R., & Schaller, M. (2008). Pathogen prevalence predicts human cross-cultural variability in individualism/collectivism. *Proceedings of the Royal Society B: Biological Sciences, 275,* 1279–1285.

Fitch, K. L. (1998). *Speaking relationally: Culture, communication and interpersonal connection.* New York: Guilford Press.

Flew, A. (1984). *A dictionary of philosophy* (2nd ed.). St. Martin's Griffin.

Fogarty, S. (2005). Binary oppositions. *The literary encyclopedia.* 15 February, 2005.

Retrieved from http://www.litencyc.com/php/stopics.php?rec=true&UID=122.

Forsyth, C. (2008). *The crisis in healthcare in rural Bolivia: Cross-cultural barriers between doctors and indigenous patients.* Retrieved from http://latinamcaribbeanaffairs.suite101.com/article.cfm/the_crisis_in_healthcare_in_rural_bolivia

Foster, W. (1986). *Paradigms and promises: New approaches to education administration.* Amherst, NY: Prometheus Books.

Freeman, S. (2003). *The Cambridge companion to Rawls (Cambridge companions philosophy).* Cambridge: Cambridge University Press.

Freud, S. (1933). *Lecture XXXV: A philosophy of life.* Richmond, UK: Hogarth Press.

Fried, C. (1978). *Right and wrong.* Cambridge, MA: Harvard University Press.

Fritzche, D., & Becker, H. (1984). Linking management behaviour to ethical philosophy: an empirical investigation. *Academy of Management Journal, 27*(1), 166-75.

Fritzsche, D. J. et al. (1995). Exploring the ethical behaviour of managers: A comparative study of four countries. *Asia Pacific Journal of Management, 12*(2), 37–61.

Gamarra, E. A. (2003). *Conflict vulnerability assessment Bolivia.* Latin American and Caribbean Center, Florida International University.

García Linera, A., Stefanoni, P., & Ramirez, F. (2009). *Las Vías de emancipación en Bolivia: Conversaciones con Álvaro García Linera.* Coyoacán, México: Ocean Sur.

Geertz, C. (1973). *The interpretation of culture.* New York: Basic Books.

Geisler, N. L., & Watkins, W. D. (1984). *Worlds Apart.* Grand Rapids, MI: Baker Book House.

Glaser, B., & Strauss, A. (1967). *The discovery of grounded theory.* New York: Aldine.

Goitia, R. (2010). Intentan linchar a presunto kharisiri en Bolívar. *Los Tiempos, 17/02/2010.* Cochabamba, Bolivia.

Gold, T., Guthrie, D., & Wank, D. (Eds.). (2002). *Social connections in China: Institutions, culture, and the changing nature of guanxi.* Cambridge: Cambridge University Press.

Goldstein, D. M. (2007). Human rights as culprit, human rights as victim: Rights and security in the state of exception. In M. Goodale & S. E. Merry (Eds.) *The practice of human rights* (pp. 48–77). New York: Cambridge University Press.

Goldstein, D., Mignolo, W., & Silverblatt, I. (2004). *The spectacular city: Violence and performance in urban Bolivia.* Durham, NC: Duke University.

Griffin, C. (1991). The researcher talks back: Dealing with power relations in studies of young people's entry into the job market. In W. B. Shaffir & R. A. Stebbins (Eds.),

196

Experiencing fieldwork: An inside view of qualitative research (pp. 109-119). Newbury Park, CA: Sage.

Gromm, R., Hammersley, M., & Foster, P. (2000). Case study and generalization. In R. Gromm, M. Hammersley & P. Foster (Eds.), *Case study method: Key issues, key texts* (pp. 98–115). London: SAGE Publications.

Grove, C. N. (2005). *Introduction to the GLOBE research project on leadership worldwide.* Grovewell Global Leadership Solutions LLC. Retrieved from http://www.grovewell.com/pub-GLOBE-intro.html

Guba, E. G., & Lincoln, Y. S. (1982). *Advantages of naturalistic methods.* San Francisco: Jossey-Bass Publishers.

Gudykunst, W. B., & Nishida, T. (2000). Theoretical perspectives for studying intercultural communication (pp. 17–46). In M. K. Asante & W. B. Gudykunst, (Eds.). *Handbook of International and Intercultural Communication.* London: Sage.

Habermas, J., & Dews, P. (1992). *Autonomy and solidarity: interviews with Jürgen Habermas* (2nd ed.). London: Verso.

Hall, E. T. (1981). *Beyond culture.* New York: Anchor Books.

Hallinger, P., & Leithwood, K. (1996). Culture and educational administration: A case of finding out what you don't know you don't know. *Journal of educational administration, 34*(5), 98–116.

Hammond, A. (2003, June 28). *Comical Ali resurfaces.* Sydney Morning Herald. Retrieved from http://www.smh.com.au/articles/2003/06/27/1056683906541.html

Hareli, S., Shomrat, N., & Biger, N. (2005). The role of emotions in employees' explanations for failure in the workplace. Journal *of Managerial Psychology, 20*(8), 663–680

Harris, N., Walgrave, L., & Braithwaite, J. (2004). Emotional dynamics in restorative conferences, *Theoretical criminology, 8*(1), 191–210.

Hart, H. (1985). Dooyeweerd's Gegenstand theory of theory. In *The legacy of Herman Dooyeweerd* (pp. 144–166). Lanham: University Press of America.

Hayward, R. (2005). *Naïve experience and differentiated practices.* Retrieved 26 February, 2007 from http://www.aspecten.org/teksten/IS2005/Hayward_Workshop.pdf

Healy, K. (1994). The shape of things to come: CEMSE and the reinvention of Bolivian public education. *Grassroots Development, 18*(2), 32–42.

Heck, R. H. (1996). Leadership and culture Conceptual and methodological issues in comparing models across cultural settings. *Journal of Educational Administration, 34*(5), 74.

Hegel, G. W. F. (1975). *Lectures on the philosophy of world history,* translated by H. B. Nisbet. Cambridge: Cambridge University Press.

Hegeman, B. (2006a). *The four hidden faces of our deepest cultural values: The proposal of a missiological rubric for inner and cultural values.* Unpublished paper.

Hegeman, B. <Ben.Hegeman@houghton.edu> (2006b, 31 January). Emailing final chapter Shame and Glory. [Personal email].

Heidegger, M. (1975). *Heraklit. Gesamtausgabe, 55* Frankfurt am Main: Vittorio Klostermann.

Heidegger, M. (1982). *The basic problems of phenomenology.* Translation by Albert Hofstadter. Studies in phenomenology and existential philosophy. Bloomington. IN: Indiana University Press.

Heine, S. J., & Norenzayan, A. (2006). Towards a psychological science for a cultural species. *Perspectives on Psychological Science, 1*(3), 251–269.

Herskovits, M. J. (1972). *Cultural relativism perspectives in cultural pluralism.* New York: Vintage Books.

Hofstede, G. (1984). *Cultures consequences: International differences in work-related values.* Newbury Park, CA: Sage Publications, Inc.

Hofstede, G. (2006). *Geert Hofstede cultural dimensions: Peru.* Retrieved 5th October, 2009 from http://www.geert-hofstede.com/hofstede_peru.shtml

Hodgkinson, C. (1999). The triumph of the will. In P. Begley & P. Leonard (Eds.). *The values of educational administration* (pp. 6–21). New York: Garland.

Hollander, E. (1978). *Leadership dynamics.* New York: The Free Press.

Holloway, I. (1997). *Basic concepts for qualitative research.* London: Blackwell Publishing.

Hollway, W., & Jefferson, A. (2000). *Doing qualitative research differently: Free association, narrative and the interview method.* London: Sage Publications.

Hoover, S. R., Petrosko, J. M., & Schulz, R. R. (1991). *Transformational and transactional leadership: An empirical test of a theory.* ERIC DIGEST ED221177.

Horn, P. R. (2005). *Gadamer and Wittgenstein on the unity of language: reality and discourse without metaphysics.* Aldershot, UK: Ashgate Publishing.

House, R. J. (1988). Leadership research: Some forgotten, ignored, or overlooked findings. In J. G. Hunt, B. R. Baliga, H. P. Dachler, H. P., & C. A. Schriessheim (Eds.), *Emerging Leadership Vistas* (pp. 245–260). Toronto: Lexington Books.

House, R. J., Hanges, P. J., Javidan, M., Dorfman, P. W., & Gupta, V., (Eds.). (2004). *Culture, leadership, and organizations: The GLOBE study of 62 societies.* Thousand Oaks, CA: Sage.

House, R. J., Wright, N., & Aditya, R. N. (1996). *Cross cultural research on organizational leadership: A critical analysis and a proposed theory.* A Working Paper of the Reginald H. Jones Center: The Wharton School University of Pennsylvania.

Huff, L. C., & Kelley, L. (1999). *Trust formation in collectivist and individualist societies.* Retrieved from
> http://marketing.byu.edu/htmlpages/ccrs/proceedings99/huff.htm.

Huff, L. C., & Kelley, L. (2003). Levels of organizational trust in individualist versus collectivist societies: A seven-nation study. *Organizational Science, 14*(1), 81–90.

Hume, D. (1997). Enquiry concerning human understanding. In L. Alanen, S. Heinämaa & T. Wallgren, *Commonality and particularity in ethics.* Bassingstoke: Macmillan Press.

Husén, T. (1988). Research paradigms in education. *Interchange, 19*(1), 2–13.

Husted, B. W., Dozier, J. B., McMahon, T. J., & Kattan, M. W. (1996). The impact of cross-national carriers of business ethics on attitudes about questionable practices and form of moral reasoning of different socio-cultural groups. *Journal of International Business Studies, 27*(2), 391-411.

Jagger, A. M. (2000). Feminist ethics. In H. LaFollette, *The Blackwell guide to ethical theory* (pp. 348–374). Malden, MA: Blackwell Publishers Ltd.

Jenkins, O. B. (1979). *What is worldview?* Retrieved 30 November, 2006 from http://endor.hsutx.edu/~obiwan/worldview/worldvwhat.html

Jezewski, M. A., & Sotnik, P. (2001). *Culture brokering: Providing culturally competent rehabilitation services to foreign-born persons.* Retrieved 15th August, 2006 from http://cirrie.buffalo.edu/monographs/cb.pdf.

Jung, D. I., & Avolio, B. J. (1999). Effects of leadership style and followers' cultural orientation on performance in group and individual task conditions. *The Academy of Management Journal*, 42(2), 208–218.

Jung, D., Bass, B., & Sosik, J. (1995). Bridging leadership and culture: A theoretical consideration of transformational leadership and collectivistic cultures. *Journal of Leadership Studies, 2*, 3–18.

Kearney, M. (1984). *Worldview.* Novato, CA: Chandler & Sharp Publishers.

Keen, B., & Hayes, K. (2009)., *A brief history of Latin America.* Boston: Houghton Mifflin.

Kilmann, R. H. (1981). Toward a unique/useful concept of values for interpersonal behaviour: A critical review of the literature on value. *Psychological Reports, 48*, 939-959.

King, A. Y. C. (1985). The individual and group in Confucianism: A relational perspective. In D. J. Munro (ed.), *Individualism and holism: Studies in Confucian and Taoist values* (pp. 57–70). Ann Arbor, MI: Center for Chinese Studies, the University of Michigan.

Klein, S. (2003). *A concise history of Bolivia.* Cambridge: Cambridge University Press.

Kienpointner, M. (1996). Whorf and Wittgenstein: Language, world view and argumentation. *Argumentation, 10*(4), 475–494.

Kohlberg, L. (1969). Stage and sequence: The cognitive moral developmental approach in socialization. In D. Goslin (Ed.). *Handbook of socialization theory and research* (pp. 247–480). Chicago, IL: Rand MacNally.

Kraft, C. H. (1979). *Christianity in culture.* New York: Orbis.

Kushner, H. W. (2003). *Encyclopedia of terrorism.* Thousand Oaks, CA: SAGE.

La Barre, W. (1966). The Aymara: History and worldview. *The Journal of American Folklore, 79*(311), 130-144.

Laniak, T. S. (1998). *Shame and honour in the book of Esther.* Atlanta, GA: Scholars Press/Society of Biblical Literature.

Lang, S., Catzikiris, A., et al. (n. d.). Practical implications: The law and the lore. *Working with Aboriginal and Torres Strait Islanders and their communities.* Retrieved from http://www.workingwithatsi.info/content/PI_laws.htm

Lavaud, J-P. (1998) *El embrollo boliviano: Turbulencias socialises y despalzamientos políticos.* Ann Arbor, MI: IEFA.

LeCompte, M. D., Preissle, J., & Tesch, R. (1993). *Ethnography and qualitative design in educational research* (2nd ed.). San Diego, CA: Academic Press.

Leiland, R. (2001). A "Good Conscience": Differences between honour and justice orientation. *Missiology, 29*(2), 131–141.

Leung, T. K. P., & Wong, Y. H (2001). The ethics and positioning of guanxi in China. *Marketing Intelligence & Planning, 19*(1), 55–64.

Lieber, E., Fung, H., & Leung, P. W. (2006). Child rearing beliefs: Key dimensions and contributions to the development of culture-appropriate assessment. *Asian Journal of Social Psychology, 9*(2), 140–147.

Lincoln, Y. S., & Guba, E. G. (1985). *Naturalistic inquiry.* Newbury Park, CA: Sage Publications Inc.

Littrell, R. F. (2002). Desirable leadership behaviours of multi-cultural managers in China. *Journal of Management Development, 21*(1), 5–74.

Los Tiempos. (2006). *Recogen propuestas para una nueva Reforma Educativa: Gobierno inaugura proceso para "secolonizar" la educación.* Cochabamba, Bolivia: Author.

Los Tiempos. (2008a). *Barómetro: los bolivianos, ¿campeones en protestar?*Cochabamba, Bolivia. Retrieved from http://www.lostiempos.com/noticias/08-09-08/08_09_08_nac1.php.

Los Tiempos. (2008b). *Las condiciones estaban dadas para una guerra civil.* Cochabamba, Bolivia. Retrieved from http://www.lostiempos.com/noticias/16-11-08/16_11_08_nac1.php.

Los Tiempos. (2010). *García Linera admite "dificultad" para aplicar leyes ordinarias con justicia originaria.* 30 de agosto del 2010.

Lotman, J., & Uspensky, B. (1978). On the semiotic mechanism of culture. *New*

Literary History, 9(2), pp. 211–232.

Lupyan, G. (2008a). The conceptual grouping effect: Categories matter (and named categories matter more). *Cognition, 108*, 566–577.

Lupyan, G. (2008b). From chair to "chair": A representational shift account of object labeling effects on memory. *Journal of Experimental Psychology: General, 137*(2), 348–369.

Luykx, A. (1999) *The citizen factory. Schooling and cultural production in Bolivia.* New York: State University of New York Press.

Lynch, M. F. (2002). The dilemma of international counsellor education: Attending to cultural and professional fits and misfits. *International Journal for the Advancement of Counselling, 24*, 89–100.

Macfarlane, A. (1970). *The family life of Ralph Josselin.* New York: W. W. Norton and Company.

Machicado, J. (2009). *Historia del derecho penal boliviano y sus reformas.* La Paz, Bolivia: CED@, *Centro de Estudios de Derecho.* Retrieved from http://h1.ripway.com/ced/dpb.htm

Maclean, K. (2009). Re-conceptualising desert landscapes: unpacking historical narratives and contemporary realities for sustainable livelihood development in central Australia. *GeoJournal, 74*(5), 451–463.

Magolda, P., & Weems, L. (2002). Doing harm: An unintended consequence of qualitative inquiry? *Journal of college student development, 43*(4), 490–507.

Man, C. F., & Cheng, C. Y (1996). *The Chinese guanxiology.* Hong Kong: Institute of Asian Pacific Studies, Chinese University of Hong Kong.

Manos Fuera de Venezuela (2008). ¡No a golpes de estado! ¡No al imperialismo americano! *Militante: Corriente Marxista Interncional.* Retrieved from http://bolivia.elmilitante.org/content/view/96/29/

Markus H. R., Kitayama S. (1991). Culture and the self: Implications for cognition, emotion, and motivation. *Psychological Review*, 98, 224–253.

Marzano, R. J., & Kendell, R. S. (2007). *The new taxonomy of educational objectives.* Thousand Oaks, CA: Corwin.

Maykut, P. S., & Morehouse, R. (1994). *Beginning qualitative research: A philosophic and practical guide.* London: The Falmer Press.

Maxwell, J. (2007). *The 21 irrefutable laws of leadership: Follow them and people will follow you.* Nashville, TN: Thomas Nelson.

Maxwell, J. (2010). *Everyone communicates, few connect: What the most effective people do differently.* Nashville, TN: Thomas Nelson.

McClelland, D. C., Koestner,R., & Weinberger, J. (1989). How Do Self-Attributed and Implicit Motives Differ? *Psychological Review, 96*(4), 690–702.

McElwain, A. K., & Korabik, K. (2005). *Work-family guilt: A Sloan work and family*

encyclopedia entry.
http://wfnetwork.bc.edu/encyclopedia_entry.php?id=270&area=All. Retrieved 28th August, 2006.

McNabb, D. E. (2004). *Research methods for political science: Quantitative and qualitative methods*. Armonk, NY: M. E. Sharpe.

McSweeney, B. (2002). Hofstede's model of national cultural differences and their consequences: A triumph of faith–a failure of analysis. *Human relations, 55*(1), 89–118.

Mead, G. H. (1932). *The philosophy of the present*. Chicago, IL: Open Court Pub.

Mead, M. (1959). Ruth Benedict, Anthropology and the Abnormal. In *An anthropologist at work*. Boston: Houghton Mifflin.

Mei, Y. P. (1967). The status of the individual in Chinese thought and practice. In C. A. Moore (Ed.). *The Chinese mind: Essentials of Chinese philosophy and culture* (pp. 323–339). Honolulu, East-West Center Press.

Merriam, S. (1998). *Qualitative research and case study applications in education: Revised and expanded from case study research in education*. San Francisco: Jossey-Bass.

Merriam, S. B. (2002). *Qualitative research in practice: Examples for discussion and analysis*. San Francisco: Jossey-Bass.

Merriam-Webster Online (2006). Retrieved from http://www.m-w.com/cgi-bin/nytmaps.pl?bolivia

Meteyard, L., Bahrami, B., & Vigliocco, G. (2007). Motion detection and motion verbs: Language affects low-level visual perception. *Psychological Science, 18*, 1007–1013.

Miller, B. (2004). *Crime prevention and socio-legal reform on Aboriginal communities in Queensland*. Retrieved from http://www.aic.gov.au/publications/previous%20series/proceedings/1-27/~/media/publications/proceedings/05/miller.ashx

Ministerio de Educación. (1994). *Ley 1565 de reforma educativa, del 7 de julio de 1994*. La Paz, Bolivia: Author.

Mintz, S. W., & Wolf, E. R. (1950). An analysis of ritual co-parenthood (compadrazgo). *Southwestern Journal of Anthropology, 6*(4), 341–368.

Mintz, S. W., & Wolf, E. R. (1977). An analysis of ritual co-parenthood (compadrazgo). In S. W. Schmidt, J. C. Scott, C. Lande, & L Guasti (Eds.). *Friends, followers and factions: A reader in political clientelism*. Los Angeles: University of California Press.

Mishler, E. (1986). *Research interviewing: Narrative and context*. Cambridge, MA: Harvard.

Mojab, C. G. (2000). The Cultural Art of Breastfeeding. *LEAVEN, 36*(5), 87-91.

Retrieved 15 August, 2006 from
http://www.lalecheleague.org/llleaderweb/LV/LVOctNov00p87.html

Mok, E., & Martinson, I. (2000). Empowerment of Chinese patients with cancer through self-help groups in Hong Kong. *Cancer Nursing, 23*(3), 206–213.

Montero-Sieburth, M. (1992). Models and practice of curriculum change in developing countries. *Comparative Education Review, 36*(2), 175–193.

Muller, R. (2000). *Honour and shame: Unlocking the door.* Bloomington, IN: Xlibris.

Muller, R. (2006a). *The messenger, the message and the community: Three critical issues for the cross-cultural church planter.* Langley, BC: CanBooks.

Muller, R. <rolandmuller@canbooks.com> (2006b, 19 April). Re: Leadership research. [Personal email].

Munro, R. (2005). Partial organization: Marilyn Strathern and the elicitation of relations. *The Sociological Review, 53*(1), 245–266

Murphy, E., & Dingwall, R. (2001). The ethics of ethnography. In P. Atkinson, A. Coffey, S. Delamont, J. Lofland & L. Lofland (Eds.), *Handbook of ethnography* (pp. 339–351). Thousand Oaks, CA: Sage.

Murra, J. V. (1970). Current research and prospects in Andean ethnohistory. *Latin American research review, 5*(1), 3–36.

Myers, M. (2000). Qualitative research and generalizability questions: Standing firm with Proteus. *The Qualitative Report, 4*(3/4), March, 2000. Retrieved 25th April, 2007 from http://www.nova.edu/ssss/QR/QR4-3/myers.html

Naugle, D. K. (2002). *Worldview: The history of a concept.* Grand Rapids, MI: William B. Eerdmans Publishing Company.

Nietzsche, F. (1980). *On the advantage and disadvantage of history for life.* Translated by P. Preuss. Indianapolis, MN: Hackett.

Nisbett, R. E., & Cohen, D. (1996). *Culture of honour: The psychology of violence in the South.* Boulder, CO: Westview Press.

November, J. (2000). *Klaus Barbie: Criminal in absentia (1945-1983).* Retrieved 12 December, 2006 from http://members.aol.com/voyl/barbie/4chapter.htm

Ocampo Flórez, E. (1999). *Liderazgo Educativo: Una respuesta o una necesidad? In Educación para la paz: Una pedagogía para consolidar la democracia social y participativa.* Bogotá, Colombia : Cooperativa Editorial Magisterio,

Ogliastri, E. (1998) *Culture and Organizational Leadership in Colombia.* Retrieved from www.haskayne.ucalgary.ca/GLOBE/Public/Links/colombian.pdf.

Olivera, O., & Lewis, O. (2004). *Cochabamba! Water war in Bolivia.* Cambridge, MA: South End Press.

Olthius, J. (1985). On worldviews. *Christian Scholars Review, 14,* 153–164.

O'Neill, P. (2007). *Glossary of Terminology of the Shamanic & Ceremonial Traditions*

of the Inca Medicine Lineage. Retrieved from
http://www.incaglossary.org/intro.html

Orr, J. (1893). *The Christian view of God and the world as centering in the incarnation*. Edinburgh: Andrew Elliot.

O'Toole, M. <Mitch.OToole@newcastle.edu.au> (2008, 10 April). Re: Collectivism. [Personal email].

Owens, R. G. (1991). *Organisation behaviour in education*. Englewood Cliffs, NJ: Prentice Hall.

Oxfam America. (2005). *Preserving Bolivia's ancient culture*. Retrieved from http://www.oxfamamerica.org/whatwedo/where_we_work/south_america/news_publications/art3981.html

Oyserman, D., Sorensen, N., Reber, R., & Chen S. X. (2009). *Connecting and separating mindsets: Culture as situated cognition*. To be published. Retrieved from
http://sitemaker.umich.edu/nicholas.sorensen/files/connecting_and_separating_mindsets.pdf

Pachón, C. O. (1995). *Administración y desarollo de comunidades educativas*. Bogatá, Columbia: Mesa Rodonda Magisterio.

Palomino de Aoki, A. (1993). *Runasimi I: Manual de Quechua Crusqueño*. Latin American Documentation Center—Japan.

Parsons, T., & Shills, E. A. (Eds.). (1962). *Towards a general theory of action*. New York: Harper.

Paton, M. P. (2002). *Qualitative research and evaluation methods* (3rd ed.). Thousand Oaks, CA: Sage.

Paulson, R. G., & Tidwell, D. (1990). Education in Latin America. In H. J. Walberg & G. D. Haertel (Eds.) *The International Encyclopedia of Educational Evaluation*. Oxford: Pergamon.

Paulson, S. (2000). Gender, ethnicity and class in Bolivian politics: Transformation or paternalism? *I simpósio internacional: Articulando gênero, raça e classe*. Bahia, Brazil: NEHP-CPD-UFBA. Retrieved from http://www.desafio.ufba.br/gt7-005.html

Pecorino, P. A. (2000). *Introduction to philosophy: An online textbook*. Retrieved from http://www2.sunysuffolk.edu/pecorip/SCCCWEB/ETEXTS/INTRO_TEXT/Chapter%208%20Ethics/Relativism.htm.

Pedraza Arpasi, J. (n.d.). *An introduction to the language, history, religion and culture of the Aymara people*. English version by Sarai Coteron. Retrieved from http://www.aymara.org/histo_eng.php.

Peirce, C. S. (1867/1960). *Collected papers of Charles Sanders Peirce, Volume 5*. Cambridge: Harvard University Press.

Peterson, P. (2001). Religion as orienting worldview. *Zygon, 36*(1), 5–19.

Phillips, D. *Building a "culture index" to world airline safety.* The Washington Post, P. A8, August 21, 1994.

Plank, D. N., & Boyd, W. L. (1990). Politics and Governance of Education. In H. J. Walberg & G. D. Haertel (Eds.)*The International Encyclopedia of Educational Evaluation.* Oxford: Pergamon.

Plantinga, A. (2000). *Warranted Christian belief.* Oxford: Oxford University Press.

Plantinga, T. (1980). *Historical understanding in the thought of Wilhelm Dilthey.* Toronto: University of Toronto Press.

Plueddemann, J. E. (2009). Leading across cultures. Downers Grove, IL: IVP Academic.

Pojman, L. P. (2002). *Ethical theory: Classic and contemporary readings.* Belmont, CA: Wadsworth Thompson Learning.

Prieto, L. B. (1960). *El concepto del líder. El Maetsro como líder.* Caracas: Editorial Arte.

Ramet, S. (2007.) The Denial Syndrome and Its Consequences: Serbian Political Culture since 2000. *Communist and post-communist studies, 40*(1), 41–58.

Randall, D. M., & Gibson, A. M. (1990). Methodology in business ethics research: A review and critical assessment. *Journal of Business Ethics, 9*(6), 457-471.

Rawwas, M. Y. A., Vitell, S. J., &Al-Khatib, J. A. (1994). Consumer ethics: The possible effects of terrorism and civil unrest on the ethical values of consumers. *Journal of Business Ethics, 13*, 223–231.

Regalsky, P., & Laurie, N. (2007). 'The school, whose place is this'? The deep structures of the hidden curriculum in indigenous education in Bolivia. *Comparative Education, 43*(2), 231–251.

Restall, M. (2003). *Seven myths of the Spanish conquest.* New York: Oxford University Press.

Rey, C. E. C. (1995). *El centro docente como proyecto educativo institutional.* Bogatá, Colombia: Instituto Lumen Gentium.

Reyes, M., &Mendieta, E.(2001). Thinking in Spanish: Memory of Logos?*Nepantla: Views from South, 2*(2), 247–264.

Richardson, D. (2007). *Eternity in Their Hearts: Startling Evidence of Belief in the One True God in Hundreds of Cultures Throughout the World.* Ventura, CA: Regal Books.

Rivera Cusicanqui, S. (1990). Liberal Democracy and Ayllu Democracy in Bolivia: The Case of Northern Potosí. *The Journal of Development Studies, 26*(4), 97–121.

Rivers, C. (2004). *Ethical decision making in negotiation: A Sino-Australian study of the influence of culture* (Chapter 5). Unpublished PhD thesis.

Rosa, J. de la (1995). *Nataniel Aguirre.* (S. G. Waisman, Trans.). New York: Oxford University Press.

Rossman, G. B., & Rallis, S. F. (2003.) *Learning in the field: An introduction to qualitative research.* Thousand Oaks, CA: Sage Publications.

Roubiczek, P. (1969). *Ethical values in the age of science.* Cambridge: The University Press.

Rubenstein, H. (2003). *Ethical Leadership: The State of the Art.* Growth Strategies, Inc: http://growth-strategies.com/subpages/articles/069.html

Sabine, H. (2006). Strathern's Melanesian dividual and the Christian individual: a perspective from Vanua Lava, Vanuatu. *Oceania, 76*(3), 285–296.

Sabini, J., & Silver, M. (1997). In defence of shame: Shame in the context of guilt and embarrassment. *Journal for the theory of social sciences, 27*(1), 1–15.

Sandberg, J. (2000). Understanding human competence at work: An interpretative approach, *Academy of Management Journal, 43*(1), 9.

Sanders, J. E., Hopkins, W. E., & Geroy, G. D. (2003) From transactional to transcendental: Toward an integrated theory of leadership. *Journal of leadership & organizational studies, 9*(4), 21–31.

Sandóval, G. (1998). *Grassroots organizations and local development in Bolivia: A study of the municipalities of Tiahuanacu, Mizque, Villa Serrano and Charagua.* Washington: The World Bank.

Sarason, S. B. (1984). If it can be studied or developed, should it be. *American Psychologist, 37*(5), 477–485.

Sarros, J. C., & Santora, J. C. (2001). *Personal values and executive leadership: Global comparisons and practical implications.* Paper presented at the 2001 Academy of Business and Administrative Sciences International Conference, Quebec City, Canada, 12-14 July 2001.

Schaedel, R. P. (1988). Andean World View: Hierarchy or Reciprocity, Regulation or Control? *Current Anthropology, 29*(5), 768-775. Retrieved from http://links.jstor.org/sici?sici=0011-3204%28198812%2929%3A5%3C768%3AAWVHOR%3E2.0.CO%3B2-4

Scheff, T. J. (2003). Shame in self and society. *Symbolic Interactio, 26*(2), 239–262.

Schlecht, N. E. (2004). *Frommer's Peru: With the most intriguing Incan ruins.* Hoboken, NJ: Wiley Publishing Inc.

Schram, T. H. (2006). *Conceptualizing qualitative inquiry.* Upper Saddle River, NY: Pearson Education, Inc.

Schwartz, S. H. (1994). Are there universal aspects in the structure and contents of human values? *Journal of Social Issues, 50*, 19–45.

Schwartz, S. H. (2006). A theory of cultural value orientations: Explication and applications. *Comparative Sociology, 5*(2-3), 137–182.

Seed, P. (1992). *To love, honor, and obey in colonial Mexico: Conflicts over marriage choice, 1574-1821*. Palo Alto, CA: Stanford University Press.

Seidel, J. (1991). Methods and madness in the application of computer technology to qualitative data analysis. In N. Fielding & R. Lee (Eds.), *Using computers in qualitative research*, (pp. 107–116). London: Sage.

Sergiovanni, T. J. (1984). Leadership and excellence in schooling, *Educational Leadership, 41*(5), 4–13.

Sergiovanni, T. J. (1990). Adding value to leadership gets extraordinary results. *Education Leadership, 47*(8), 23-7.

Shults, F. L. (1997). Rationality in Science and Theology: Overcoming the Postmodern Dilemma. PSCF 49 (December 1997): 228-237. Retrieved 27th April, 2007 from http://www.asa3.org/ASA/PSCF/1997/PSCF12-97Shults.html#15

Shweder, R. A., Mahapatra, M., & Miller, J. G. (1987). Culture and moral development. In J. Kagen & S. Lamb (Eds.), *The emergence of morality in young children* (pp. 1–82). Chicago, IL: University of Chicago Press.

Silins, H. C. (1992). Effective leadership for school reform. *The Alberta journal of educational research, 38*(4), 317–334.

Sire, J. (2004). *Universe next door: A basic worldview catalog*. InterVarsity Press.

Slater, C. L., Boone, M., Ivarez, I. et al. (2006). Ideal images of educational leadership in Mexico City and South Texas. *The Educational Forum, 70*(2), 154–170.

Smith, D. W., & McIntyre, R. (1982). *Husserl and intentionality: A study of mind, meaning, and language*. Dordecht and Boston: D. Reidel.

Snyder, K. A. (2002). Modern cows and exotic trees: Identity, personhood, and exchange among the Iraqw of Tanzania. *Ethnology, 42*(2), 155–174.

Sokoya, S. K. (1998). Hofstede's Cultural Dimensions of Values and Personal Value Orientation of Nigerian Managers: Implications for Management Practice. *International Journal of Value Based Management, 11*, 225–235.

Soltis, J. F. (1990). The ethics of qualitative research. In E. Eisner & A. Peshkin (Eds.), *Qualitative inquiry in education* (pp. 247–257). New York: Teachers College Press.

Srnka, K. J. (2004). Culture's role in marketers' ethical decision making: An integrated theoretical framework. *Academy of Marketing Science Review, 2004*(1). Retrieved 23rd October, 2006 from http://www.amsreview.org/articles/srnka01-2004.pdf

Stables, A. (2002). On the making and breaking of frames in pursuit of sustainability. *The trumpeter*. Retrieved from http://trumpeter.athabascau.ca/index.php/trumpet/article/view/119/1271

Stake, R. E. (1978). The Case Study Method in Social Inquiry. *Educational Researcher, 7*(2), 5–8.

Stake, R. E. (2005). Qualitative case studies. In N. K.; Denzin & Y. S. Lincoln (Eds.), *The SAGE handbook of qualitative research* (3rd ed., pp. 443–466). Thousand Oaks, CA: Sage.

Starratt, R. J. (2004). *Ethical leadership.* San Franciscio, CA: Jossey-Bass.

Starratt, R. J. (2005). Ethical leadership. In B. Davies (Ed.). *The essentials of school leadership* (pp. 61–74). Thousand Oaks, CA SAGE.

Stine, P. C. (2004). *Let the words be written: The lasting influence of Eugene A. Nida.* Atlanta, GA: Society for Biblical Literature.

Strathern, M. (1988). *The gender of the gift: Problems with women and problems with society in Melanesia.* Berkley, CA: University of California Press.

Strauss, A., & Corbin, J. (1990). *Basics of qualitative research: Grounded Theory procedures and techniques.* Newbury Park, CA: Sage.

Strobele-Gregor, J. (1996). Culture and Political Practice of the Aymara and Quechua in Bolivia: Autonomous Forms of Modernity in the Andes. *Latin American Perspectives, 23*(2), 72–90.

Sturman, A. (1997). Case study methods. In J. P. Keeves (Ed.), *Educational research, methodology, and measurement: An international handbook.* (2nd ed., pp. 61–66). New York: Pergamon.

Sue, D. W. (1981). *Counseling the culturally different: Theory and practice.* New York: Wiley.

Swineyard, W. R., Rinne, H., & Keng Kau, A. (1990). The morality of software piracy: A cross-cultural analysis. *Journal of Business Ethics, 9,* 655–664.

Swoyer, C. (2003). Relativism. *Stanford encyclopaedia of philosophy.* Retrieved 13 March, 2007 from http://plato.stanford.edu/entries/relativism/#1.2

Tamayo Flores, A-M. (1992). *Derecho en los Andes: Un estudio de antropología jurídica.* Lima: Centro de Estudios País y Región.

Tangney, J. P., & Dearing, R. L. (2002). *Shame and guilt.* New York: Guilford.

Tapia, E. (2002). *Liderazgo: Manual de lideres.* Bolivia: Ediciones Qhananchawi.

Tapia, G. (2008). *Las condiciones estaban dadas para una guerra civil.* Cochabamba, Bolivia: Los Tiempos. Retrieved from http://www.lostiempos.com/noticias/16-11-08/16_11_08_nac2.php

Thatcher, O. J. (Ed.). (1907). *The library of original sources, Vol. III: The Roman world.* Milwaukee: University Research Extension Co.

Thayer, J. H. (2007). *Thayer's Greek-English Lexicon of the New Testament: Coded with Strong's concordance numbers.* Peabody, MA: Hendrickson Publishers.

Thiselton, A. (1992). *New horizons in hermeneutics: The theory and practice of transforming biblical reading.* Grand Rapids, MI: Zondervan.

Thomas, H. (2003). *Cultural themes, worldview perspectives, and Christian conversion among urbanizing Evangelical Aymaras.* (Doctoral dissertation, Fuller Theological Seminary, Pasadena, CA, 2003).

Thomas, H. <hthomas@prodola.org> (2010a, April 17). Re: Reporting [Personal Email].

Thomas, H. <hthomas@prodola.org> (2010b, April 20). Re: Reporting [Personal Email].

Thomas, H. <hthomas@prodola.org> (2010c, April 22). Re: Reporting [Personal Email].

Thomas, H. <hthomas@prodola.org> (2010d, April 23). Re: Reporting [Personal Email].

Tiznado, J. G. (2001) Globalización, calidad y liderazgo educativo. Notas introductorias. *Acción Educativa Revista Electrónica del Centro de Investigaciones y Servicios Educativos.* Universidad Autónoma de Sinaloa. Volumen I, Número 1, Febrero del 2001. Culiacán, Sin. México. Retrieved from http://uas.uasnet.mx/cise/rev/Num1/

Torres, J. B., Solberg, V. S. H., & Carlstrom, A. H. (2002). The myth of sameness among Latino men and their machismo. *American Journal of Orthopsychiatry, 72*(2), 163–181

Transparency International (2004). *CPI Table.* Retrieved from http://www.transparency.org/policy_research/surveys_indices/cpi/2004

Transparency International (2009). *CPI Table.* Retrieved from http://www.transparency.org/news_room/in_focus/2008/cpi2008/cpi_2008_table

Triandis, H. C. (1988). Collectivism and individualism: A reconceptualization of a basic concept in cross-cultural psychology. In C. Bagley & G. Verma (Eds.), *Personality, cognition, and values: Cross-cultural perspectives of childhood and adolescence* (pp. 60–95). London: Macmillan.

Triandis, H. C., Bontempo, R., Villareal, M. J., Asai, M., & Lucca, N. (1988). Individualism and collectivism: Cross-cultural perspectives on self-ingroup relationships. *Journal of Personality and Social Psychology, 54,*323–338.

Triandis, H. C. et al. (1993). An etic-emic analysis of individualism and collectivism. *Journal Of Cross-Cultural Psychology, 24*(3), 366–383.

Triplett, C. (2002). *Postmodern Approaches to Knowledge: Finding a Starting Place for Faith and Learning after Foundationalism.* Retrieved from http://www.mobap.edu/academics/fl/journal/1.1/triplett.asp

Trugden, R. (2000). *Why Warriors lie down and die.* Nhulunbuy, NT: Aboriginal Resource and Development Services.

Uskul, A. K., Oyserman, D., & Schwarz, N. (in press, 2009). Cultural emphasis on honour, modesty or self-enhancement: Implications for the survey response process. To appear in J. Harkness et al. (Eds.), *Survey methods in multinational, multiregional and multicultural contexts.* New York: Wiley.

Van Manen, M. (1990). *Researching lived experience: Human science for an action sensitive pedagogy.* New York: State University of New York.

Vargas Rivas, G. (n.d.) *Asamblea constituyente: Historia de las constituciones de Bolivia.* Retrieved from http://www.laconstituyente.org/?q=node/53

Vásquez, K. (2009). La Pachamama tiene hambre. *Los Tiempos, 9 Aug 09.* Cochabamba, Bolivia. Retrieved from http://www.lostiempos.com/diario/actualidad/local/20090809/la-pachamama-tiene-hambre_29421_47205.html.

Vila de Prado, R. (2003). Liberal thought and Bolivian political culture (1899–1934). Translated by J. H. Cole from *Revista de Humanidades y Ciencias Sociales* 9(1–2), pp. 79–118.

Walsh. B. J., & Middleton, R. (1984). *Transforming the vision: Shaping a Christian worldview.* Downers Grove, IL: InterVarsity Press.

Weidjers, I. (2000). Punishment and upbringing: Considerations for an educative justification of punishment. *Journal of moral education, 29*(1), 61–73.

Weiler, K. (1988). *Women teaching for change: Gender, class & Power.* New York: Bergin & Garvey.

Weiner, B. (1986), *Attribution theory of motivation and emotion.* New York: Springer-Verlag.

Weinsheimer, J., & Marshall, D. G. (1998). Translators' Preface. In H. Gadamer. *Truth and Method.* New York: Continuum.

Weissberg, R. (2004). Mr. Pinocchio goes to Washington: Lying in politics. *Social Philosophy and Policy, 21*(1), 167–201. Retrieved from http://proquest.umi.com.ezproxy1.acu.edu.au/pqdweb?index=17&did=626401821&SrchMode=1&sid=1&Fmt=6&VInst=PROD&VType=PQD&RQT=309&VName=PQD&TS=1268440553&clientId=18921

Wei-Ting, J., & Gutierrez, W. P. (2003). *How Asian/Asian North American women theological educators negotiate power dynamics.* Retrieved 20 February, 2007 from http://www.coe.uga.edu/leap/adulted/pdf/Jannette_Wei_ting_Gutierroz.pdf

Wellington, J. J. (2000). *Educational research: Contemporary issues and practical approaches.* London: Continuum International Publishing Group.

Wilde, M. (2007). *Who wanted what and why at the Second Vatican Council? Toward a general theory of religious change.* Retrieved from http://www.sociologica.mulino.it/journal/articlefulltext/index/Article/Journal:ARTICLE:33

Williams, R. A. (1992). *The American Indian in western legal thought: The discourses of conquest.* New York: Oxford University Press.

Willower, D. (1992). Educational administration: Intellectual trends. In *Encyclopaedia of educational research*, (6th ed.) Toronto: Macmillan.

Wilson, S. (2002.) Face, norms and instrumentality. In T. Gold, D. Guthrie & D. Wank, (Eds.), *Social connections in China: Institutions, culture, and the changing nature of guanxi* (pp. 163–178). Cambridge: Cambridge University Press.

Wittgenstein, L. (1969). *On certainty.* Oxford: Basil Blackwell.

Wolf, E. R. (1956). Aspects of Group Relations in a Complex Society: Mexico. *American Anthropologist, 58*(6), 1065–1078.

Wright, W. (1998). *Cultural issues in mediation: A practical guide to individualist and collectivist paradigms.* The Association of Attorney-Mediators. Retrieved from http://www.attorney-mediators.org/wright.html.

Yau-fai Ho, D. (1976). On the concept of face. *American Journal of Sociology, 81*(4). (Jan., 1976), 867–884.

Yin, R. K. (2003). *Case study research: Design and methods* (3rd ed.). Thousand Oaks, CA: Sage Publications.

Yu, C. H. (1994). *Abduction? Deduction? Induction? Is there a logic to exploratory data analysis?* Paper presented at the annual meeting of the American Research Association (New Orleans, LA, April 4–8, 1994).

Yu, C. H. (2006). *Abduction, deduction, and induction: Their implications to quantitative methods.* Paper submitted to AERA 2006. Retrieved 12 May, 2007 from http://www.creative-wisdom.com/teaching/WBI/abduction5.pdf.